Prentice Hall LITERATURE

PENGUIN EDITION

Unit Two
Resources

Grade Six

Upper Saddle River, New Jersey
Boston, Massachusetts
Chandler, Arizona
Glenview, Illinois

BQ Tunes Credits
Keith London, Defined Mind, Inc., Executive Producer
Mike Pandolfo, Wonderful, Producer
All songs mixed and mastered by Mike Pandolfo, Wonderful
Vlad Gutkovich, Wonderful, Assistant Engineer
Recorded November 2007 – February 2008 in SoHo, New York City, at
Wonderful, 594 Broadway

ISBN–13: 978-0-13-366430-0
ISBN–10:   0-13-366430-9

4 5 6 7 8 9 10   V011   12 11 10

CONTENTS

For information about the Unit Resources, assessing fluency, and teaching with BQ Tunes, see the opening pages of your Unit One Resources.

"Becky and the Wheels-and-Brake Boys" by James Berry

"The Southpaw" by Judith Viorst

Writing Workshop: Response to Literature—Review

Writing Workshop: Errors with Verbs

Benchmark Test 3

Skills Concept Map 2

"The Circuit" by Francisco Jiménez

"The All-American Slurp" by Lensey Namioka

"The Fun They Had" by Isaac Asimov

"Feathered Friend" by Arthur C. Clarke

BQ Tunes

Into the Light, performed by DogDay

We **challenge** and engage the contest
The **battle** to be fought
The storm gathers at the horizon
Life's not a **game** played at any cost
There's no glory in test of wills
We **compete**, but the race is lost
I **defend** against your abuses
In roiling seas, the ship is tossed
In roiling seas, the ship is tossed

In the end I reach the conclusion
I'm not **convinced** the fight's worth the price
Resist, refuse to accept it
Bring a new way into the light, into the light, into the light

We **argue**, force our points of view
But the **issue** isn't what's at stake
The problem is who's in control
Your pound of flesh is mine to take
Win, success is how you see it
Does it pay to **negotiate**?
To share some common ground
Peace lies far before heaven's gate
Peace lies far before heaven's gate

In the end I reach the conclusion
I'm not convinced the fight's worth the price
Resist, refuse to accept it
Bring a new way into the light, into the light, into the light

We can gamble with our survival
But to live is to win
Once we **lose**, all is lost

Continued

A failure paid with life and limb

Resolve that peace is the answer

Decide that's where to begin

It's the key to all our questions

All tears are shed in vain

All tears are shed in vain

In the end I reach the conclusion

I'm not convinced the fight's worth the price

Resist, refuse to accept it

Bring a new way into the light, into the light, into the light

---

Song Title: **Into the Light**
Artist / Performed by DogDay
Vocals & Guitar: Joe Pascarell
Lyrics by Keith London
Music composed by Keith London, Joe Pascarell & Mike Pandolfo
Produced by Mike Pandolfo, Wonderful
Executive Producer: Keith London, Defined Mind

x

Name _____ Date _____

Unit 2: Short Stories
Big Question Vocabulary—1

The Big Question: Is conflict always bad?

It is impossible to have relationships with people without some conflict arising. One kind of conflict is an argument between friends. The following words are used to talk about arguments.

argue: to disagree with someone in words, often in an angry way

conclude: to bring something to an end

convince: to get another person to think the same way as you

issue: a problem or subject that people discuss

resolve: to find an acceptable way to deal with a problem or difficulty

DIRECTIONS: *Write about a disagreement that you have had with a friend or family member, using the words in parentheses.*

1. **Description of the disagreement:**

(argue, issue)

2. **How did each party to the disagreement try to get the other person to change his or her thinking?**

(convince)

3. **What was the end result?**

(resolve, conclude)

Unit 2: Short Stories
Big Question Vocabulary—2

The Big Question: Is conflict always bad?

One kind of conflict is games or sports, which are played according to rules. Most people agree that games or sports are "good" conflict.

challenge: *n.* something that tests a person's strength, skill or ability; *v.* to question whether something is fair or right

compete: to try to gain something, or to be better or more successful at something than someone else

game: an activity or sport in which people play against one another according to agreed rules

lose: to not be best or first at something

win: to be best or first at something

DIRECTIONS: *Using the words in parentheses, describe a game or sport that you are familiar with.*

1. How do you play?

(game, challenge)

2. Who plays?

(compete)

3. What is the end result?

(win, lose)

Unit 2: Short Stories
Big Question Vocabulary—3

The Big Question: Is conflict always bad?

Sometimes conflict can lead to violent battles or wars between opposing groups. The following words can help you talk about these kinds of conflict.

battle: encounter in which opposing groups compete, fight, or argue to try to win

defend: to act in support of someone being hurt or criticized

negotiate: to discuss something to reach an agreement

resist: to stop yourself from doing something you would very much like to do

survival: the state of continuing to exist when there is a risk that you might die

DIRECTIONS: *Answer the questions below using the words in parentheses in the boxes.*

When the early settlers came to America, the Native Americans were already living here.

1. What were two ways the settlers could have dealt with the problem of sharing land with the Native Americans?

2. What are possible results of each decision?

1.

(negotiate)   **(battle)**

2.

(survival)   **(defend)**

Name _____ Date _____

Unit 2: Short Stories
Applying the Big Question

 Is conflict always bad?

DIRECTIONS: *Complete the chart below to apply what you have learned about the "pros and cons" of conflict. One row has been completed for you.*

Example	Type of Conflict	How the conflict is resolved	What is bad about the conflict	What is good about the conflict	What I learned
From Literature	In "The Circuit," a boy wants to stay in one place, but his family must often move.	Panchito must accept the hardships of his family's life.	Panchito feels uncomfortable in school; he has to leave a new friend.	Panchito sees how others live; he learns something new with each new experience.	Some conflicts cannot be resolved; conflicts can be a source of courage.
From Literature					
From Science					
From Social Studies					
From Real Life					

Name _____

Unit 2: Short Stories Skills Concept Map—1
Is conflict always bad?

Words you can use to discuss the Big Question

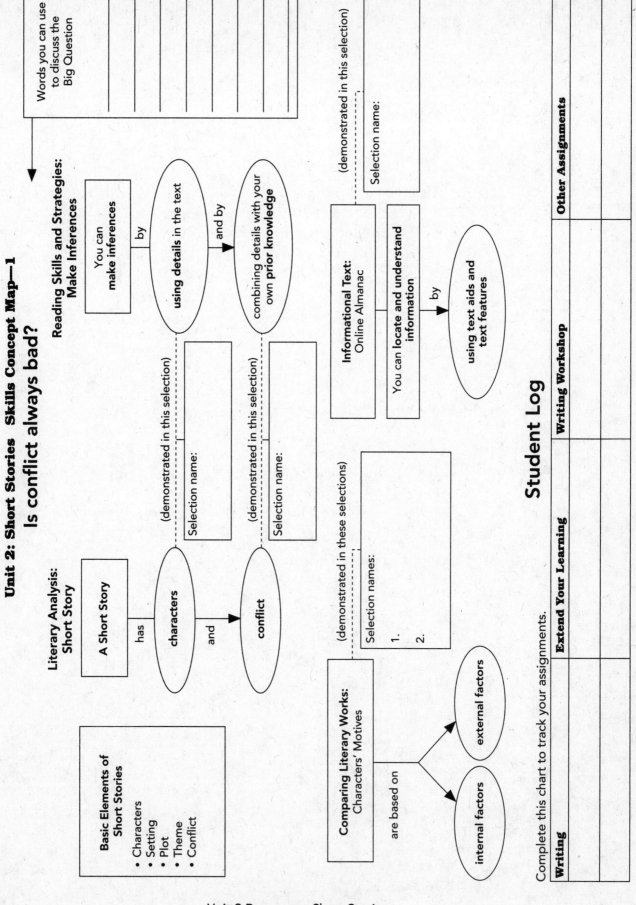

Reading Skills and Strategies: Make Inferences

You can make inferences

by

using details in the text

and by

combining details with your own prior knowledge

Literary Analysis: Short Story

A Short Story

has

characters

and

conflict

(demonstrated in this selection)

Selection name: _____

(demonstrated in this selection)

Selection name: _____

Basic Elements of Short Stories
- Characters
- Setting
- Plot
- Theme
- Conflict

Informational Text: Online Almanac

You can locate and understand information

by

using text aids and text features

(demonstrated in this selection)

Selection name: _____

Comparing Literary Works: Characters' Motives

are based on

external factors

internal factors

(demonstrated in these selections)

Selection names:
1.
2.

Student Log

Complete this chart to track your assignments.

Writing	Extend Your Learning	Writing Workshop	Other Assignments

Vocabulary Warm-up Word Lists

Study these words from "The Wounded Wolf." Then, complete the activities.

Word List A

blinding [BLYN ding] *adj.* so bright as to make it hard to see
The <u>blinding</u> lights from the cameras made it hard to see people's faces.

clan [KLAN] *n.* a large group of families
My aunts, uncles, cousins, and the rest of the <u>clan</u> are coming over for dinner.

flesh [FLESH] *n.* the meat of an animal
Vegetarians do not eat animal <u>flesh</u>.

gulps [GUHLPS] *v.* drinks or eats quickly or greedily
After running ten miles, he <u>gulps</u> the water as if he hasn't had a drink for days.

lunges [LUHN jez] *v.* moves forward very quickly
Nancy <u>lunges</u> for the softball but just misses catching it.

presence [PREZ ens] *n.* a being or body
It was so dark I couldn't see, but I felt a nearby <u>presence</u> in the room.

squints [SKWINTS] *v.* partially closes the eyes
When it's sunny, Ted always <u>squints</u>, trying to block out the sun so he can see.

whimpers [WIM perz] *v.* makes a soft crying sound
When the baby <u>whimpers</u>, her voice is so soft I can barely hear it.

Word List B

barren [BA ruhn] *adj.* empty or lifeless
After fire burned down all the trees, the land looked <u>barren</u>.

boldly [BOHLD lee] *adv.* bravely, without fear or caution
The soldier ran <u>boldly</u> into the battle, not worrying what might happen to him.

flits [FLITS] *v.* moves quickly from one place to another
The fly <u>flits</u> around the room, never staying in one place for more than a second.

foes [FOHZ] *n.* enemies
Cats and dogs are not always <u>foes</u>; sometimes they like each other.

frigid [FRIJ id] *adj.* extremely cold
This weather is so <u>frigid</u>, I can't seem to get warm no matter what I wear.

massive [MA siv] *adj.* huge; large and impressive
Lindsey's house is <u>massive</u>; it must have fifty rooms in it.

shatters [SHAT erz] *v.* breaks into small pieces
If the mirror <u>shatters</u>, there will be tiny pieces of glass everywhere.

starvation [stahr VAY shuhn] *n.* suffering or dying from lack of food
After a week with no food on the desert island, the sailor was facing <u>starvation</u>.

"The Wounded Wolf" by Jean Craighead George
Vocabulary Warm-up Exercises

Exercise A *Fill in each blank in the paragraph below with an appropriate word from Word List A. Use each word only once.*

I could sense a [1] _____ outside the door. It was Uncle Henry, the first to arrive. The whole [2] _____ comes to our house for the holidays, and it makes me a little crazy. Uncle Henry is the worst. He [3] _____ around the kitchen like a wild cat, looking for food and [4] _____ it down greedily when he finds some. Aunt Abigail, on the other hand, refuses to eat the [5] _____ of animals. "Henry knows that I don't like vegetables either," she [6] _____.

Cousin Hugo always [7] _____ with his eyes. "The lights are [8] _____," he says, no matter how dark or light it is. I can't wait for the holidays to end!

Exercise B *Revise each sentence so that the underlined vocabulary word is used in a logical way. Be sure to keep the vocabulary word in your revision.*

Example: There's so much food in the fridge that we are at risk of <u>starvation</u>.
    There's so little food in the fridge that we are at risk of <u>starvation</u>.

1. This lamp <u>shatters</u> easily, so I'm very careless moving it.
   _____

2. The mountain is <u>massive</u>; it will take a minute or two to climb it.
   _____

3. The wind is <u>frigid</u>; I'll wear shorts and a tee shirt when I go outside.
   _____

4. Terrence gets along with everyone, so we're not surprised that he has <u>foes</u>.
   _____

5. The fish <u>flits</u> through the water so slowly that it's easy to catch.
   _____

6. J.J. walked by the pit bull so <u>boldly</u> that I guessed he was afraid of dogs.
   _____

7. This desert is a <u>barren</u> place, full of trees, plants, and animals.
   _____

"The Wounded Wolf" by Jean Craighead George
Reading Warm-up A

Read the following passage. Pay special attention to the underlined words. Then, read it again, and complete the activities. Use a separate sheet of paper for your written answers.

Like most baby animals, a newborn wolf is nearly helpless at first. The baby wolf, called a pup, is born in a den. The wolf's mother will have built the den a few weeks before. She may have dug it out of the ground, or she may have found a den that had already been built by another animal. In this den, the wolf pup begins its life. It <u>squints</u> its eyes, but it cannot see. When it can open its eyes completely, light will be <u>blinding</u>. The pup <u>whimpers</u>, making small soft sounds. It senses a <u>presence</u> next to him, a brother or sister pup. Wolves are not born alone; they arrive into a ready-made <u>clan</u>. Mother wolves give birth to several pups at a time. The average-size group is five.

The pup is small, weighing just about a pound. It is hungry, though, and it <u>gulps</u> down its mother's milk. It will grow bigger with help. This pup is part of a pack, and pack members will bring food to the baby and its mother.

In time, the pup will grow to weigh a hundred pounds or more. It will become fast and strong, with long legs and powerful leg muscles. It will be able to run at speeds of up to 35 miles an hour for short periods. Often, these bursts of speed come during the hunt. They will end with the moment when the wolf <u>lunges</u> after its prey. This pup will grow into a hunter. Wolves feed on the <u>flesh</u> of other animals such as deer, elk, and caribou.

The pup will stay with the pack until it is several years old. Then it may leave, find a new pack, or even start its own.

1. Underline the words that tell what the pup <u>squints</u>. Then write a sentence explaining what might make you *squint*.

2. Circle the words that tell what is <u>blinding</u>. Then tell what *blinding* means.

3. Circle the words that tell what it sounds like when the pup <u>whimpers</u>. Then name something else that *whimpers*.

4. Underline the words that tell what <u>presence</u> the pup feels beside it. Write a sentence using the word *presence*.

5. Write a sentence telling who is included in the pup's <u>clan</u>.

6. Underline the words that tell what the pup <u>gulps</u> down. Then tell what *gulps* means.

7. Circle the words that tell what the wolf <u>lunges</u> toward. Then tell what *lunges* means.

8. Circle the words that tell what kind of <u>flesh</u> wolves eat. Then tell what *flesh* means.

Name _____ Date _____

Reading Warm-up B

Read the following passage. Pay special attention to the underlined words. Then, read it again, and complete the activities. Use a separate sheet of paper for your written answers.

The Arctic Circle is the northernmost region of the world. It includes all the land and water within an imaginary circle centered around the North Pole. It is a <u>frigid</u> region, home to some of the coldest days and nights on the planet. Yet it is a wondrous place to visit. Many people look forward all their lives for a chance to go. Despite the cold, many companies offer boat trips into the area.

The sights are amazing. In the water, you may see hundreds of icebergs, some of them <u>massive</u>, as tall as apartment buildings. You may see whales, wolves, or even polar bears. On land, you may catch sight of a small chicken-like bird as it <u>flits</u> across the snow.

The sounds are also incredible. There are few sounds as impressive as the crack of an iceberg as it <u>shatters</u>. You may also hear the roars of polar bears or the howls of wolves.

Indeed, it is the wildlife that draws many visitors here. Although pictures may make it look like a <u>barren</u> place, the Arctic Circle is full of life. Many different species live here. There is the snowy owl, found only in the Arctic. It can change its looks with the seasons: white in winter, brown in summer. To human visitors, snowy owls may appear friendly. To the smaller birds that owls hunt, however, the snowy owls are <u>foes</u>. Life in the Arctic is a struggle to stay alive. Animals are always on the hunt. Those that cannot find food face <u>starvation</u>.

No animal knows this better than the Arctic seal. The seal is always on the hunt for fish, such as cod. Still, it can't afford to go <u>boldly</u> wherever it wants. It must always be on the lookout. Its enemy, the polar bear, is always waiting, hoping for a meal.

1. Underline the words that tell what the weather is like in a <u>frigid</u> region. Then name the season most likely to have *frigid* weather.

2. Circle the words that tell how <u>massive</u> icebergs are. Then tell what *massive* means.

3. Circle the words that tell what <u>flits</u> across the snow. Then tell what *flits* means.

4. In your own words, write a sentence telling what happens to an iceberg when it <u>shatters</u>.

5. Circle the nearby words that mean the opposite of <u>barren</u>. Then tell what *barren* means.

6. Underline the words that tell who are <u>foes</u> of snowy owls. Then tell what *foes* means.

7. Underline the words that tell what kind of animals face <u>starvation</u>. Then write a sentence telling what *starvation* means.

8. Write a sentence telling why a seal can't go <u>boldly</u> anyplace it wants.

Jean Craighead George
Listening and Viewing

Segment 1: Meet Jean Craighead George
• Why do you think Jean Craighead George chose to write about nature?

_____

_____

_____

_____

Segment 2: Short Story
• How does Jean Craighead George determine when to use the short-story form? Why did she choose to write the story about the wolf?

_____

_____

_____

_____

Segment 3: The Writing Process
• Why do you think research is such an important part of Jean Craighead George's writing?

_____

_____

_____

_____

Segment 4: The Rewards of Writing
• What reward does Jean Craighead George hope to receive from writing? How is her audience also rewarded?

_____

_____

_____

_____

Learning About Short Stories

The short story is a form of fiction. This chart outlines its basic elements.

Elements of Short Story	Examples
CHARACTERS The characters are the people or animals in the story.	A character's **traits** are his or her qualities, such as honesty. A character's **motives** are the reasons he or she acts, such as a desire to be liked.
PLOT The plot is the series of events.	The plot contains a **conflict,** or problem, between opposing forces. One or more characters must solve the conflict. An **internal conflict** takes place inside a character's mind, such as when a man struggles to make a decision. An **external conflict** is one in which a character struggles with an outside force.
SETTING The setting is the time and place of the story's action.	An example of setting might be a small village in England in the winter of 1765.
THEME The theme is a message about life.	A **stated theme** is expressed directly by the author, such as when a fable ends with the moral "Look before you leap." An **implied theme** is suggested by what happens to the characters, such as when a thief ends up in jail. The implied theme is that crime doesn't pay.

DIRECTIONS: *The following are examples of short story elements. Underline the term that correctly identifies each.*

1. A deer tries to survive a forest fire.

       internal conflict   external conflict

2. A character says, "Honesty is very important."

       stated theme   implied theme

3. A man always turns everything into a joke.

       character trait   character motive

4. Relax and make discoveries during a vacation.

       theme   setting

5. A man must find a way to return from outer space.

       character   plot

Name _____ Date _____

"The Wounded Wolf" by Jean Craighead George
Model Selection: Short Story

Like other fiction, a short story contains plot, characters, setting, and theme. The plot contains a **conflict,** or problem, that one or more characters must solve. An **internal conflict** occurs inside a character's mind. The character struggles to make a decision or overcome an obstacle. An **external conflict** is one in which a character struggles with an outside force or enemy.

As the conflict deepens, the plot builds to a **climax.** This is the point of greatest tension. Then there is a **resolution,** the solving of the problem. Then the story ends.

Characters have certain **character traits,** or qualities. For example, a character might be brave. They also have **character motives.** These are the reasons why they act. For example, a character might do something in order to win a prize.

The **setting** is the time and place in which the story takes place. Often, the setting plays an important role. For example, the setting of a burning building would certainly affect the characters' actions.

A. DIRECTIONS: *"The Wounded Wolf" is a short story. Answer these questions about its plot, characters, and setting.*

1. What character traits does Roko have? _____

2. What character motives lead him to act in certain ways?

   _____

3. Does Roko face an internal or an external conflict? Explain.

   _____

   _____

4. What is the setting of the story? _____

5. How does the setting affect Roko's actions?

   _____

   _____

B. DIRECTIONS: *Many short stories carry a **theme,** a message about life. It might be stated by the author or a character. Or, it might be suggested by the characters' actions. Answer the questions about theme.*

1. Does "The Wounded Wolf" have a stated theme or a suggested theme? Explain.

   _____

   _____

2. What might the theme of "The Wounded Wolf" be? Support your answer with details from the story. _____

   _____

   _____

Name _____ Date _____

"The Wounded Wolf" by Jean Craighead George
Open-Book Test

Short Answer *Write your responses to the questions in this section on the lines provided.*

1. Plot is the sequence of events in a story that are linked by cause and effect. Explain how the plot builds to the climax.

   _____

   _____

2. A conflict is a problem between opposing forces. Explain the difference between an internal conflict and an external conflict.

   _____

   _____

3. In a short story, a boy learns to follow his true feelings. Explain which short story element matches this description.

   _____

   _____

4. "The Wounded Wolf" is a short story about a brave young wolf. Explain which short story element matches this description.

   _____

   _____

5. In each circle of the word web, write a phrase from "The Wounded Wolf" that describes the setting of the story. Then, on the line, tell how the setting is important to the story.

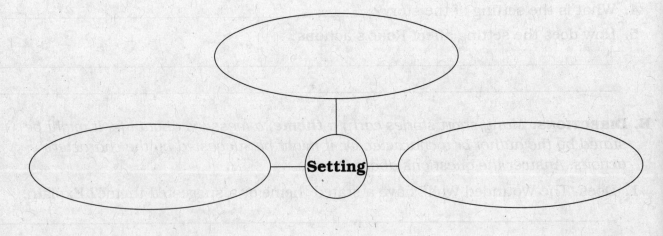

   _____

   _____

6. The author of "The Wounded Wolf" writes that the herd of musk-ox forms a "fort of heads and horns and fur." Explain why this is a good description for their circle.

_____

_____

_____

7. In "The Wounded Wolf," the other animals begin to attack Roko. The wolf wedges himself between a rock and the ground. Explain why he does this.

_____

_____

8. The wolves in "The Wounded Wolf" are organized as a pack that exists to help its members survive. Identify two events in the story that show this organization.

_____

_____

_____

9. When Kiglo brings Roko food in "The Wounded Wolf," the young wolf "gnashes, gorges, and shatters bits upon the snow." What does the word *gnashes* tell you about how he is eating?

_____

_____

_____

10. At the end of "The Wounded Wolf," what is the reason for "the sound of whoops and yips and barks and howls"? Support your answer with details from the story.

_____

_____

_____

Essay

Write an extended response to the question of your choice or to the question or questions your teacher assigns you.

11. After fighting off his foes in "The Wounded Wolf," Roko is too weak to answer the roll call. He waits for hours and sees his enemies get closer. How do you think he feels when he sees Kiglo trotting around the knoll? In an essay, describe how Roko feels when he sees his leader and the food he brings. Support your answer with examples from the story.

12. If readers know a character's traits, they can better understand why he or she acts in certain ways. In an essay, discuss how Roko's character traits help you understand his actions in "The Wounded Wolf." Focus on the thoughts, feelings, or desires that lead him to act in certain ways. Use details from the story in your answer.

13. In an essay, explain how the setting of "The Wounded Wolf" helps play an important role in the events of the story.

14. **Thinking About the Big Question: Is conflict always bad?** In "The Wounded Wolf," Roko struggles to survive against the cold and his foes. In an essay, discuss if Roko's conflict is a bad thing. Consider what positive and negative things come from the conflict. Use examples from the story to support your ideas.

Oral Response

15. Go back to question 2, 6, 7, or 10 or to the question your teacher assigns to you. Take a few minutes to expand your answer and prepare an oral response. Find additional details in "The Wounded Wolf" that will support your points. If necessary, make notes to guide your response.

"The Wounded Wolf" by Jean Craighead George
Selection Test A

Learning About Short Stories *Identify the letter of the choice that best answers the question.*

____ 1. What is the setting of a story?
A. a problem to be solved
B. the reasons for characters' actions
C. the time and place of the story's action
D. a message about life

____ 2. What is the *best* definition of a character's traits?
A. problems that take place inside his or her mind
B. forces of nature that cause a struggle
C. personal qualities such as honesty or courage
D. the point in the story when the action builds

____ 3. At what point in a plot does the greatest tension occur?
A. the climax
B. the introduction
C. the story
D. the motive

____ 4. Which statement is true about the plot of a short story?
A. Most often, it contains a conflict.
B. Most often, it contains an internal conflict.
C. Most often, it contains an external conflict.
D. Most often, it does not contain a conflict.

____ 5. Which word names a message about life that short stories often provide?
A. setting
B. conflict
C. theme
D. character

Critical Reading

____ 6. Which of the following *best* describes the setting of "The Wounded Wolf"?
A. a wildlife park during the summer
B. an icy Arctic valley in the winter
C. a den where a grizzly bear has slept
D. a wooded plain in Africa

___ 7. Which statement *best* describes Roko in "The Wounded Wolf"?
   A. He is the leader of a pack of wolves.
   B. He is a bear that was wounded by a wolf.
   C. He is a raven that was wounded by a wolf.
   D. He is a wolf that has been wounded.

___ 8. Which animal is the first to see Roko's signal in "The Wounded Wolf"?
   A. a raven
   B. a fox
   C. a grizzly bear
   D. a musk-ox

___ 9. When the author introduces the owl in "The Wounded Wolf," she says that the owl "joined the deathwatch." What does she mean?
   A. The owl tried to protect other animals from dying.
   B. The owl was watching when the wolves were hunting caribou.
   C. The owl will stand by and watch, expecting the wolf to die.
   D. Being a wise owl, the owl knows when the wolf will die.

___ 10. What motives lead the ravens and other animals to follow Roko in "The Wounded Wolf"?
   A. They are lonely.
   B. They are hungry.
   C. They are lost.
   D. They are frightened.

___ 11. In "The Wounded Wolf," why does Roko wedge himself between a rock and the ground?
   A. He is cold and needs protection from the wind.
   B. He is hungry and hopes to catch a raven in his trap.
   C. He hopes that Kiglo will remember this special place.
   D. He wants to protect himself from the other animals.

___ 12. Which character trait *best* describes Roko from "The Wounded Wolf"?
   A. playful
   B. confused
   C. brave
   D. gentle

_____ 13. In "The Wounded Wolf," after Kiglo barks in the roll call, why are the other wolves silent?

A. They are waiting for Roko to take his turn barking.

B. They can't hear Kiglo's bark because of the icy winds.

C. They are trying to sneak up on the herd of musk-ox.

D. They are frightened when they sense a grizzly bear nearby.

_____ 14. Which term names the point in "The Wounded Wolf" when the ravens and other animals inch closer and closer to Roko?

A. motive

B. setting

C. climax

D. internal conflict

_____ 15. Which sentence *best* summarizes the resolution of "The Wounded Wolf"?

A. Roko is injured during a hunt for caribou.

B. Kiglo arrives with food for Roko.

C. The musk-ox herd forms a circle.

D. The raven calls out, "Kong, kong, kong."

Essay

16. Think about the theme of "The Wounded Wolf." Then, read this statement: *Like people, many animals benefit from teamwork and cooperation.* How is this statement supported by at least two details from "The Wounded Wolf"?

17. How do you think Roko feels when he sees Kiglo trotting around the knoll in "The Wounded Wolf"? Suppose you were Roko. Explain how you would feel when you see your leader and the food he brings.

18. **Thinking About the Big Question: Is conflict always bad?** In "The Wounded Wolf," Roko struggles to survive against the cold and the other animals. In an essay, discuss whether the conflict Roko faces is a bad thing. Think about the good and bad things that come from the conflict. Use examples from the story to support your ideas.

"The Wounded Wolf" by Jean Craighead George
Selection Test B

Learning About Short Stories *Identify the letter of the choice that best completes the statement or answers the question.*

_____ 1. What are a character's personal qualities, such as stubbornness or bravery, called?
    A. motives
    B. traits
    C. resolutions
    D. conflicts

_____ 2. Which is the *best* definition for an internal conflict in a short story?
    A. a problem faced by all of the characters
    B. a problem with an outside force or enemy
    C. a problem that takes place in the mind of a character
    D. a problem that involves the story's setting

_____ 3. Which is the *best* description of the climax in a short story?
    A. the point of greatest tension in the plot
    B. the time and place of the action
    C. the reasons for a character's actions
    D. the point at which the conflict is solved

_____ 4. Which statement is true about the theme of a short story?
    A. Most often, it is directly stated by the author.
    B. Most often, it is directly stated by a character in the story.
    C. Sometimes, it is suggested by what happens to characters.
    D. Sometimes, it includes the year or the time of day.

_____ 5. Which is the *best* definition of the resolution of a short story?
    A. a problem that a character must overcome
    B. the moment that the conflict begins
    C. the point at which the conflict is solved
    D. the message the story offers about life

_____ 6. Which of the following is an example of a character trait?
    A. winter and summer
    B. a person the character dislikes
    C. a terrible storm
    D. honesty

Critical Reading

_____ 7. Which statement is true about "The Wounded Wolf"?
    A. It has a stated theme.
    B. It has a cold and icy setting.
    C. It has an internal conflict.
    D. It has humans and animals.

____ 8. Which statement is true about the main character in "The Wounded Wolf"?
A. It is a wolf named Toklat.
B. It is a wolf named Roko.
C. It is a wolf named Kiglo.
D. It is a wolf named Kong.

____ 9. At the beginning of "The Wounded Wolf," how does the wolf become wounded?
A. He has been bitten by a raven.
B. He has been attacked by a hungry fox.
C. He has been struck by the hoof of a caribou.
D. He has been hit by the claws of a grizzly bear.

____ 10. Which statement is true about the setting of "The Wounded Wolf"?
A. It is the end of winter, and there is little food for the ánimals.
B. It is the end of summer, and the harvest has not been gathered.
C. It is the middle of winter, and the wolves are heading south.
D. It is hunting season, and the wolves must hide to avoid being shot.

____ 11. In "The Wounded Wolf," why does the raven cry, "Kong, kong, kong"?
A. to frighten the wounded wolf
B. to drive away the white fox
C. to alert other ravens that he has found food
D. to tell animals that the grizzly bear is awake

____ 12. The author of "The Wounded Wolf" says that the herd of musk-ox forms a "fort of heads and horns and fur." What does she mean?
A. They have gathered behind the shelter rock.
B. They have circled into a ring to protect themselves.
C. They have formed a ring to protect young Roko.
D. They have leaped across the walls of the outpost fort.

____ 13. Based on "The Wounded Wolf," which statement describes one of Roko's character traits?
A. He has little courage.
B. He is determined to survive.
C. He is angry with other wolves.
D. He can find food easily.

____ 14. Which statement is the *best* description of Roko's conflict in "The Wounded Wolf"?
A. It is an internal conflict involving a difficult decision he must make.
B. It is an external conflict involving his competition to be leader of the pack.
C. It is an external conflict involving his being lost in the wilderness.
D. It is an external conflict involving his being followed by other animals.

____ 15. What happens at the climax of "The Wounded Wolf"?
A. The wounded wolf wags his tail.
B. The wounded wolf is wounded while hunting with his pack.
C. The ravens and other animals inch closer to the wounded wolf.
D. The grizzly bear awakens from his sleep and joins the ravens.

____ 16. How do the other wolves in "The Wounded Wolf" discover that the wounded wolf is in trouble?
A. The wounded wolf whimpers softly, and they hear him.
B. The wolves hear the raven's message that something is dying.
C. The wolves hear the icy winds blowing on Toklat Ridge.
D. The bear is missing from his den, and they know he is hungry.

____ 17. When does the resolution of "The Wounded Wolf" occur?
A. when the wolf pack sings the "hunt's end" song
B. when the storm ends and the sun comes out
C. when the grizzly bear attacks the white fox
D. when Kiglo arrives with food for Roko

____ 18. Why does Kiglo put his mouth around Roko's nose in "The Wounded Wolf"?
A. to protect Roko from the ravens
B. to try to keep Roko warm and dry
C. to tell Roko that Roko will become the leader
D. to tell Roko that Kiglo is the wolves' leader

____ 19. At the end of "The Wounded Wolf," why does the wolf pack bark and howl?
A. They want to permanently frighten away the grizzly bear.
B. They have had a successful, satisfying hunt.
C. They want to choose Roko as their new leader.
D. They are pleased that Roko has regained his strength.

____ 20. Which statement is the *best* choice as a theme for "The Wounded Wolf"?
A. Winters are harsh in the Arctic region.
B. Animals rarely protect each other.
C. Ravens are fearful animals that should be avoided.
D. Courage and determination are tools for survival.

Essay

21. A character's traits help readers understand the character and his or her actions. A character acts in certain ways because of his or her motives. In "The Wounded Wolf," what do Roko's character traits tell you about him that help you understand his actions? What motives lead him to act in certain ways? Use details from the story to help you respond.

22. A character often learns a lesson by facing and solving the conflict in a story. What lesson or lessons do you think Roko might have learned from his experience in "The Wounded Wolf"? Use at least two details from the story to support your response.

23. **Thinking About the Big Question: Is conflict always bad?** In "The Wounded Wolf," Roko struggles to survive against the cold and his foes. In an essay, discuss whether Roko's conflict is a bad thing. Consider the positive and negative things that come from the conflict. Use examples from the story to support your ideas.

Vocabulary Warm-up Word Lists

Study these words from "The Tail." Then, apply your knowledge to the activities that follow.

Word List A

centuries [SEN chuh reez] *n.* time periods of one hundred years
   Three <u>centuries</u> equals three hundred years.

elderly [EL dur lee] *adj.* old
   My cat is fifteen years old; that's <u>elderly</u> for a cat!

entrance [EN trens] *n.* the way in to a place
   The <u>entrance</u> to the theater was crowded with people trying to buy tickets.

filthy [FIL thee] *adj.* very dirty
   That shirt is <u>filthy</u> with mud; you need to wash it.

hiking [HY king] *n.* an outdoor activity in which you walk in the countryside
   I don't enjoy <u>hiking</u> because I get out of breath when I take long walks.

overlooking [oh ver LOOK ing] *adv.* with a view of
   The window is <u>overlooking</u> the tracks so it is easy to see trains.

ridiculous [ri DIK yuh lus] *adj.* silly, almost unbelievable
   He can't eat ten hot dogs; that's <u>ridiculous</u>.

stoop [STOOP] *n.* a set of steps in front of a building
   It's hot inside; let's go sit on the <u>stoop</u> outside the door where it's cooler.

Word List B

annual [AN yoo uhl] *adj.* happening one time each year
   June is the month for our <u>annual</u> end-of-the-year picnic.

blackmail [BLAK mayl] *v.* to threaten a person to make them do what you want
   Go ahead and tell Mom that I was late; you can't <u>blackmail</u> me into doing your chores.

dimples [DIM puhlz] *n.* tiny hollow places on a person's cheek
   You can only see her <u>dimples</u> when she smiles.

monstrous [MAHN struhs] *adj.* horrible and scary looking
   When Tracy put on her Frankenstein costume she really looked <u>monstrous</u>.

obedience [oh BEE dee ens] *n.* doing what you are told to do
   <u>Obedience</u> is important in class; always do what your teacher tells you to do.

responsibilities [ri spahn suh BIL i teez] *n.* things you have a duty to do
   My after-dinner <u>responsibilities</u> include clearing the table and doing the dishes.

spasm [SPAZ uhm] *n.* a burst of emotion or activity, such as fear or laughter
   When the cake went down the wrong way, it caused me to have a coughing <u>spasm</u>.

torment [TAWR ment] *v.* to bother or cause suffering
   My sore throat hurts when I laugh, so don't <u>torment</u> me by telling me jokes.

Name _____ Date _____

"The Tail" by Joyce Hansen
Vocabulary Warm-up Exercises

Exercise A *Fill in each blank in the paragraph below with an appropriate word from Word List A. Use each word only once.*

I love [1] _____ in the woods. When we stay in the city, however, I enjoy

sitting on the [2] _____ in front of the [3] _____ to our

house. From the steps [4] _____ the street, I can see everything that

goes on. I clean them off before sitting down; they get [5] _____ with dirt.

No sooner do I sit down than a man wearing a [6] _____ elephant costume

walks by. Is it Halloween? Then, an [7] _____ lady, at least 90 years old,

rides by on a skateboard. I think I could sit here for [8] _____ without

ever getting bored!

Exercise B *Decide whether each statement below is true or false. Circle T or F. Then, explain your answers.*

1. It is an act of friendship to *blackmail* someone.
   T / F _____

2. Breaking a rule is an example of *obedience*.
   T / F _____

3. Most kittens look *monstrous*.
   T / F _____

4. Putting out fires and saving lives are two of a fireman's *responsibilities*.
   T / F _____

5. If you give a hungry person food, you *torment* that person.
   T / F _____

6. A really funny joke can cause you to have a *spasm* of laughter.
   T / F _____

7. *Dimples* are found on a person's face.
   T / F _____

8. An *annual* event happens twice a year.
   T / F _____

"The Tail" by Joyce Hansen
Reading Warm-up A

Read the following passage. Pay special attention to the underlined words. Then, read it again, and complete the activities. Use a separate sheet of paper for your written answers.

Today, Manhattan is the busy center of New York City, one of the least "natural" places in the world. It is covered with concrete, steel, and cement. Cars and trucks jam the streets. Skyscrapers fill the air. However, some <u>centuries</u> ago—just a few hundred years—Manhattan was completely different. Crossing the island didn't mean getting into a taxi or taking the train. Instead, it meant <u>hiking</u> through the woods. The island was covered with trees, not buildings. Deer and foxes roamed through the forests.

Back in the early seventeenth century, the Dutch had just settled on the island. They had bought it for a <u>ridiculous</u> price, paying about $25 in goods to the Native Americans who lived there. They had just built a small city at Manhattan's southern tip. The city grew and grew. Over time, it took over the whole island and beyond.

In today's Manhattan, sitting on the <u>stoop</u> of a building is a lot easier than taking a walk in the woods. Still, there are a few places left where trees outnumber the buildings. One of them is Fort Tryon Park. You'll find it on the island's northern tip, <u>overlooking</u> a highway. In the park, you'll find the Cloisters, a famous museum. You'll find playgrounds filled with kids and benches near the <u>entrance</u>, where <u>elderly</u> people can relax and enjoy good weather. You will also find lots of green spaces filled with trees and birds. If you ignore the sounds of the highway below, you may be able to imagine how Manhattan used to be. The park is beautiful. Though some years ago it was <u>filthy</u>, the city has been hard at work. Employees of the parks department have been working to keep it clean and garbage-free.

1. Underline the words that tell you what <u>centuries</u> means. Then tell if you were alive *centuries* ago.

2. Circle the words that tell you where <u>hiking</u> is performed. Then tell what *hiking* means.

3. Circle the words that tell what the <u>ridiculous</u> price was. Then tell why that price might seem *ridiculous*.

4. Underline the words that tell what a <u>stoop</u> is part of. Then tell what *stoop* means.

5. Circle the words that tell what the park is <u>overlooking</u>. Then tell what your classroom window is *overlooking*.

6. Underline the words that tell what you can find by the <u>entrance</u> to the park. Then tell what *entrance* means.

7. Circle the words that tell what <u>elderly</u> people do in the park. Then tell what *elderly* means.

8. Underline the nearby words that mean the opposite of <u>filthy</u>. Then tell what *filthy* means.

"The Tail" by Joyce Hansen
Reading Warm-up B

Read the following passage. Pay special attention to the underlined words. Then, read it again, and complete the activities. Use a separate sheet of paper for your written answers.

"These are your <u>responsibilities</u>," said my mother, looking sternly at my sister Rebecca and me. "First, the two of you must clean all your old stuff out of the attic. Then, you will help your father and me in the basement. Finally, the two of you will bring all the stuff over to the thrift shop."

It was our <u>annual</u> spring-cleaning Sunday. That meant a full day of nonstop chores: cleaning, sweeping, sorting, and organizing. Rebecca and I knew that it was hopeless to object. Any lack of <u>obedience</u> would result in a week without dessert, or worse, permanent grounding. Nobody fooled around on spring-cleaning Sunday.

The only pleasure I had was the knowledge that the work would <u>torment</u> Rebecca more than it would me. She hates getting her hands dirty, let alone her precious face. Dirt might spoil those cute little <u>dimples</u> she was so proud of. Why would anyone be proud of little dents in her face? I'll never understand Rebecca.

We began in the attic. Actually it wasn't as terrible as I had feared. Apparently, we had gotten rid of most of the old junk during last year's spring-cleaning event. We collected some bags of old clothes, swept out some cobwebs, and dusted the furniture. Rebecca had one <u>spasm</u> of fear when she thought she had broken a nail. Aside from that, she didn't seem to mind her tasks.

Neither of us, however, was looking forward to working in the basement. The basement was petrifying, filled with <u>monstrous</u> shadows and creepy dark corners. When I was younger, Rebecca used to <u>blackmail</u> me with the basement. She would threaten to lock me in there if I didn't obey her commands. Surprisingly, by the time we got downstairs, our parents were already finishing up. One quick drive to the thrift shop and this year's spring cleaning would be over.

1. Underline the sentences that tell what the girls' **responsibilities** are. Then, write a sentence naming one of your **responsibilities**.

2. Circle the words that tell what the **annual** event is. Then tell how often this family does this event.

3. Circle the words that tell what will happen if the sisters don't show **obedience**. Then tell what **obedience** means.

4. Write a sentence telling why the work would **torment** Rebecca.

5. Circle the nearby words that tell in what part of the body **dimples** are found. Then tell what **dimples** are.

6. Underline the word that tells what type of **spasm** Rebecca had. Then tell what **spasm** means.

7. Underline the words that tell what **monstrous** things are found in the basement. Then write a sentence telling what else might appear **monstrous** to people.

8. Underline the sentence that tells how Rebecca used to **blackmail** her sister. Then tell what **blackmail** means.

"The Tail" by Joyce Hansen

Writing About the Big Question

Is conflict always bad?

Big Question Vocabulary

argue	battle	challenge	compete	conclude
convince	defend	game	issue	lose
negotiate	oppose	resolve	survival	win

A. *Use one or more words from the list above to complete each sentence.*

1. One way to entertain a child is to play a _____ with him or her.

2. Parents and children are likely to _____ with each other.

3. It often seems important to both sides to _____ an argument.

4. Sometimes it is possible to _____ an outcome that makes everyone happy.

B. *Respond to each item with a complete sentence.*

1. Describe two arguments you have had with someone in your family.

   _____

   _____

2. Explain how you managed to negotiate an agreement in one of the arguments you had. Use at least two of the Big Question vocabulary words.

   _____

   _____

C. *Complete this sentence. Then, write a brief paragraph in which you connect this sentence to the Big Question.*

Conflicts between kids and their parents can have positive outcomes when

_____

_____

_____

_____

_____

"The Tail" by Joyce Hansen
Reading: Use Details to Make Inferences

When you **make inferences,** you make logical assumptions about something that is not directly stated in the text. To make inferences, use the **details** that the author provides.

Details in the text + What you know = Inference

Look at the details, shown in italics, in the following sentence.

Arnie *ran* to the mailbox *as fast as he could* to see if Jim's letter had *finally* arrived.

You can make two inferences from the details and from what you know.

- From *finally,* you can infer that Arnie has been waiting to hear from Jim.
- Because Arnie runs fast, you can infer that he is eager to get the letter.

DIRECTIONS: *As you read "The Tail," find details that help you make three inferences. Write two details and your logical inference in each row of boxes below.*

A.

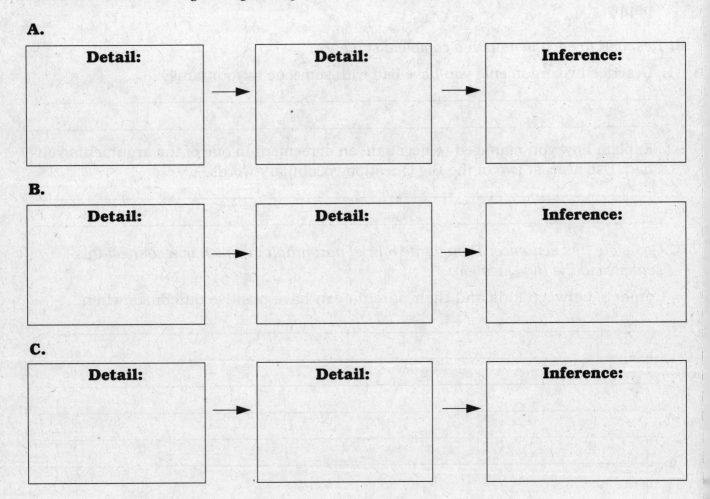

| Detail: | Detail: | Inference: |

B.

| Detail: | Detail: | Inference: |

C.

| Detail: | Detail: | Inference: |

Name _____ Date _____

Literary Analysis: Characterization

Characterization is the way writers develop and reveal information about characters.

- **Direct characterization:** a writer makes direct statements about a character.
- **Indirect characterization:** a writer suggests information through a character's thoughts, words, and actions as well as what other characters say and think about the character.

In this passage from "The Tail," the writer uses Tasha's thoughts to give an indirect characterization that Junior is cute, but very troublesome.

> Junior held her hand and stared up at her with an innocent look in his bright brown eyes, which everyone thought were so cute. Dimples decorated his round cheeks as he smiled and nodded at me every time Ma gave me an order. I knew he was just waiting for her to leave so he could torment me.

DIRECTIONS: *In each part of the pyramid below, jot down direct statements as well as Tasha's and other characters' words, thoughts, and actions that tell about Tasha in "The Tail."*

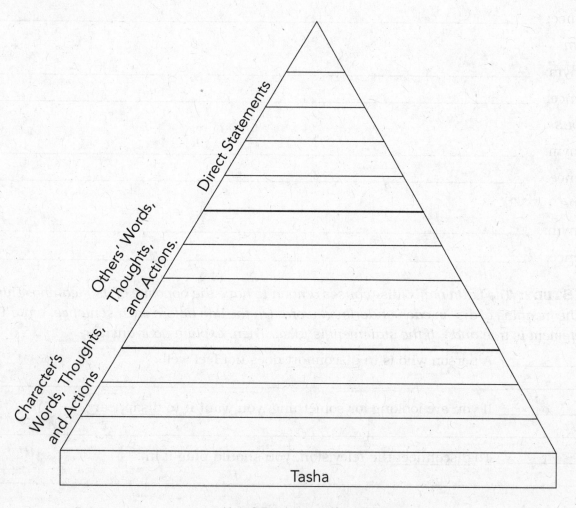

Name _____ Date _____

"The Tail" by Joyce Hansen
Vocabulary Builder

Word List

anxious   gnawing   mauled   routine   spasm   vow

A. DIRECTIONS: *Synonyms are words that are similar in meaning. Find and write a synonym for each vocabulary word. Then, use each synonym in a sentence that makes the meaning of the word clear. The first one has been done for you.*

1. *gnawing*

   Synonym: <u>chewing</u>

   Sentence: Rodents have been chewing on the bark of this tree.

2. *mauled*

   Synonym: _____

   Sentence: _____

3. *vow*

   Synonym: _____

   Sentence: _____

4. *spasm*

   Synonym: _____

   Sentence: _____

5. *anxious*

   Synonym: _____

   Sentence: _____

6. *routine*

   Synonym: _____

   Sentence: _____

B. WORD STUDY: *The Latin prefix* dis- *causes a noun to have the opposite of its meaning. Think about the meaning of* dis- *in each underlined word. On the line before each sentence, write* T *if the statement is true and* F *if the statement is false. Then, explain your answer.*

1. _____ A person who is in <u>discomfort</u> does not feel well.

   _____

2. _____ If you are looking for something, you want it to <u>disappear.</u>

   _____

3. _____ To <u>disconnect</u> the television, you should plug it in.

   _____

Name _____ Date _____

"The Tail" by Joyce Hansen
Enrichment: The Cloisters

In "The Tail," Tasha offers to take Junior to the Cloisters Museum. This Manhattan museum overlooks the Hudson River. It contains medieval and Renaissance art.

DIRECTIONS: *Use library or Internet resources to find out more about the Cloisters. Information can also be found in a New York City guidebook or a book about medieval art or museums. Focus on the Cloisters' famous set of woven tapestries titled* The Hunt of the Unicorn. *On the lines below, write three facts about the Cloisters and three facts about the Unicorn Tapestries. Then, use these facts to write two or three paragraphs telling what Tasha and Junior might experience in a visit to the Cloisters.*

Facts About the Cloisters

1. _____

2. _____

3. _____

Facts About the Unicorn Tapestries

1. _____

2. _____

3. _____

_____

_____

_____

_____

_____

_____

_____

_____

_____

_____

_____

_____

"The Tail" by Joyce Hansen

Open-Book Test

Short Answer *Write your responses to the questions in this section on the lines provided.*

1. In "The Tail," you can infer that Junior has no playmates of his own nearby. What details does the narrator give you near the beginning of story that allow you to infer this?

    _____

    _____

2. Explain what the following passage from "The Tail" tells about Junior.

    Dimples decorated his round cheeks as he smiled and nodded at me every time Ma gave me an order. I knew he was just waiting for her to leave so he could torment me.

    _____

    _____

3. Think about what you learn about Ma in the first two pages of "The Tail." Describe Ma's character. Use details from the story.

    _____

    _____

    _____

    _____

4. When Junior is lost in "The Tail," Tasha feels that a part of her is gone. Think about what she is feeling at the time. Explain what you can infer, or assume, about her feelings for her brother.

    _____

    _____

5. In "The Tail," Tasha sends Naomi away so she will not be mauled by the dog. What would a toy mouse look like after being mauled by a cat? Explain your answer.

    _____

    _____

    _____

6. In "The Tail," why does Tasha continue to climb up the steps in the park even though she sees a big brown and gray monstrous thing? Support your answer with details from the story.

    _____

    _____

    _____

7. Think about the trick that Junior plays on his sister in "The Tail." How would you describe his personality? Use details from the story to support your answer.

_____

_____

8. Describe the relationship between Tasha and Junior in "The Tail." Use examples from the story to support your answer.

_____

_____

_____

9. The author of "The Tail" uses both direct and indirect characterization. The first column of the chart contains an example of characterization from the story. In the second column, tell if the sentence is an example of direct or indirect characterization. Then, in the last column, explain what the sentence reveals about Junior.

Characterization	What Kind?	What Is Revealed?
"I'm going to tell Ma you didn't stay on the block."		
He wasn't as pesty as he used to be, because now he had Thunder.		

10. In "The Tail," Junior follows Tasha "like a tail." At the end of the story, Tasha says that you never miss a tail until you almost lose it. Explain what she has learned about her feelings for her brother.

_____

_____

Essay

Write an extended response to the question of your choice or to the question or questions your teacher assigns you.

11. Tasha changes in "The Tail." Think about her feelings toward Junior at the beginning of the story. Then, think about how they are different at the end of the story. In an essay, explain how and why she changes. Use examples from the story to support your ideas.

12. The author of "The Tail" uses indirect characterization to develop the character of Tasha. The reader learns about her through her thoughts, words, and actions. In an essay, explain what you learn about Tasha, focusing on the traits that make up her character.

13. Imagine "The Tail" rewritten from Junior's point of view. How would this affect what the reader knows about the characters? In an essay, explain how the story would change and whether you think it would work as well.

14. **Thinking About the Big Question: Is conflict always bad?** In "The Tail," Tasha has the responsibility of taking care of a younger brother when she wants to be carefree for the summer. In an essay, discuss whether this conflict is bad or good for Tasha. Consider what problems the conflict causes, how she deals with them, and what she learns from them. Support your ideas with details from the story.

Oral Response

15. Go back to question 4, 6, 7, or 8 or to the question your teacher assigns to you. Take a few minutes to expand your answer and prepare an oral response. Find additional details in "The Tail" that will support your points. If necessary, make notes to guide your response.

"The Tail" by Joyce Hansen
Selection Test A

Critical Reading *Identify the letter of the choice that best answers the question.*

____ 1. Why does Tasha, the narrator in "The Tail," think that her summer is ruined?
  A. She has to take summer classes.
  B. She has to get a summer job.
  C. Her best friend is moving away.
  D. She has to take care of her little brother.

____ 2. Which statement from "The Tail" is the *best* example of indirect characterization?
  A. Mama went to work that next morning.
  B. I knew he was just waiting for her to leave so he could torment me.
  C. I went into the kitchen to start cleaning, when the downstairs bell rang.
  D. I knew that it was Naomi, ready to start our big, fun summer.

____ 3. Which detail from "The Tail" helps you infer that Junior is lonely?
  A. Junior doesn't have a regular babysitter.
  B. Tasha says there are no other kids his age on the block.
  C. Junior acts very sweet and innocent around his mother.
  D. He likes to play a game of checkers.

____ 4. In "The Tail," what does Naomi, Tasha's friend, think of Junior?
  A. She thinks he is cute.
  B. She doesn't like him.
  C. She thinks he is a pest.
  D. She thinks he acts like a baby.

____ 5. Why are Tasha and Naomi scared to go into the woods in the park?
  A. It is evening, and it is getting dark outside.
  B. There is a rumor about wild dogs in the park.
  C. They are afraid of the caves.
  D. They are afraid of getting lost.

____ 6. Where is Junior hiding?
  A. in the park
  B. in a tree
  C. at the apartment
  D. at the Cloisters

_____ 7. Which word *best* describes how Junior behaves in "The Tail"?

A. innocent

B. sweet

C. troublesome

D. cruel

_____ 8. Which sentence from "The Tail" is the *best* example of direct characterization of Junior?

A. He wasn't as pesty as he used to be, because now he had Thunder.

B. He grinned as she pinched his cheeks.

C. Junior clutched some comic books and his checkers game.

D. Suddenly, there was an unbelievable growl.

_____ 9. Which statement helps you infer that Tasha loves her brother?

A. She complains about him a lot.

B. She refuses to play checkers with him.

C. When he is lost, she feels that a part of her is gone.

D. She tells him to get lost when he embarrasses her.

_____ 10. What does Tasha mean when she says that you never miss a tail until you almost lose it?

A. A dog does not need a tail to be a good pet.

B. She didn't know how good a friend Naomi was until Junior was lost.

C. She didn't know how much she would miss her freedom.

D. She didn't realize how she felt about her brother until he was missing.

_____ 11. What lesson does Tasha learn in "The Tail"?

A. Responsibility can be fun.

B. She truly loves her brother.

C. She should always tell the truth.

D. Friends are more important than family.

Vocabulary and Grammar

_____ 12. When Naomi first sees the dog, she has a spasm of laughter. Which statement *best* describes her laugh?

A. It is a chuckle.

B. It is musical.

C. It is silent

D. It is a burst.

___ 13. When Tasha made a vow to watch her brother, what did she do?

   A. She promised to watch him.

   B. She lied to her mother.

   C. She made a joke about Junior.

   D. She wrote down directions.

___ 14. Which possessive pronoun correctly completes this sentence?

   Tasha and Junior never told _____ mother what happened.

   A. mine

   B. ours

   C. their

   D. theirs

___ 15. In which sentence is the personal pronoun *I* used correctly?

   A. Dad and I went shopping for school supplies.

   B. The teacher spoke to Jamie and I about our project.

   C. This jump rope is I.

   D. Tomas played catch with I in the park.

Essay

16. In "The Tail," the author uses indirect characterization to tell the reader about Tasha. In an essay, describe Tasha's character. Explain what you learn about her through her thoughts, statements, and actions.

17. In "The Tail," Tasha changes in her feelings and actions toward her brother, Junior. Write an essay explaining how and why she changes. Use details from the story to support your explanation.

18. **Thinking About the Big Question: Is conflict always bad?** In "The Tail," Tasha has to take care of her younger brother when all she wants is to be free for the summer. In an essay, discuss whether this conflict is bad or good for Tasha. Consider what problems she faces and what she learns from them. Support your ideas with details from the story.

"The Tail" by Joyce Hansen
Selection Test B

Critical Reading *Identify the letter of the choice that best completes the statement or answers the question.*

____ 1. When the narrator says that there are no kids Junior's age on the block, you can infer that
A. other kids don't like Junior.   C. Tasha doesn't like younger kids.
B. Junior has no one to play with.   D. Tasha likes to play with Junior.

____ 2. What does this passage from "The Tail" tell you about Junior?
    Dimples decorated his round cheeks as he smiled and nodded at me every time Ma
    gave me an order. I knew he was just waiting for her to leave so he could torment me.
A. Junior loves Tasha very much.
B. Junior can be very troublesome.
C. Junior likes to follow orders.
D. Junior will do just what he is told.

____ 3. What inference can you make from this passage in "The Tail"?
    "Tasha," my ma broke into my happy thoughts, "your father and I decided that you're
old enough now to take on certain responsibilities."
    My heart came to a sudden halt. "Responsibilities?"
A. Tasha is looking forward to her new responsibilities.
B. Tasha has just had a heart attack and needs to go to the hospital.
C. Tasha doesn't know what the word "responsibilities" means.
D. Tasha doesn't want any new responsibilities.

____ 4. Ma's many orders to Tasha are an indirect characterization that reveals which fact about the mother?
A. She is mean and critical.   C. She is strict but caring.
B. She is kind and gentle.   D. She doesn't trust Tasha at all.

____ 5. You can infer that when Tasha takes Junior to the park, she is hoping that
A. Junior will not tell their mother.
B. Junior will jump rope with the girls.
C. she will lose him in the park.
D. Junior will find a friend.

____ 6. Tasha breaks one of her mother's rules when she
A. washes the dishes.   C. plays on the block.
B. leaves the block.   D. helps Junior vacuum.

____ 7. In the park, Tasha gets very angry with Junior when he
A. trips her as she is jumping rope.
B. threatens to tell their mother about getting lost.
C. begs repeatedly to play with the older kids.
D. runs back to the apartment to hide.

___ 8. What can you infer about Tasha's feelings for her brother from this passage in "The Tail"?

"... please let me find him. I will play any kind of game he wants. I'll never yell at him again."

A. Tasha resents her brother.   C. Tasha loves her brother deeply.

B. Tasha is afraid of her brother.   D. Tasha is annoyed by her brother.

___ 9. What can you infer from this passage in "The Tail"?

We heard a rustling in the bushes and grabbed each other. "Probably just a bird," I said, trying to sound brave.

A. Tasha is frightened.   C. Junior is hiding in the bushes.

B. Tasha is not afraid.   D. Naomi is more scared than Tasha.

___ 10. The big brown and gray shape that frightens Tasha is

A. a wild dog.   C. a lost child.

B. a dead tree trunk.   D. a flock of birds.

___ 11. Which sentence *best* expresses the relationship between Tasha and Junior?

A. They are best friends.

B. They resent each other.

C. They put up with each other to keep peace in their family.

D. They fight and tease each other, but they are very close.

___ 12. Which word *best* describes the personality of Junior in "The Tail"?

A. unkind   C. intellectual

B. mischievous   D. thoughtful

___ 13. Which lesson does Tasha learn from her experiences in "The Tail"?

A. If you don't succeed at first, you must try again.

B. A true friend sticks with you through thick and thin.

C. Losing someone can teach you the depth of your love for that person.

D. Danger can bring out the best in people.

Vocabulary and Grammar

___ 14. When a cat has *mauled* a toy mouse, it has

A. played gently with it.   C. hidden it.

B. torn it up.   D. lost it.

___ 15. Which sentence is *best* completed with the word *refer*?

A. Carla had to _____ the book to the library because it was overdue.

B. The bell sounded so that students would _____ to their classrooms.

C. A good speaker will _____ to his notes to be sure his facts are correct.

D. I could _____ that the girl was scared by the way she trembled.

___ 16. Which possessive pronoun best completes this sentence?

The girls won _____ first jump-rope contest.

A. his   C. theirs

B. mine   D. their

____ **17.** Which sentence contains a personal pronoun?
   A. She was very good at jumping rope.
   B. Tasha looked for Junior for hours.
   C. Mother gave Tasha specific instructions.
   D. Naomi helped Tasha look for Junior.

Essay

18. In "The Tail," the writer uses indirect characterization of thoughts, words, actions, and what other characters say and think to develop the character of Tasha. Write an essay to tell what you learned about Tasha. Focus your essay on the traits and qualities that make up this character.

19. In some important ways, Tasha has become a different person by the end of "The Tail." In an essay, describe how she has changed. What lessons did she learn? How have the lessons changed her? Use details from the story to support your claims.

20. Thinking About the Big Question: Is conflict always bad? In "The Tail," Tasha has the responsibility of taking care of a younger brother when she wants to be carefree for the summer. In an essay, discuss whether this conflict is bad or good for Tasha. Consider the problems the conflict causes, how she deals with them, and what she learns from them. Support your ideas with details from the story.

Vocabulary Warm-up Word Lists

Study these words from "Dragon, Dragon." Then, complete the activities that follow.

Word List A

labored [LAY berd] *v.* worked hard
  Ahmed <u>labored</u> for hours on the decorations; now he needs a rest.

lair [LAIR] *n.* home or resting place for a person or animal
  Zoo workers tried to make the bear's cage like its <u>lair</u> in the wild.

maidens [MAY duhnz] *n.* young women
  In fairy tales, young unmarried women are often called <u>maidens</u>.

merely [MEER lee] *adv.* only, just
  He was <u>merely</u> joking when he said that; he didn't want to hurt anyone's feelings.

novels [NAHV uhlz] *n.* books that tell a story about made-up people and events
  The teacher assigned the students <u>novels</u>, which took longer to read than short stories.

poems [POH uhmz] *n.* pieces of writing that often include rhythm and rhyme
  I like the way <u>poems</u> sound, but I don't always understand their meanings.

slicing [SLY sing] *v.* cutting
  <u>Slicing</u> bread is easy with this new, sharp knife.

strolled [STROHLD] *v.* walked in a slow, relaxed way
  June and Jim weren't in a hurry as they <u>strolled</u> through the park.

Word List B

annoyed [uh NOYD] *v.* feeling bothered
  Elvin hated to wait and was <u>annoyed</u> that the bus was late.

decent [DEE sent] *adj.* honest and good
  He's a very <u>decent</u> boy, and you can trust him.

eldest [EL dist] *adj.* oldest person in a group
  My <u>eldest</u> daughter is eleven; my youngest daughter is six.

impression [im PRESH uhn] *n.* effect something has on people, or feeling it gives
  The song made a big <u>impression</u> on those who heard it; everyone felt sad.

patience [PAY shens] *n.* the ability to wait calmly without getting upset
  Show some <u>patience</u>; wait until we get home to open the present.

prefer [pree FER] *v.* like one thing more than another
  I <u>prefer</u> chocolate, but if I really have to, I'll eat the vanilla cone.

slay [SLAY] *v.* kill
  In the horror movie, the hero used a special weapon to <u>slay</u> the monsters.

tempted [TEMP tid] *v.* to consider doing something that might not be smart or good.
  I was <u>tempted</u> to eat all the cookies myself, instead of bringing them to the party.

"Dragon, Dragon" by John Gardner
Vocabulary Warm-up Exercises

Exercise A *Fill in each blank in the paragraph below with an appropriate word from Word List A. Use each word only once.*

Ray loves reading [1] _____, but he also likes the rhythm and the rhyme of great [2] _____. He thinks of the porch as his own special place, his [3] _____ for resting and reading. He [4] _____ hard to make it that way. First, he put up a hammock. Then, he made a sign for his sisters that said, "NO [5] _____ allowed!" They got angry, pulling it down and [6] _____ it in half. Still, they [7] _____ away and didn't come back. Ray didn't mean to be nasty; he [8] _____ needed a quiet place to read.

Exercise B *Write a complete sentence to respond to each item below. For each one, use a word from Word List B to replace the underlined word or phrase without changing its meaning.*

1. Who is the <u>oldest</u> person who lives in your house?

   _____

2. Name a book or story in which someone has to <u>kill</u> a monster.

   _____

3. Describe a time when you had to show <u>an ability to wait without getting upset</u>.

   _____

4. Name a movie you saw that had a big <u>effect</u> on you.

   _____

5. Describe the last time you were <u>feeling bothered</u> and explain why.

   _____

6. Will people still like you if you don't act in a <u>good and honest</u> way?

   _____

7. Which do you <u>like more than the other</u>, pizza or chicken?

   _____

8. What made the mouse <u>consider</u> walking into the mousetrap?

   _____

Name _____   Date _____

Read the following passage. Pay special attention to the underlined words. Then, read it again, and complete the activities. Use a separate sheet of paper for your written answers.

You'll read about dragons in stories and longer works like <u>novels</u>. You'll watch dragons in cartoons, coming out of their homes to breathe fire. By the way, a dragon's home is usually called a <u>lair</u>. In movies, you'll see princes and warriors <u>slicing</u> off dragons' heads, but you'll hardly ever see one in real life. In fact, you'll never see one! That's because dragons don't really exist. They are <u>merely</u> make-believe. In ancient times, people believed in dragons, but none have ever been found.

Dragons aren't the only make-believe creatures around. Many other creatures besides dragons live only in legends and fairy tales. One good example is the mermaid. Mermaids are <u>maidens</u> of the sea. They are half-women and half-fish. A mermaid has a woman's head and body but a fish tail in place of legs. Mermaids are usually beautiful. There are many stories in which sailors chasing mermaids walk off their boats and drown in the sea.

One especially famous mermaid tale is "The Little Mermaid." In it, a mermaid gives up her life at sea. She goes to live on land with a prince. Many people have <u>labored</u> hard to find a real mermaid, but without any luck. Half-women, half-fish creatures simply don't exist.

Another famous make-believe creature is the unicorn. A unicorn is an animal that looks something like a horse. It is usually colored white and thought to be very beautiful. What makes a unicorn special is its horn. In stories, <u>poems</u>, and pictures, it always has a single long horn sticking out of its forehead. It often appears in paintings from the Middle Ages. Like the dragon, the unicorn was thought to be real by people of earlier times. However, no unicorn has ever <u>strolled</u> on Earth.

1. Underline the word that names texts that are shorter than <u>novels</u>. Then tell what *novels* are.

2. Underline the words that explain what a <u>lair</u> is.

3. Circle the words that tell what princes and warriors are <u>slicing</u> off. Then tell what *slicing* means.

4. Rewrite the sentence using the word <u>merely</u>, replacing *merely* with a synonym.

5. Underline the word that tells who are <u>maidens</u> of the sea. Then tell what *maidens* means.

6. Circle the words that tell what people have <u>labored</u> hard to do. Then write a sentence telling about something you *labored* to do.

7. Underline the words that tell how unicorns are described in <u>poems</u>. What do you like best about *poems*?

8. Circle the words that tell what has never <u>strolled</u> the earth. Then tell what *strolled* means.

"Dragon, Dragon" by John Gardner
Reading Warm-up B

Read the following passage. Pay special attention to the underlined words. Then, read it again, and complete the activities. Use a separate sheet of paper for your written answers.

When the king heard that a dragon had been seen in the fields across the river, he was <u>tempted</u> to send his knights to <u>slay</u> it. In general, dragons produced problems in the kingdom. They burned down whole fields with their fiery breath, devoured helpless villagers, and created all sorts of difficulties.

Instead of sending out the knights, however, the king called his sons and daughters together for a meeting. He relied on the advice of his children for making big decisions, and his <u>eldest</u> son spoke first.

"I think we should kill it," said Harry. "Dragons make a terrible <u>impression</u> on the villagers. It makes them believe that we are not providing for their safety." Most of the others nodded their head in agreement. Then, Attila, the youngest son, spoke up.

"I'd <u>prefer</u> to handle this in a different way," he said. "We always try to kill the dragons, and although we usually succeed, it is often exceedingly costly. We lose ten or twelve knights for every dragon that we destroy. It seems to me that dragons are probably <u>decent</u> creatures, all in all. The fires are probably accidental. It's not easy having flaming breath. As for eating the villagers, well, it's probably a question of hunger."

Harry was <u>annoyed</u> that his younger brother didn't agree with his suggestion. The king, however, seemed interested.

"So how do you propose we handle these 'decent' creatures?" asked the King.

"By feeding them," answered Attila. "I will try to find some large amounts of dragon food. We will deliver it to the dragon and see if he leaves us alone."

"Very well," said the King. "We will show some <u>patience</u> with this dragon before killing it. Let's give your idea the opportunity to work. If the dragon doesn't eat any villagers, we will let him live."

1. Underline the words that tell what the king was <u>tempted</u> to do. Then write a sentence using the word *tempted*.

2. Write a sentence telling whom the knights would <u>slay</u>.

3. Does the king have any children older than the <u>eldest</u> son? Explain.

4. Circle the word that tells what kind of <u>impression</u> the dragon makes. Then describe something that made a big *impression* on you.

5. Tell what Attila would <u>prefer</u> *not* to do.

6. Rewrite the sentence using a replacement word or phrase for <u>decent</u>.

7. Underline the words that tell why Harry was <u>annoyed</u>. Then tell what *annoyed* means.

8. Circle the words that tell with whom the king will show <u>patience</u>. Then tell what *patience* means.

"Dragon, Dragon" by John Gardner
Writing About the Big Question

Is conflict always bad?

Big Question Vocabulary

argue	battle	challenge	compete	conclude
convince	defend	game	issue	lose
negotiate	oppose	resolve	survival	win

A. *Use one or more words from the list above to complete each sentence.*

1. In fairy tales, a knight or king often has to _____ his land against an enemy.

2. The hero must _____ the enemy to a fight.

3. The hero and the enemy meet in a terrible _____ that only one can _____.

4. The one to _____ the fight is not usually the hero.

B. *Respond to each item with a complete sentence.*

1. Describe a time when you had to challenge someone or defend someone.

   _____

   _____

2. Explain what the outcome of the conflict was and what you learned from it. Use at least two of the Big Question vocabulary words in your response.

   _____

   _____

C. *Complete this sentence. Then, write a brief paragraph in which you connect this sentence to the Big Question.*

If there was someone terrorizing my neighborhood, I would _____

_____

_____

_____

_____

Name _____ Date _____

Reading: Use Details to Make Inferences

When you **make inferences,** you make logical assumptions about something that is not directly stated in the text. To make inferences, use the **details** that the author provides.

Details in the text + What you know = Inference

Look at the details, shown in italics, in this sentence:

Irene *dragged her feet* as she *slowly walked* to the bus that would take her home from summer camp.

You can make two inferences from the details and from what you know.

- From *dragged her feet,* you can infer that Irene is reluctant to leave camp.
- Because Irene walked slowly, you can infer that she is not eager to leave camp.

DIRECTIONS: *As you read "Dragon, Dragon," find details that help you make three inferences. Write two details and your logical inference in each row of boxes below.*

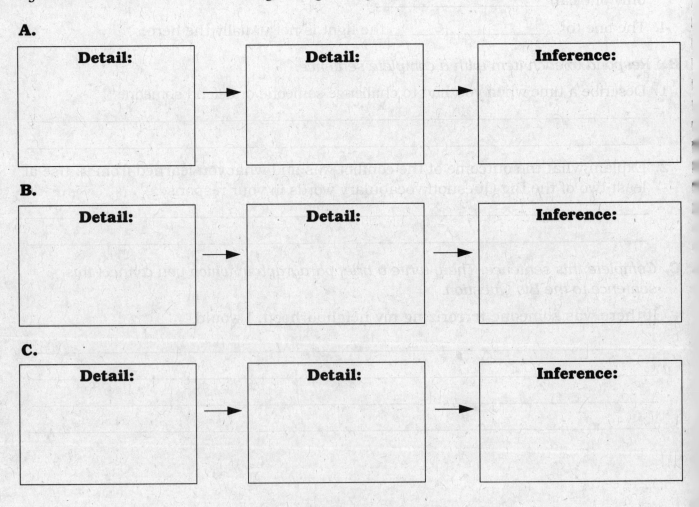

A.

| Detail: | → | Detail: | → | Inference: |

B.

| Detail: | → | Detail: | → | Inference: |

C.

| Detail: | → | Detail: | → | Inference: |

Name _____ Date _____

Literary Analysis: Characterization

Characterization is the way writers develop and reveal information about characters.

- **Direct characterization:** A writer makes direct statements about a character.
- **Indirect characterization:** A writer suggests information through a character's thoughts, words, and actions as well as what other characters say and think about the character.

In this passage from "Dragon, Dragon," the writer uses direct characterization to tell the reader that the cobbler is wise. He uses indirect characterization to tell the reader that the cobbler is humble.

> Now it happened that there lived in the kingdom a wise old cobbler who had a wife and three sons. The cobbler and his family came to the king's meeting and stood way in back by the door, for the cobbler had a feeling that since he was nobody important there had probably been some mistake, . . .

DIRECTIONS: *In each part of the pyramid below, jot down direct statements as well as the eldest son's and other characters' words, thoughts, and actions that tell about the cobbler's eldest son in "Dragon, Dragon."*

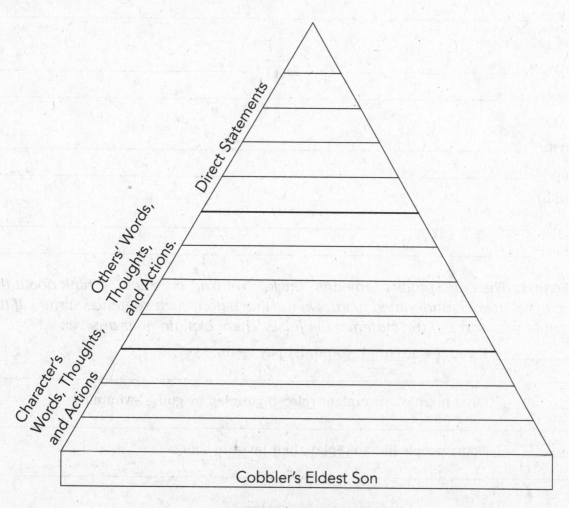

"Dragon, Dragon" by John Gardner

Vocabulary Builder

Word List

craned   enviously   plagued   ravaged   reflecting   tyrant

A. DIRECTIONS: *Synonyms* *are words that are similar in meaning. Find and write a synonym for each vocabulary word. Then, use each synonym in a sentence that makes the meaning of the word clear. The first one has been done for you.*

1. *plagued*

   Synonym: <u>tormented</u>

   Sentence: Clouds of locusts tormented the farmers and ate the crops.

2. *reflecting*

   Synonym: _____

   Sentence: _____

3. *ravaged*

   Synonym: _____

   Sentence: _____

4. *craned*

   Synonym: _____

   Sentence: _____

5. *tyrant*

   Synonym: _____

   Sentence: _____

6. *enviously*

   Synonym: _____

   Sentence: _____

B. WORD STUDY: *The Latin prefix* re- *means "back," "return," or "anew." Think about the meaning of* re- *in each underlined word. On the line before each sentence, write* T *if the statement is true and* F *if the statement is false. Then, explain your answer.*

1. _____ If you get a <u>refund</u>, you must pay again.

   _____

2. _____ On a hot day, you might <u>refresh</u> yourself by going swimming.

   _____

3. _____ Some people like to <u>replay</u> their favorite songs.

   _____

Unit 2 Resources: Short Stories
48

Name _____ Date _____

"Dragon, Dragon" by John Gardner
Enrichment: Fairy Tales

"Dragon, Dragon" follows a basic formula for a certain kind of fairy tale. A dragon or other monster threatens a kingdom, usually by killing people and destroying the land. No one can kill the monster or make it go away. The king offers a prize to a hero who can kill the dragon. Several would-be heroes try and fail until the true hero succeeds, often with the help of a magic charm or object. The hero claims his prize and lives happily ever after.

A. DIRECTIONS: *Refer back to "Dragon, Dragon" to answer the questions below.*

1. What kind of creature threatens the kingdom? _____

2. What prize does the king offer? _____

3. Who tries unsuccessfully to kill the monster? _____

4. Who is the hero? _____

5. What is the magic charm or object? _____

6. How does the fairy tale end? _____

B. DIRECTIONS: *Work with a partner to plan and tell an original fairy tale. Use the formula described above or your own variation. Begin by jotting down ideas on the lines below. On a separate sheet of paper, organize your story in an outline. Rehearse your original fairy tale with your partner, and then tell your story to another pair of students.*

_____

_____

_____

_____

_____

_____

_____

_____

_____

_____

_____

_____

_____

"The Tail" by Joyce Hansen
"Dragon, Dragon" by John Gardner
Integrated Language Skills: Grammar

Verbs

A **verb** is a word that expresses the action or condition of a person, place, or thing. No sentence is complete without a verb. The two main kinds of verbs are action verbs and linking verbs.

Action verbs express physical or mental action (*walk, sit, think*).

Panchito's family <u>picks</u> fruit for a living.

Linking verbs express a state of being. They tell what the subject of a sentence is or is like by linking the subject to a word that further describes or identifies it. The most common linking verb is a form of *be* (*is, am, are,* and so on).

The family <u>is</u> very poor.

Other linking verbs include *appear, become, seem, grow, look.*

A. PRACTICE: *Underline the verbs in the following sentences. Then, above each one, write A if it is an action verb and L if it is a linking verb.*

1. It was that time of year again.
2. When I opened the front door to the shack, I stopped.
3. No sooner had he said that than I felt sick to my stomach.
4. I knew he was sad.
5. I still felt a little dizzy when we took a break to eat lunch.

B. Writing Application: *Follow the directions below to write sentences about the specified topics.*

1. Use the verb *feels* in a sentence about Roberto.

   _____

2. Use the verb *struggle* in a sentence about working as a fruit picker.

   _____

3. Use the verb *reads* in a sentence about Panchito's experience at school.

   _____

4. Use the verb *seems* in a sentence about the weather during the picking season.

   _____

5. Use the verb *moves* in a sentence about Panchito's family.

   _____

Name _____ Date _____

"**The Tail**" by Joyce Hansen
"**Dragon, Dragon**" by John Gardner
Integrated Language Skills: Support for Writing a Help-Wanted Advertisement

DIRECTIONS: *Use this chart to help you write a help-wanted ad. On the chart, list the responsibilities of the job and the character traits, abilities, and knowledge the applicant should possess.*

Job Responsibilities	Character Traits	Abilities	Knowledge

Now, use the information from your chart to write a help-wanted ad.

"The Tail" by Joyce Hansen
"Dragon, Dragon" by John Gardner

Integrated Language Skills: Support for Extend Your Learning

Research: "The Tail"

Fill out a Venn diagram for two outdoor children's games. Label each circle with the name of one game. In the part of the circles that overlap, write details that the games share. In the parts of the circles that do not overlap, write details that are different for each game.

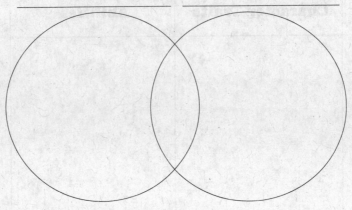

Research: "Dragon, Dragon"

Fill out a Venn diagram for two dragon tales from various cultures. Label each circle with a culture you have chosen. In the part of the circles that overlap, write characteristics about dragons that the cultures share. In the parts of the circles that do not overlap, write characteristics about dragons that are different in each culture.

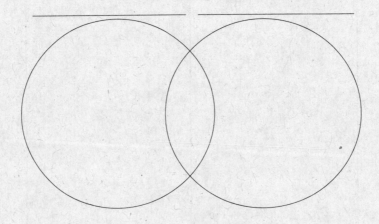

"Dragon, Dragon" by John Gardner

Open-Book Test

Short Answer *Write your responses to the questions in this section on the lines provided.*

1. What inference, or logical assumption, can you make about the Dragon in "Dragon, Dragon"? Use details from the first page.

    _____

    _____

2. Think about the qualities of a good wizard. In "Dragon, Dragon," the wizard turns the queen into a rosebush while practicing a spell. What does this tell you about his abilities?

    _____

    _____

3. In "Dragon, Dragon," the cobbler stays at the back during the meeting with the king. He asks what the reward is for slaying the dragon. What does his response to the king's offer tell you about the character of the cobbler?

    _____

    _____

4. Think about what happens to the two oldest sons in "Dragon, Dragon." What can you infer about how *not* to slay the dragon? Use details from the story to support your answer.

    _____

    _____

5. Think about why the older brothers in "Dragon, Dragon" do not succeed while their younger brother does. What lesson do they learn from the success of their younger brother?

    _____

    _____

6. In "Dragon, Dragon," the youngest son knows he is no match for the dragon. Yet, he goes off to slay the creature. What character traits does this action reveal? In each circle of the web, write one of these traits. Then, on the line, tell if these traits match what the narrator says about him.

    _____

    _____

7. Toward the end of "Dragon, Dragon," the dragon is reflecting that patience seldom goes unrewarded. What might the youngest son be reflecting at that same moment?

_____

_____

_____

8. In "Dragon, Dragon," the dragon craned his neck. If a short man craned his neck at a parade, what was he probably trying to do? Explain.

_____

_____

_____

9. When the dragon laughs at the poem in "Dragon, Dragon," why does the youngest son become angry? Explain your answer.

_____

_____

_____

10. In "Dragon, Dragon," what character trait of the Dragon's leads to his defeat? Use details from the story to support your answer.

_____

_____

_____

Essay

Write an extended response to the question of your choice or to the question or questions your teacher assigns you.

11. The author of "Dragon, Dragon" uses humor in his fairy tale. Think about three events in the story that are funny. In an essay, discuss why the events are funny and how they differ from those in traditional fairy tales. Use details from the story to support your ideas.

12. Think about what the characters and the reader learn from what happens in "Dragon, Dragon." In an essay, discuss a moral, or lesson, that could fit at the end of the story. Explain why this message is appropriate, using details from the story as support.

13. The author of "Dragon, Dragon" uses both direct and indirect characterization. In an essay, give an example from the story of each type of characterization. Then, explain why John Gardner used this particular type of characterization for each example.

14. **Thinking About the Big Question: Is conflict always bad?** In "Dragon, Dragon," there is a conflict between the people of the kingdom and the dragon that plagues them. In an essay, first discuss in what ways this conflict is bad for the kingdom. Then, discuss how the solution to the conflict turns out to be a good thing. Use details from the story to support your ideas.

Oral Response

15. Go back to question 1, 5, 9, or 10 or to the question your teacher assigns to you. Take a few minutes to expand your answer and prepare an oral response. Find additional details in "Dragon, Dragon" that will support your points. If necessary, make notes to guide your response.

"Dragon, Dragon" by John Gardner
Selection Test A

Critical Reading *Identify the letter of the choice that best answers the question.*

____ 1. What can you conclude about the character of the dragon in "Dragon, Dragon" after reading about his deeds in the countryside?
   A. He will become more dangerous over time.
   B. He is more of a pest than a danger.
   C. He threatens the lives of everyone in the kingdom.
   D. He is completely harmless and should be ignored.

____ 2. Which excerpt is an indirect characterization of the king in "Dragon, Dragon"?
   A. There was once a king whose kingdom was plagued by a dragon.
   B. The king was at his wit's end.
   C. "I'm not a tyrant. . . ."
   D. . . . the king smiled, pleased with the impression he had made.

____ 3. Which word *best* describes the wizard in "Dragon, Dragon"?
   A. powerful
   B. incompetent
   C. wicked
   D. skillful

____ 4. Which detail from "Dragon, Dragon" is the funniest action of the wizard?
   A. He used to do spells and chants.
   B. He misplaced his wizard's book.
   C. He turns the queen into a rosebush.
   D. He gives the king bad advice.

____ 5. In "Dragon, Dragon," which detail helps you infer that the cobbler is very sensible?
   A. He sends his sons out to try to kill the dragon.
   B. He objects to the king's offers because they require too much responsibility.
   C. His work involves repairing shoes and boots.
   D. He tries to convince his sons to recite a poem to the dragon.

____ 6. Which excerpt is a direct characterization of the middle son in "Dragon, Dragon"?
   A. The middle son was very strong. . . .
   B. "What an odd thing to say," thought the middle son.
   C. . . . the middle son spurred his horse to a gallop. . . .
   D. . . . the dragon swallowed the middle son in a single gulp. . . .

_____ 7. In "Dragon, Dragon," who follows the wise old cobbler's advice?
   A. the eldest son
   B. the middle son
   C. the youngest son
   D. the king

_____ 8. What happens when the youngest son recites his father's poem to the dragon?
   A. The dragon falls down dead.
   B. The dragon begins to laugh.
   C. The dragon tries to kill him.
   D. The dragon runs away.

_____ 9. How does the dragon in "Dragon, Dragon" die?
   A. The dragon dies of laughter.
   B. The middle son stabs the dragon in the heart.
   C. The sword falls of its own weight and cuts off the dragon's head.
   D. The eldest son cuts off the dragon's head.

_____ 10. What happens to the cobbler's two older sons in "Dragon, Dragon"?
   A. Their lives are saved when they crawl out of the dead dragon.
   B. They are eaten and never seen again.
   C. They run off to hide in another kingdom.
   D. They live happily ever after with the princess.

_____ 11. What lesson do the two older brothers learn in "Dragon, Dragon"?
   A. Always take your father's advice.
   B. Always say no when a king offers you half his kingdom.
   C. To slay a dragon, charge toward it on horseback.
   D. Much will be gained when you sell brushes to a dragon.

Vocabulary and Grammar

_____ 12. Which of the following describes someone who is *plagued* by bad luck?
   A. lucky
   B. playful
   C. very unlucky
   D. hopeful

Unit 2 Resources: Short Stories
57

___ 13. Which phrase describes the job of an *inspector*?
   A. looks closely at something
   B. talks to customers
   C. judges performers
   D. builds bridges and tunnels

___ 14. What is the action verb in this sentence?
   "The kingdom is mine," said the cobbler's son.

   A. The
   B. is
   C. said
   D. cobbler's

___ 15. Which sentence contains a linking verb?
   A. The sword looked very heavy.
   B. My father gave me some advice that I ignored.
   C. The dragon bothered my family and me.
   D. My brother and I tried to slay the dragon.

Essay

16. Write an essay describing the character traits of one character from "Dragon, Dragon." Give as much information about the character as you can. Use details from both direct and indirect characterizations in the story in your description.

17. "Dragon, Dragon" is a humorous version of a traditional fairy-tale form. In an essay, tell why the events in "Dragon, Dragon" are funny and how they are different from traditional fairy-tale events.

18. **Thinking About the Big Question: Is conflict always bad?** In "Dragon, Dragon," the main conflict is between the people of the kingdom and the dragon that bothers them. In an essay, discuss how this conflict is bad for the kingdom and how the solution to the conflict is good. Use details from the story to support your ideas.

"**Dragon, Dragon**" by John Gardner
Selection Test B

Critical Reading *Identify the letter of the choice that best completes the statement or answers the question.*

_____ 1. When the dragon ravages the kingdom in "Dragon, Dragon," you can infer that the dragon wants to
   A. kill everyone in the kingdom.
   B. cause confusion and trouble.
   C. chase the people from the kingdom.
   D. find himself a bride.

_____ 2. In "Dragon, Dragon," the king calls a meeting of everyone in the kingdom to
   A. praise his knights and his wizard.
   B. find a way to stop the dragon.
   C. find a husband for his daughter.
   D. announce his intention to retire.

_____ 3. In "Dragon, Dragon," what are the cobbler's thoughts at the beginning of the king's meeting?
   A. He thinks he is the only one who knows the dragon cannot be killed.
   B. He thinks he has brave children who will face the dragon.
   C. He thinks he has the best plan for solving the king's problem.
   D. He thinks he is too unimportant to attend the meeting.

_____ 4. In "Dragon, Dragon," the king says, "I'm not a tyrant." What does he mean?
   A. He is not the rightful ruler.
   B. He is not a cruel, unjust ruler.
   C. He is not an outlaw king.
   D. He did not inherit the throne.

_____ 5. What inference can be made from this passage in "Dragon, Dragon"?
   "Why doesn't the wizard say a magic spell?" asked the cobbler.
   "He's done the best he can," said the king.

   A. The king knows the wizard can't vanquish the dragon.
   B. The king hopes the wizard can vanquish the dragon.
   C. The wizard is secretly working to vanquish the dragon.
   D. Magic will not work on the dragon.

_____ 6. In "Dragon, Dragon," which phrase *best* describes the personality of the wizard?
   A. talented and clever
   B. helpless and bumbling
   C. fearful and hesitant
   D. outspoken and bossy

___ 7. Read the following passage. Then, choose the statement that *best* explains why the author of "Dragon, Dragon" included this detail in his story.

"Oh yes," said the king. "I'll tell you what I'll do. I'll give the princess's hand in marriage to anyone who can make the dragon stop."

"It's not enough," said the cobbler. "She's a nice enough girl, you understand. But how would an ordinary person support her? Also, what about those of us that are already married?"

A. It adds suspense to the story.
B. It adds humor to the story.
C. It shows how powerful the king is.
D. It tells how beautiful the princess is.

___ 8. What does this passage from "Dragon, Dragon" tell you about the cobbler's middle son?

He felt perfectly sure he could slay the dragon by simply laying into him, but he thought it would be only polite to ask his father's advice.

A. He is very clever.
B. He is confident.
C. He is a coward.
D. He is easily confused.

___ 9. When the two oldest sons are eaten by the dragon in "Dragon, Dragon," you can infer that
A. their father will have to defeat the dragon himself.
B. trickery and brute force will not defeat the dragon.
C. the father will feel terribly guilty.
D. the dragon will apologize.

___ 10. What inference can be made from this sentence in "Dragon, Dragon"?

The dragon, who had seen the cobbler's youngest son while he was still a long way off, was seated up above the door, inside the cave, waiting and smiling to himself.

A. The dragon hopes the youngest son won't find him.
B. The dragon is much smarter than the youngest son.
C. The dragon will be killed by the youngest son.
D. The dragon expects to surprise the youngest son.

___ 11. When the youngest son in "Dragon, Dragon" recites his poem, the dragon
A. turns into a mouse.
B. trembles with fear.
C. becomes helpless with laughter.
D. admires the young man's talent.

___ 12. Which quality is the youngest son's secret to his success?
A. strength
B. cleverness
C. courage
D. trust

_____ 13. What lesson do the three sons in "Dragon, Dragon" learn?
   A. Listen to a wise person's advice, even if the advice makes no sense.
   B. Never listen to anyone's advice, no matter now wise and useful it may seem.
   C. Never confront a dragon in its lair.
   D. People who have confidence in themselves always succeed.

Vocabulary and Grammar

_____ 14. Someone who is *reflecting* on a plan is
   A. thinking seriously about it.
   B. rejecting it.
   C. raising money for the plan.
   D. putting the plan into effect.

_____ 15. Where would you most likely see a *ferry*?
   A. on water
   B. in a zoo
   C. at the top of a high building
   D. in an amusement park

_____ 16. How many action verbs are in the following sentence?
   The king said, "You can marry my daughter if you vanquish the dragon."
   A. 3
   B. 5
   C. 1
   D. 4

_____ 17. Which sentence contains a linking verb?
   A. The guards were all nervous.
   B. The dragon said, "Why are you bothering me?"
   C. The king asked them to get rid of the dragon.
   D. The dragon laughed as he circled above us.

Essay

18. Think about what the cobbler's sons, the king, the wizard, and the reader all learn from the events of "Dragon, Dragon." In an essay, write a moral, or lesson, for the story. Use details from the story to illustrate your moral.

19. Write an essay in which you compare and contrast "Dragon, Dragon" with a traditional fairy tale that you know, such as "Little Red Riding Hood" or "Beauty and the Beast." Point out the similarities and differences in the problems the characters face and how they solve their problems. Cite specific events and details from the stories to support your comparison.

20. **Thinking About the Big Question: Is conflict always bad?** In "Dragon, Dragon," there is a conflict between the people of the kingdom and the dragon that plagues them. In an essay, first discuss in what ways this conflict is bad for the kingdom. Then, discuss how the solution to the conflict turns out to be a good thing. Use details from the story to support your ideas.

Study these words from "Zlateh the Goat." Then, complete the activities.

Word List A

blanketed [BLANG ki tid] *v.* thickly covered
The field was <u>blanketed</u> with flowers of a rich orange-red.

blizzard [BLIZ erd] *n.* heavy snowstorm
The <u>blizzard</u> left over three feet of snow in less than 24 hours.

cuddled [KUH duhld] *v.* held someone closely in your arms
The mother <u>cuddled</u> her daughter to comfort her during the thunderstorm.

dense [DENS] *adj.* crowded or thick
Rita couldn't see through the <u>dense</u> fog and rain.

experienced [eks PEER ee uhnst] *v.* lived through something, had it happen to you
When I first <u>experienced</u> a school cafeteria, I was overwhelmed by all the choices for a meal.

flakes [FLAYKS] *n.* small, thin pieces of something
Tiny <u>flakes</u> of paint chipped off the wall of the old clubhouse.

mighty [MY tee] *adj.* having great strength or force
The weightlifter raised the barbell with his <u>mighty</u> arms.

mild [MYLD] *adj.* moderate and not too harsh
Instead of being spicy, the soup had a <u>mild</u> flavor.

Word List B

accustomed [uh KUS tuhmd] *adj.* used to something
Doug was <u>accustomed</u> to sitting in the same seat every day.

bleating [BLEET ing] *v.* crying by a goat or a sheep
The farmer listened to his herd of goats <u>bleating</u>.

consisted [kuhn SIS tid] *v.* made up of
Maria's favorite sandwich <u>consisted</u> of whole wheat bread, peanut butter, and jelly.

frequently [FREE kwent lee] *adv.* often
Since my mom often works late, I <u>frequently</u> make my own dinner.

hesitation [hez uh TAY shuhn] *n.* pause before doing something
Jamie had a moment of <u>hesitation</u> before she came to a decision.

regained [ri GAYND] *v.* got back; recovered
The racer <u>regained</u> his lead near the finish line.

resist [ri ZIST] *v.* refuse to accept; oppose
Omar tried to <u>resist</u> going to kindergarten on the first day.

satisfaction [sa tis FAK shuhn] *n.* feeling of contentment
Luis felt a sense of <u>satisfaction</u> after getting an A on a test.

"Zlateh the Goat" by Isaac Bashevis Singer
Vocabulary Warm-up Exercises

Exercise A *Fill in each blank in the paragraph below with an appropriate word from Word List A. Use each word only once.*

Angela woke up to find the ground [1] _____ with snow. Yesterday, the weatherman had predicted warm and [2] _____ winter weather. He had been wrong. Angela looked at the tiny [3] _____ of snow falling and knew her town was in for a [4] _____. She had never [5] _____ one before. She stepped outside. The snowfall was so [6] _____ Angela could barely see the houses across the street. The [7] _____ chill turned her fingers numb. She went inside and [8] _____ with her dog to warm up.

Exercise B *Decide whether each statement below is true or false. Circle T or F. Then, explain your answers.*

1. If you <u>resist</u> doing something, you are happy to do it.
   T / F _____

2. A sense of <u>satisfaction</u> comes after a poorly done job.
   T / F _____

3. When a goat wants to communicate, it makes a <u>bleating</u> sound.
   T / F _____

4. <u>Hesitation</u> means acting without pausing.
   T / F _____

5. A person who has <u>regained</u> his health feels very sick.
   T / F _____

6. I go shopping almost every day, which means I go shopping <u>frequently</u>.
   T / F _____

7. Harry's salad <u>consisted</u> of lettuce and tomatoes.
   T / F _____

8. When you are <u>accustomed</u> to doing something, you do it very rarely.
   T / F _____

Name _____ Date _____

"**Zlateh the Goat**" by Isaac Bashevis Singer
Reading Warm-up A

Read the following passage. Pay special attention to the underlined words. Then, read it again, and complete the activities. Use a separate sheet of paper for your written answers.

The most famous <u>blizzard</u> in U.S. history was known as the Great White Hurricane. In March of 1888, this heavy snowstorm left the northeastern United States covered in tons of snow. This snow stretched from Maine south to Virginia.

The Great White Hurricane was not the coldest snowstorm in history. It was also not the heaviest snowfall ever in the country. Still, it was one of the most destructive natural disasters in American history.

The days before the Great White Hurricane struck were warm and <u>mild</u>. Temperatures were between 40 and 50 degrees Fahrenheit. At first, the individual <u>flakes</u> of snow fell slowly. After a few hours, the snow began falling very quickly. The snow fell so fast that in places like Connecticut, over four feet of snow fell in thirty-six hours. The snowfall was so <u>dense</u> that people could barely see through it.

Cities across the northeast were paralyzed by the storm. Strong winds snapped telephone poles with their <u>mighty</u> force. Boston, New York, and Philadelphia had no telephone service. Thousands of people were stuck in their homes as the snow piled higher. As the temperature dropped, people <u>cuddled</u> together, pressing their bodies up against each other to stay warm. In the cities, major streets were shut down. People could not even go outside to get food.

After two days, the snow stopped falling. The entire northeast of America was <u>blanketed</u> in a thick covering of snow. It took weeks to repair the 25 million dollars' worth of damage caused by the storm. It was definitely the worst snowstorm most people had ever <u>experienced</u>. It took the lives of over four hundred people. When the snow finally melted, the Great White Hurricane would always be remembered for its destructive force.

1. Circle the words that explain what a <u>blizzard</u> is. Then write a sentence about a *blizzard*.

2. Underline the sentence that describes the word <u>mild</u>. Then, tell what *mild* weather is like.

3. Circle the words that tell you what <u>flakes</u> mean. Describe two things that come in *flakes*.

4. Underline the words that tell you what <u>dense</u> means. Write a sentence containing the word *dense*.

5. Circle the words that explain what <u>mighty</u> means. Write a sentence about something you would describe as *mighty*.

6. Underline the words that describe the word <u>cuddled</u>. How does it feel to be *cuddled*?

7. Underline the words that show what the blizzard <u>blanketed</u> the northeast with. Use the word *blanketed* in a sentence.

8. Why was the Great White Hurricane the worst snowstorm most people had ever <u>experienced</u>? What is something enjoyable that you have *experienced*?

Name _____   Date _____

"Zlateh the Goat" by Isaac Bashevis Singer
Reading Warm-up B

Read the following passage. Pay special attention to the underlined words. Then, read it again, and complete the activities. Use a separate sheet of paper for your written answers.

Victor was not <u>accustomed</u> to being around farm animals. In fact, the only animals he was used to seeing were the squirrels and pigeons in the park near his house. Here in his mama's village in rural Guatemala, however, life was very different. Mama's brother Miguel raised herds of animals—pigs, chickens, and goats. It made Victor uncomfortable to be around so many strange creatures.

The goats were the strangest because they made bizarre <u>bleating</u> sounds and seemed to enjoy chewing on everything in sight. They were friendly animals, but even Miguel complained about their annoying behavior. One morning, when Miguel told Victor that his responsibility for the day was to watch the goats, Victor began to <u>resist</u>. He tried to refuse because he thought watching the goats was too scary. He soon changed his mind and resolved to help his uncle.

Miguel's herd of goats <u>consisted</u> of one ram, three nannies, and two kids. This group was also made up of some stubborn personalities. One of the younger goats, named Lechuga, was the most mischievous. She was <u>frequently</u> quarreling with the others and trying to get away from her herd. Once, when Victor tried to chase after her, he clumsily tripped and fell. He <u>regained</u> his feet but noticed that Lechuga had managed to run far. When Victor overtook the stubborn goat, he realized that he was lost. Worried, Victor stopped to think. After a moment of <u>hesitation</u>, he figured out in which direction he needed to go to get back to the farm. He threw his arms around Lechuga's neck and carried her back to the rest of the herd.

When Victor returned home that evening, he told Miguel about his day with Lechuga. Strangely, he smiled as he thought of the runaway. Had he actually enjoyed his adventure with the troublesome goat? Victor laughed to himself with <u>satisfaction</u> as he realized he wasn't afraid of goats anymore.

1. Circle the words that tell you what <u>accustomed</u> means. What are things you are *accustomed* to?

2. Write a sentence about what an animal sounds like when it is <u>bleating</u>.

3. What was Victor trying to <u>resist</u>? Why?

4. Underline the words that tell you what <u>consisted</u> means. Describe what the herd of goats *consisted* of.

5. What was Lechuga <u>frequently</u> doing? What is something you do *frequently*?

6. Write a sentence telling what Victor <u>regained</u>. Tell what *regained* means.

7. Circle the words that describe what <u>hesitation</u> means. How often do you have moments of *hesitation*?

8. Why did Victor have a sense of <u>satisfaction</u>? Write a sentence using the word *satisfaction*.

Name _____ Date _____

"**Zlateh the Goat**" by Isaac Bashevis Singer
Writing About the Big Question

Is conflict always bad?

Big Question Vocabulary

argue	battle	challenge	compete	conclude
convince	defend	game	issue	lose
negotiate	oppose	resolve	survival	win

A. *Use one or more words from the list above to complete each sentence.*

1. Many people _____ homes and belongings in natural disasters.

2. The forces of nature can make _____ difficult.

3. Blizzards, hurricanes, wildfires, and floods can _____ even the strongest person.

4. To _____ nature, you have to be both strong and determined.

B. *Respond to each item with a complete sentence.*

1. What is the worst weather situation you have ever faced? Describe it.

   _____

   _____

2. Use at least two Big Question vocabulary words to tell how the forces of nature challenged you and how you reacted.

   _____

   _____

C. *Complete this sentence. Then, write a brief paragraph in which you connect this idea to the Big Question.*

One positive outcome of hardship or conflict can be _____

   _____

   _____

   _____

   _____

   _____

   _____

   _____

66

"**Zlateh the Goat**" by Isaac Bashevis Singer
Reading: Use Prior Knowledge to Make Inferences

An **inference** is a logical assumption about information that is not directly stated. An inference is based on information you are given and your own thoughts. To make an inference, combine clues from the text with your own **prior knowledge,** or what you already know.

Clues in the text + What you know = Inference

Read this passage from "Zlateh the Goat."

   For Reuven the furrier it was a bad year, and after long hesitation he decided to sell Zlateh the goat.

- The passage tells you that Reuven hesitates before making his decision.
- Your prior knowledge tells you that people might hesitate before making difficult decisions.
- You can infer that Reuven's decision to sell the goat was not an easy decision for him to make.

DIRECTIONS: *The chart below lists story details from "Zlateh the Goat" and prior knowledge that you can use to make inferences. In the third box in each row, use the detail and the prior knowledge to make and write an inference.*

1.

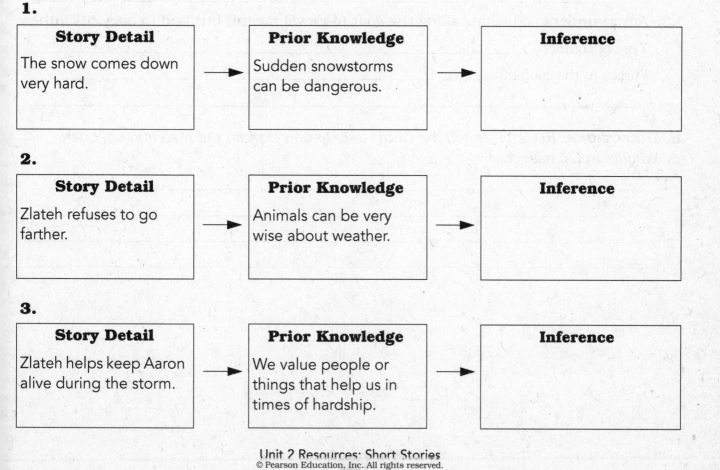

Story Detail	Prior Knowledge	Inference
The snow comes down very hard.	Sudden snowstorms can be dangerous.	

2.

Story Detail	Prior Knowledge	Inference
Zlateh refuses to go farther.	Animals can be very wise about weather.	

3.

Story Detail	Prior Knowledge	Inference
Zlateh helps keep Aaron alive during the storm.	We value people or things that help us in times of hardship.	

"Zlateh the Goat" by Isaac Bashevis Singer
Literary Analysis: Conflict and Resolution

A **conflict** is a struggle between opposing forces. In a short story, the conflict, or struggle, drives the action. Events contribute to the conflict or to the **resolution.** The resolution is the way in which the conflict is settled. Conflicts can be *external* or *internal.*

- **External conflict:** a character struggles against an outside force, such as another person or an element of nature. An example of external conflict is a fire that threatens the safety of a family and their home.
- **Internal conflict:** a character struggles within himself or herself to make a choice, take an action, or overcome a feeling. An example of internal conflict is a girl's desire to go skating with her friends when she knows she should stay home to do her homework.

A. DIRECTIONS: *Read the following sentences. On the lines, write* internal *or* external *to describe the conflict. Then, explain the opposing forces that cause the conflict.*

1. The peasants complained that because of the dry weather there would be a poor harvest of winter grain.

    Type of conflict: _____

    Forces in the conflict: _____

    _____

2. Aaron understood what taking the goat to Fievel meant, but had to obey his father.

    Type of conflict: _____

    Forces in the conflict: _____

    _____

B. DIRECTIONS: *Review "Zlateh the Goat" to help you explain the resolution of each conflict in Exercise A.*

1. _____

    _____

2. _____

    _____

"Zlateh the Goat" by Isaac Bashevis Singer
Vocabulary Builder

Word List

astray   bound   exuded   flickering   rapidly   splendor   trace

A. DIRECTIONS: *On the line before each sentence, write T if the statement is true or F if the statement is false. Then, explain your answer. The first one has been done for you.*

1. __F__ Aaron *bound* the snow to his jacket.
   Bound means "to tie," and Aaron cannot tie snow to his jacket.

2. _____ Someone who *exuded* a sense of despair would soon be happy.
   _____
   _____

3. _____ A sheep that has gone *astray* is with the other sheep.
   _____
   _____

4. _____ Most civilizations leave a *trace* of their existence behind.
   _____
   _____

5. _____ People in a family are often *bound* by affection and shared values.
   _____
   _____

6. _____ A candle flame would be *flickering* in a breeze.
   _____
   _____

7. _____ A person might be awed by the *splendor* of a huge palace.
   _____
   _____

B. WORD STUDY: *The Latin prefix ex- means "out," "from," or "beyond." Think about the meaning of the prefix ex- in each underlined word. Then, write an answer to each question.*

1. When might you <u>explain</u> an idea?
   _____

2. What kind of animal has an <u>external</u> shell?
   _____

3. What kind of sports are called <u>extreme</u> sports?
   _____

"Zlateh the Goat" by Isaac Bashevis Singer
Enrichment: A Map of Poland

Many of Isaac Bashevis Singer's stories, including "Zlateh the Goat," take place in Poland, where the author was born and grew up. Below is a map of Poland and the area surrounding it.

DIRECTIONS: *Answer the following questions on the lines provided.*

1. Isaac Bashevis Singer spent much of his childhood in the capital city of Poland. What is the name of this city? **Hint:** On this map, as on most maps, the capital city is labeled with a star.

   _____

2. A novel by Singer called *The Magician of Lublin* takes place in the Polish city of Lublin. Find Lublin on the map. About how far is it in miles from Lublin to the capital city? **Hint:** There is a scale of miles on the map that will help you estimate the distance.

   _____

3. Some of Singer's funniest stories take place in the town of Chelm. About how far is it in miles from Lublin to Chelm?

   _____

4. What is the name of the body of water that borders part of Poland?

   _____

5. What are the names of at least three of the seven countries that border Poland?

   _____

"Zlateh the Goat" by Isaac Bashevis Singer
Open-Book Test

Short Answer *Write your responses to the questions in this section on the lines provided.*

1. In "Zlateh the Goat," Feivel is the town butcher. Aaron understands what taking the goat to Feivel means. Use details from the story and your own prior knowledge to explain what Aaron understands.

   _____

   _____

   _____

2. In "Zlateh the Goat," all the family members love Zlateh. Why then does Aaron obey his father and set out to deliver her to Feivel? Use details from the story to support your answer.

   _____

   _____

   _____

3. In "Zlateh the Goat," Aaron bound a rope around the goat's neck. Explain in what way the boy and goat are bound by their experiences in the snowstorm.

   _____

   _____

   _____

4. You can infer in "Zlateh the Goat" that Aaron is confused and surprised by the strength of the blizzard that roars up. What detail from the story supports this inference?

   _____

   _____

   _____

5. In "Zlateh the Goat," Aaron is caught in a terrible snowstorm with Zlateh. They are very cold and the goat is in need of food. Explain how finding the haystack solves these conflicts with nature.

   _____

   _____

   _____

6. After finding the haystack in "Zlateh the Goat," Aaron faces a new conflict with the storm. In the conflict diagram, write the conflict and Aaron's solution. On the line, explain whether this is an internal or external conflict.

Conflict		Solution
	→	

_____

_____

7. Think about the ways that Aaron and Zlateh work together to survive the storm in "Zlateh the Goat." What kind of relationship do they have? Use examples from the story to support your answer.

_____

_____

_____

8. While Aaron is in the haystack in "Zlateh the Goat," he feels "that there could never have been summer, that the snow has always fallen." Explain what he feels and why he feels this way.

_____

_____

_____

9. In "Zlateh the Goat," Aaron's family found no trace of the boy and the goat during the storm. Explain what trace a person might leave in the snow. Use the definition of trace.

_____

_____

10. One conflict in "Zlateh the Goat" is the family's distress at having to sell a beloved animal. What two events from the story help resolve this conflict?

_____

_____

_____

_____

ESSAY

Write an extended response to the question of your choice or to the question or questions your teacher assigns you.

11. In "Zlateh the Goat," both Aaron and Zlateh struggle to survive the storm. Think of the problems that each one has. Which character has a more difficult time during the three days in the haystack? In an essay, explain your choice. Use details from the story to support your answer.

12. Near the beginning of "Zlateh the Goat," the reader discovers that Aaron obeys his father even if it means taking a beloved goat to the butcher. However, at the end of the story, he brings the goat home instead of taking her to the butcher. In an essay, discuss this turnabout. Explain why Aaron has a change of heart. Consider what internal conflicts he might face in making his decision.

13. In "Zlateh the Goat," Aaron comes to believe that we must accept all that we are given in life, "heat, cold, hunger, satisfaction, light, and darkness." In an essay, explain how well he accepts what he is given in all parts of the story. Think about the internal and external conflicts that Aaron faces.

14. **Thinking About the Big Question: Is conflict always bad?** In "Zlateh the Goat," Aaron and Zlateh face an external conflict with nature during the storm. In some ways this conflict is bad for the characters, but it turns out quite good in other ways. In an essay, explain whether you think the conflict is, on the whole, bad or good. Consider whether nature helps or harms the characters. Use details from the story to support your ideas.

Oral Response

15. Go back to question 1, 2, 3, or 10 or to the question your teacher assigns to you. Take a few minutes to expand your answer and prepare an oral response. Find additional details in "Zlateh the Goat" that will support your points. If necessary, make notes to guide your response.

"Zlateh the Goat" by Isaac Bashevis Singer
Selection Test A

Critical Reading *Identify the letter of the choice that best answers the question.*

____ 1. In "Zlateh the Goat," why is Reuven the furrier having a bad year?
   A. His eyesight is failing.
   B. It is a mild winter.
   C. His farm suffers from the drought.
   D. His wife and children are sick.

____ 2. In "Zlateh the Goat," why can you infer that the family is sorry to sell Zlateh?
   A. The mother and sisters cry when the goat leaves.
   B. The family will not allow Aaron to take the goat.
   C. The family will not speak to Reuven because they are so upset.
   D. Leah tells the goat that they are sorry.

____ 3. Which detail from "Zlateh the Goat" helps you infer that, before he finds shelter, Aaron is in danger?
   A. The sun was shining when Aaron left the village.
   B. At first Zlateh didn't seem to mind the change in weather.
   C. This was no ordinary storm. It was a mighty blizzard.
   D. Suddenly he made out the shape of a hill.

____ 4. How does finding the haystack solve Aaron's problem in the snowstorm?
   A. The haystack is a landmark that helps Aaron find his way home.
   B. Behind the haystack, Aaron finds shelter from the wind.
   C. Inside the haystack, Aaron finds warmth and Zlateh finds food.
   D. From on top of the haystack, Aaron sees the peasant on the sleigh.

____ 5. How does the storm continue to endanger Aaron and Zlateh after they find the haystack?
   A. The weather gets very cold, and they risk freezing.
   B. There is no food available, and they risk starving.
   C. The snow is so heavy that it threatens to crush them.
   D. The snow covers everything and makes it hard to breathe.

____ 6. How did Zlateh help Aaron during the storm?
   A. Zlateh helped him keep warm, gave him milk, and kept him company.
   B. Zlateh gave Aaron ideas for surviving the storm.
   C. Zlateh made noise so that the peasant on the sleigh heard her.
   D. Zlateh helped Aaron find his way home.

_____ 7. How does the hay help Zlateh and Aaron?
   A. It keeps them warm and gives Zlateh food.
   B. Aaron uses the hay to build a fire to keep them warm.
   C. They can both eat the hay.
   D. Aaron weaves the hay into warm blankets.

_____ 8. While in the haystack, Aaron feels "that there could never have been a summer, that the snow had always fallen." Why does he feel this way?
   A. It is very warm and summery inside the haystack.
   B. He has decided to pass the time by inventing stories.
   C. He has been in the haystack so long that life seems dreamlike.
   D. The cold and lack of food have affected his memory.

_____ 9. What kind of relationship do Aaron and Zlateh have?
   A. Aaron loves Zlateh, but she doesn't care for him.
   B. They are very fond of each other.
   C. Zlateh loves Aaron, but he doesn't care for her.
   D. They each think the other is a pest.

_____ 10. How does Aaron's family react when Aaron and Zlateh come home?
   A. They are angry with Aaron for getting lost.
   B. They are sorry that Aaron didn't sell Zlateh.
   C. They are surprised to learn that there had been a blizzard.
   D. They are overjoyed and grateful to Zlateh for saving Aaron.

_____ 11. Why did Aaron not carry out the task of taking the goat to the butcher?
   A. Zlateh ran away.
   B. The sisters convinced Reuven to change his mind about selling Zlateh.
   C. Aaron sold Zlateh to a man they met along the road.
   D. The blizzard that delayed Aaron gave Zlateh a chance to be a hero.

Vocabulary and Grammar

_____ 12. What does the word _trace_ mean in this sentence?
   Aaron's family and their neighbors had searched for the boy and the goat but had found no trace of them during the storm.
   A. location
   B. mark left behind
   C. hollow opening
   D. pattern

____ **13.** What do you do when you *infer* information?

    A. You make a guess.

    B. You support a statement with facts and statistics.

    C. You use details and prior knowledge to make an assumption.

    D. You ask other people for their opinions and then you make a judgment.

____ **14.** Which sentence uses an indefinite pronoun?

    A. Someone is talking too loudly.

    B. I never knew you had a twin sister!

    C. Jason did his homework sloppily.

    D. The Yeos and their friends had a party.

Essay

15. During the blizzard in "Zlateh the Goat," Aaron and Zlateh face an external conflict with nature. However, it is also nature that helps Aaron and Zlateh survive. Write an essay explaining how nature helps Aaron and Zlateh. Use examples and details from the story to support your ideas.

16. During the three days in the haystack, which character has a more difficult time, Aaron or Zlateh? In an essay, explain your choice and use examples from the story to support your answer.

17. Thinking About the Big Question: Is conflict always bad? In "Zlateh the Goat," Aaron and Zlateh face a conflict with the storm. In some ways this conflict is bad for the characters, but in some ways it turns out to be good. In an essay, explain whether you think the conflict with the storm is, on the whole, bad or good. Use details about what happens during and after the storm to support your ideas.

Name _____ Date _____

"**Zlateh the Goat**" by Isaac Bashevis Singer
Selection Test B

Critical Reading *Identify the letter of the choice that best completes the statement or answers the question.*

____ 1. In "Zlateh the Goat," why does the warm winter mean a bad year for Reuven the furrier?
A. No one needs a fur coat in warm weather.
B. There are no fur-bearing animals in warm winters.
C. There would be a poor harvest of winter grain that year.
D. The peasants were saving their money for Hanukkah gifts.

____ 2. What does this passage from "Zlateh the Goat" tell you about how family members feel about the selling of the goat?

> Leah, his mother, wiped the tears from her eyes when she heard the news. Aaron's younger sisters, Anna and Miriam, cried loudly.

A. The family is angry at Reuven.
B. The family is very sorry to sell Zlateh.
C. The family is very upset at Aaron.
D. The family does not need a goat.

____ 3. Even though Aaron loves Zlateh, he agrees to take her to Feivel the butcher because
A. he knows it would be wrong to disobey his father.
B. he is afraid of his father and mother.
C. he wants the money from selling Zlateh so he can buy presents.
D. he does not understand what taking the goat to Feivel means.

____ 4. Zlateh trusts Aaron and allows him to put the rope around her neck because
A. the family welcomes her into the kitchen.
B. she is treated like one of the family.
C. the family have always fed her and never harmed her.
D. she knows they need her milk.

____ 5. What can you infer about Aaron from this sentence from "Zlateh the Goat"?

> In his twelve years Aaron had seen all kinds of weather, but he had never experienced a snow like this one.

A. Aaron has never seen snow before in his life.
B. Aaron has lost all hope of surviving in a snowstorm.
C. Aaron wishes he lived in a tropical climate.
D. Aaron is surprised and perhaps bewildered by the intensity of the blizzard.

____ 6. What is the greatest conflict caused by the snowstorm in "Zlateh the Goat"?
A. Aaron can't find his way to Feivel's house in the snow.
B. Without shelter, Aaron will freeze to death.
C. Aaron cannot make Zlateh walk in the snow.
D. Aaron and Zlateh are hungry and have no food to eat.

____ 7. In "Zlateh the Goat," Aaron's conflict with the storm continues after he finds the haystack because
A. he runs out of food and risks starving.
B. the temperature drops and he risks freezing.
C. the snow piles high and makes it difficult to get enough air.
D. the snow is so heavy it threatens to crush him.

____ 8. What can you infer about Aaron from this passage from "Zlateh the Goat"?
   He was alone, cut off from his family, and wanted to talk. He began to talk to Zlateh.
A. Aaron feels silly because he is talking to a goat.
B. Aaron is beginning to feel that Zlateh is a member of the family.
C. Aaron has begun to hallucinate because he is hungry.
D. Aaron is bored and has nothing else to do.

____ 9. When Aaron and Zlateh come home, Aaron's family reacts with
A. anger at Aaron's carelessness.
B. disappointment in Aaron's disobedience.
C. joy and gratitude toward Zlateh.
D. indifference toward Aaron's situation.

____ 10. After the snowstorm, why would no one ever again think of selling Zlateh?
A. Feivel didn't want to buy Zlateh.
B. The family made enough money from selling Zlateh's milk.
C. The family was thankful that Aaron's life was saved.
D. Zlateh was too old to be sold.

____ 11. Aaron's main internal conflict in "Zlateh the Goat" is between
A. his desire to obey his father and his love for Zlateh.
B. his love for his father and his love for his mother.
C. his desire for money and his love for Zlateh.
D. his fear of his father and his fear of dying.

____ 12. Which statement *best* characterizes the relationship between Zlateh and Aaron?
A. Aaron loves Zlateh, but she only loves Reuven.
B. Aaron and Zlateh are very fond of each other.
C. Zlateh loves Aaron, but he finds Zlateh troublesome.
D. They each find the other irritating and troublesome.

____ 13. In "Zlateh the Goat," which of Reuven's problems is solved by the snowstorm?
A. The peasants will be able to grow more crops to feed his family.
B. There will be a larger supply of grain and food for his cattle.
C. There will be plenty of potatoes and snow for Hanukkah.
D. People will need to be warm and they will buy his furs.

Vocabulary and Grammar

____ 14. Aaron stayed close to Zlateh because she *exuded* warmth. This means that Zlateh
   A. gave off warmth.
   B. held in warmth.
   C. preserved heat.
   D. contained heat.

____ 15. Aaron and Zlateh are *bound* by their experiences in the snowstorm. In other words, they are
   A. repelled.
   B. made enemies.
   C. overjoyed.
   D. tied together.

____ 16. What is the indefinite pronoun in this sentence?
   Nobody ever again thought of selling Zlateh.
   A. again
   B. ever
   C. nobody
   D. of

____ 17. What is the interrogative pronoun in this sentence?
   Who had piled snow into such a huge heap?
   A. who
   B. into
   C. such
   D. heap

Essay

18. In an essay, explain the difficulties Aaron faces during his three days in the haystack. Tell how he overcomes these challenges. Use examples from the story to support your answer.

19. At the beginning of the story, we learn that Aaron never disobeys his father. Yet, at the end of the story, he brings Zlateh home instead of taking her to the butcher, as his father has asked. In an essay, explain why Aaron changed his mind. What internal conflicts did he face in making his decision?

20. **Thinking About the Big Question: Is conflict always bad?** In "Zlateh the Goat," Aaron and Zlateh face an external conflict with nature during the storm. In some ways this conflict is bad for the characters, but it turns out quite good in other ways. In an essay, explain whether you think the conflict is, on the whole, bad or good. Consider whether nature helps or harms the characters. Use details from the story to support your ideas.

Study these words from "The Old Woman Who Lived with the Wolves." Then, complete the activities.

Word List A

borders [BAWR derz] *n.* dividing lines between one region or country and another
   The United States shares its <u>borders</u> with Mexico and Canada.

considered [kuhn SID erd] *v.* believed that something was true
   Laura <u>considered</u> her teacher to be the nicest one in the school.

odor [OH der] *n.* smell
   Roquefort cheese has a strong taste and an even stronger <u>odor</u>!

pure [PYOOR] *adj.* not mixed with anything else
   The necklace was made out of <u>pure</u> gold—not gold mixed with nickel and copper.

seek [SEEK] *v.* to look or search for
   Animals <u>seek</u> shelter in a storm.

shaggy [SHAG ee] *adj.* having long, rough hair or fur
   The buffalo in the zoo had a <u>shaggy</u> coat.

territory [TER uh tawr ee] *n.* an area or region of land
   The soldier carefully crossed into enemy <u>territory</u>.

wherever [wair EV er] *conj.* in, at, or to any place
   The stray dog went <u>wherever</u> it could find food.

Word List B

determined [di TER mind] *adj.* focused on success
   Ricardo was <u>determined</u> to go to college, so he studied hard to get good grades.

elsewhere [ELS wair] *adv.* somewhere else
   Jessie looked in her locker for her gym bag, but it was <u>elsewhere</u>.

foothills [FOOT hilz] *n.* low hills at the base of a mountain range
   George drove past some <u>foothills</u> on his way to the Rocky Mountains.

journeyed [JER need] *v.* to have made a long trip
   The adventurer <u>journeyed</u> far to reach the South Pole.

offensive [uh FEN siv] *adj.* unpleasant or disagreeable
   The smell of old garbage is <u>offensive</u>.

perished [PER isht] *v.* died, was destroyed
   The last of the flowers <u>perished</u> in the frost.

throughout [throo OWT] *adv.* in every part, everywhere
   Sparrows live <u>throughout</u> the United States and Europe.

trespass [TRES pas] *v.* to enter someone's property without permission
   The children were told repeatedly not to <u>trespass</u> in the old abandoned building.

"The Old Woman Who Lived With the Wolves" by Chief Luther Standing Bear
Vocabulary Warm-up Exercises

Exercise A *Fill in each blank in the paragraph below with an appropriate word from Word List A. Use each word only once.*

Dennis liked to find adventure [1] _____ he went. He

[2] _____ his entire neighborhood to be his playground. Sometimes,

he would [3] _____ adventures outside the [4] _____

of the neighborhood where he lived. This foreign [5] _____ was

exciting to explore. One day, when he was far from home, he smelled a strange

[6] _____. He followed the smell until he found a stray dog with a

[7] _____ coat. The dog tried to follow him home! When Dennis finally

got rid of the dog, he smiled. His latest adventure had been [8] _____

excitement.

Exercise B *Answer the questions with complete explanations.*

Example: If Ellen <u>journeyed</u> to the beach this summer, does she live near or far from the beach? Explain.

It means she lives far from the beach because people who have journeyed have made a long trip.

1. How would you feel if you saw someone trying to <u>trespass</u> on your property?
   _____

2. If your favorite species of animal <u>perished</u> from the earth, would you be sad?
   _____

3. Is a <u>foothill</u> harder to climb than a mountain? Explain.
   _____

4. If you smelled a rotten odor <u>throughout</u> your kitchen, what would you do?
   _____

5. What kinds of behaviors do you find <u>offensive</u>? Explain.
   _____

6. If a person is <u>determined</u> to do something, will he or she make it happen? Explain.
   _____

7. If the park is closed, will you play <u>elsewhere</u>? Explain.
   _____

Name _____ Date _____

"The Old Woman Who Lived With the Wolves" by Chief Luther Standing Bear
Reading Warm-up A

Read the following passage. Pay special attention to the underlined words. Then, read it again, and complete the activities. Use a separate sheet of paper for your written answers.

Wolves are wild mammals that are native to North America. They are related to dogs. Unlike dogs, however, wolves cannot be domesticated. Wolves look like dogs but have thick, <u>shaggy</u> fur and large noses. There once were many wolves in North America. The gray wolf and the red wolf are two types of wolves that were once very common in the United States.

A group of wolves is called a pack. Packs are like large families. A normal-sized pack is made up of six or seven wolves. Each pack of wolves has its own <u>territory</u>. This is the land on which the pack lives and hunts. The wolves protect this area of land by marking its <u>borders</u> with their scent. When a wolf walks onto land marked by a different pack of wolves, it smells the <u>odor</u> they have left behind. This smell tells the wolf to move off the other pack's land.

Wolf packs have a strict power structure. There are always two wolves, a male and a female, in charge. They are <u>considered</u> the leaders of the pack. The leaders decide where the pack will hunt and sleep. Many wolves do not actually <u>seek</u> shelter when they sleep. Instead, they sleep in the open, <u>wherever</u> the pack's leaders decide to rest.

There are few wolves left in the United States today. Once, however, there were millions. Many wolves were hunted by ranchers for killing cattle. People also destroyed much of the <u>pure</u>, unspoiled wilderness where wolves used to roam. Fortunately, these days more is being done to protect wolves. Slowly, the number of wolves in this country is growing again.

1. Underline the words that explain the word <u>shaggy</u>. Write a sentence about something you know that is *shaggy*.

2. Circle the words that tell you what a wolf's <u>territory</u> is. What do you consider your own *territory*?

3. Underline the words that tell what <u>borders</u> are. Explain what *borders* are in your own words.

4. Circle the synonyms of the word <u>odor</u>. What is an *odor* you do not like?

5. Underline which wolves are <u>considered</u> to be leaders. Write a sentence using the word *considered*.

6. Write a sentence about some of the things wolves <u>seek</u>.

7. Circle the words that describe what <u>wherever</u> means. Use *wherever* in a sentence.

8. Underline the words that tell you what is <u>pure</u> about where the wolves live. What does *pure* mean in your own words?

"The Old Woman Who Lived With the Wolves" by Chief Luther Standing Bear
Reading Warm-up B

Read the following passage. Pay special attention to the underlined words. Then, read it again, and complete the activities. Use a separate sheet of paper for your written answers.

The Sioux are one of the oldest tribes of Native Americans. It is believed that they came to North America from Asia over thirty thousand years ago. Throughout history, the Sioux have <u>journeyed</u> from camp to camp, traveling to different locations in different parts of the year. If food supplies were running low or if the weather became too harsh, the Sioux would pick up their camp and move <u>elsewhere</u>. In the past, the Sioux lived in the <u>foothills</u> of South Dakota and Nebraska. This low, hilly land was well suited to the traditional Sioux way of life.

Sioux warriors were famous for their courage. They often fought with neighboring Native American tribes over land rights. To the Sioux, the idea of other tribes sharing their land was <u>offensive</u>. To protect their territory from invaders, they attacked those who came onto their land. The word Sioux actually means "Little Snake." This name was given to the Sioux by a rival tribe, the Chippewa.

When white settlers began to <u>trespass</u> on Sioux land, the people of the tribe became angry. <u>Determined</u> to preserve their territory, the Sioux fought many battles to save their way of life. One of the most famous was the Battle of Little Bighorn in 1876. While the Sioux won this battle against the United States Army, many great warriors <u>perished</u> in the attack. In the end, the Sioux were defeated and forced to live on reservations.

Today there are about thirty thousand Sioux tribe members in the United States. They live scattered on many reservations <u>throughout</u> South Dakota. Life on the reservations can be harsh. It is often a struggle for the Sioux to preserve their traditional ways of life.

1. Circle the words that tell you what the word <u>journeyed</u> means. Have you ever *journeyed* far from home? Explain.

2. Underline the words that tell you why the Sioux would move <u>elsewhere</u>. Use *elsewhere* in a sentence.

3. Circle the words that describe the <u>foothills</u> of South Dakota. Are there *foothills* near where you live?

4. In your own words, rewrite the sentence containing the word <u>offensive</u>. Then, write what *offensive* means.

5. Underline the words that tell you what <u>trespass</u> means. Do you think it is right to *trespass*?

6. Write a sentence describing why the Sioux were <u>determined</u> to protect their land.

7. Who <u>perished</u> at Little Bighorn?

8. Write a sentence about something that can be found <u>throughout</u> your state, using a synonym for the word *throughout*.

Name _____ Date _____

Writing About the Big Question

Is conflict always bad?

Big Question Vocabulary

argue	battle	challenge	compete	conclude
convince	defend	game	issue	lose
negotiate	oppose	resolve	survival	win

A. *Use one or more words from the list above to complete each sentence.*

1. If you ever get lost in the woods, the first thing you must do is _____ yourself to stay calm.

2. Sometimes your _____ depends on staying in one place, even though you want to keep walking.

3. If it is likely to get cold, you should _____ to find a place that is warm and protected.

B. *Respond to each item with a complete sentence.*

1. If you have ever been lost, describe what happened. If not, write a description of what you think it would be like.

_____

_____

2. Explain how you would advise a friend to act if he or she were lost. Use at least two Big Question vocabulary words.

_____

_____

C. *Complete this sentence. Then, write a brief paragraph explaining why trust can help overcome conflict.*

Sometimes when we choose to trust instead of fear something, we

_____

_____

_____

_____

84

Name _____   Date _____

Reading: Use Prior Knowledge to Make Inferences

An **inference** is a logical assumption about information that is not directly stated. An inference is based on information you are given and your own thoughts. To make an inference, combine clues from the text with your own **prior knowledge,** or what you already know.

Clues in the text + What you know = Inference

Read this passage from "The Old Woman Who Lived With the Wolves."

> The Sioux . . . liked to make their home first here and then there upon their own ground, just as they pleased. It was not like moving from one strange town to another, but wherever they settled it was home.

- The passage tells you the Sioux moved often.
- Your prior knowledge tells you that "home" is a place where people feel comfortable.
- You can infer that the Sioux feel comfortable wherever they go.

DIRECTIONS: *The chart below lists story details from "The Old Woman Who Lived With the Wolves" and prior knowledge that you can use to make inferences. In the third box in each row, use the detail and the prior knowledge to make and write an inference.*

1.

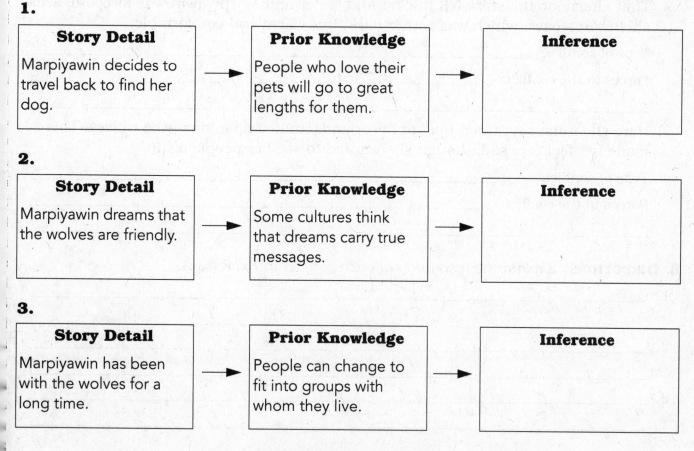

Story Detail	Prior Knowledge	Inference
Marpiyawin decides to travel back to find her dog.	People who love their pets will go to great lengths for them.	

2.

Story Detail	Prior Knowledge	Inference
Marpiyawin dreams that the wolves are friendly.	Some cultures think that dreams carry true messages.	

3.

Story Detail	Prior Knowledge	Inference
Marpiyawin has been with the wolves for a long time.	People can change to fit into groups with whom they live.	

"The Old Woman Who Lived With the Wolves" by Chief Luther Standing Bear
Literary Analysis: Conflict and Resolution

A **conflict** is a struggle between opposing forces. In a short story, the conflict, or struggle, drives the action. Events contribute to the conflict or to the **resolution**. The resolution is the way in which the conflict is settled. Conflicts can be *external* or *internal*.

- **External conflict:** a character struggles against an outside force, such as another person or an element of nature. An example of external conflict is a parent who tells a son he cannot go to a party that the son really wants to attend.
- **Internal conflict:** a character struggles within himself or herself to make a choice, take an action, or overcome a feeling. An example of internal conflict is the guilt a character feels when he or she tells a lie.

A. DIRECTIONS: *Read the following sentences. On the lines, write* internal *or* external *to describe the conflict. Then, explain the opposing forces that cause the conflict.*

1. One evening Marpiyawin missed her dog. She looked and she called, but he was not to be found.

   Type of conflict: _____

   Forces in the conflict: _____

   _____

2. That afternoon the snow fell thicker and faster and Marpiyawin was forced to seek shelter in a cave, which was rather dark, but warm and comfortable.

   Type of conflict: _____

   Forces in the conflict: _____

   _____

3. Here she must say "Good-bye" to her friends and companions—the wolves. This made her feel very sad, though she wanted to see her people again.

   Type of conflict: _____

   Forces in the conflict: _____

   _____

B. DIRECTIONS: *Explain the resolution of each conflict in Exercise A.*

1. _____

   _____

2. _____

   _____

3. _____

Name _____ Date _____

"The Old Woman Who Lived With the Wolves" by Chief Luther Standing Bear
Vocabulary Builder

Word List

coaxed   mystified   offensive   perished   scarce   traversed   trespass

A. DIRECTIONS: *On the line before the sentence, write* T *if the statement is true or* F *if the statement is false. Then, explain your answer. The first one has been done for you.*

1. ___T___ Marpiyawin and the wolves *traversed* valleys and walked up hills and down hills.
   They traveled across valleys and walked up and down hills as they crossed the land.

2. _____ Someone who *traversed* a frozen pond would have walked around the pond.
   _____
   _____

3. _____ A child who is frightened may have to be *coaxed* to come out of hiding.
   _____
   _____

4. _____ If the smell of pizza is *offensive*, a restaurant will sell more pizzas.
   _____
   _____

5. _____ Marpiyawin *perished* when she met the wolves.
   _____
   _____

6. _____ A person who planned to *trespass* would try to stay hidden.
   _____
   _____

7. _____ People are *scarce* in big cities.
   _____
   _____

8. _____ Someone who saw a person disappear might be *mystified*.
   _____
   _____

B. WORD STUDY: *The Latin prefix* in- *means "not." Think about the meaning of the prefix* in- *in each underlined word. Then, write an answer to each question.*

1. What is an <u>indecisive</u> person likely to do when choosing a flavor of ice cream?
   _____

2. Why might a view be <u>indescribable</u>?
   _____

3. If a party is <u>informal</u>, how should you dress?
   _____

Unit 2 Resources: Short Stories
© Pearson Education, Inc. All rights reserved.
87

Name _____ Date _____

Enrichment: Reintroducing Wolves

Wolves have been an endangered species since the 1930s. In the 1990s, the U.S. government began reintroducing wolves in various areas of the country. Gray wolves were released into Yellowstone National Park. Wolves were reintroduced into Idaho and Arizona. The government is considering bringing wolves to the Adirondack National Park in New York State. People have strong opinions about wolf reintroduction. Some believe wolves should be reintroduced; others believe wolves should not be reintroduced.

DIRECTIONS: *Look at the chart of pros and cons for wolf reintroduction. Choose one side of the issue to support. Use Internet and library resources to find facts to support your opinions. Then, write a brief position statement that gives your opinion and the facts that support your opinion.*

Wolf Reintroduction

Pros	Cons
• Wolves are endangered, and reintroduction will help them survive. • Reintroduction of wolves will help keep deer and other wildlife populations in balance. • Wolves are part of the world's biodiversity and should be encouraged to exist in their native habitats.	• Wolves are a threat to livestock populations. • Wolves can overhunt large animal groups such as deer and caribou. • Wolf reintroduction is costly, and government money can be better spent.

My Position Statement: _____

_____

_____

_____

_____

_____

_____

_____

_____

_____

_____

_____

"The Old Woman Who Lived With the Wolves" by Chief Luther Standing Bear
"Zlateh the Goat" by Isaac Bashevis Singer

Integrated Language Skills: Grammar

A verb is a word that expresses an action or a state of being. Every verb has four main forms, or **principal parts**. These parts show the tense of a verb. The tense lets you know when an action took place. Most verbs are **regular**, meaning that they form their principal parts in the same way. Some verbs, however, are **irregular**, meaning that the forms of their principal parts do not follow general rules. The principal parts of irregular verbs must be learned.

Principal Part	Regular Verbs	Irregular Verbs
Present tense	talk, jump, finish, expect	am/is/are, have/has, sing, become/becomes, bring
Past tense	Add *ed*: talk*ed*, jump*ed*, finish*ed*, expect*ed*	was/were, had, sang, became, brought
Present participle	Add *ing*: (am/is/are) talk*ing*, jump*ing*, finish*ing*, expect*ing*	(am/is/are) being, having, singing, becoming, bringing
Past participle	Add *ed*: (has/have/had) talk*ed*, jump*ed*, finish*ed*, expect*ed*	(has/have/had) been, had, sung, become, brought

A. PRACTICE: *For each of the following sentences, identify which principal part of the underlined verb is being used. The first one has been done as an example.*

_____past_____ 1. The sun <u>shone</u> for only a few hours the day Aaron left.

_____ 2. Aaron *is* <u>having</u> trouble finding shelter.

_____ 3. Marpiyawin <u>knows</u> that she can trust the wolves.

_____ 4. Aaron *has* <u>helped</u> protect Zlateh.

_____ 5. Marpiyawin *had* <u>found</u> her way to the foothills.

_____ 6. Aaron *was* <u>hoping</u> to dig his way through the snow.

_____ 7. Aaron's family <u>understood</u> his love for Zlateh.

B. Writing Application: *Write a sentence using the verb and principal part indicated.*

1. decide; present tense

_____

2. become; past tense

_____

"Zlateh the Goat" by Isaac Bashevis Singer
"The Old Woman Who Lived With the Wolves" by Chief Luther Standing Bear
Integrated Language Skills: Support for Writing a Persuasive Speech

Pretend that you are either Aaron or Marpiyawin. Then, in the chart below, list at least three reasons for your life-changing decision. Use details from the story to support the reasons, and explain why each reason was necessary and what either your family or tribe must do now.

Reasons	Details That Support the Reason	Why the Reason Is Convincing

Now, use the reasons you have written to write your persuasive speech.

"Zlateh the Goat" by Isaac Bashevis Singer
"The Old Woman Who Lived With the Wolves" by Chief Luther Standing Bear
Support for Extend Your Learning

Research

To prepare to make a compare-and-contrast chart about goats and wolves in world literature, write the answers to these questions.

1. What types of tales feature goats?

_____

_____

What types of tales feature wolves?

_____

_____

2. What physical features do goats have in the tales?

_____

_____

What physical features do wolves have in the tales?

_____

_____

3. What characteristics do goats have in the tales?

_____

_____

What characteristics do wolves have in the tales?

_____

_____

"The Old Woman Who Lived With the Wolves" by Chief Luther Standing Bear
Open-Book Test

Short Answer *Write your responses to the questions in this section on the lines provided.*

1. At the beginning of "The Old Woman Who Lived With the Wolves," the narrator describes how the Sioux like to move around. Think about what the Sioux take with them when they travel from place to place. Then, explain why they feel at home wherever they settle.

   _____

   _____

2. Explain how moving to a new place causes a conflict for Marpiyawin in "The Old Woman Who Lived With the Wolves."

   _____

   _____

3. Read the detail from "The Old Woman Who Lived With the Wolves." In the blank box, write what you know about a person who would set out on her own. Then write an inference about Marpiyawin based on the detail and your own prior knowledge.

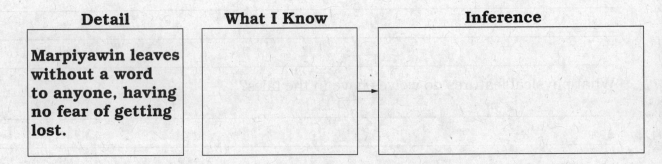

Detail	What I Know	Inference
Marpiyawin leaves without a word to anyone, having no fear of getting lost.		

4. After Marpiyawin leaves to find her dog in "The Old Woman Who Lived With the Wolves," she comes into conflict with nature. Explain the problem that she has.

   _____

   _____

5. Think about the dream Marpiyawin has about the wolves in "The Old Woman Who Lived With the Wolves." You can infer that she believes in her dreams because of the way she acts when she wakes up. Explain what she does when she awakens that would help you make the inference.

   _____

   _____

   _____

6. In "The Old Woman Who Lived With the Wolves," the tribe traversed many little valleys. If they traversed a deep river, what might they have used? Explain.

_____

_____

_____

7. In "The Old Woman Who Lived With the Wolves," the wolves find the odor of people to be offensive. What is one odor that people find offensive? Explain.

_____

_____

_____

8. In "The Old Woman Who Lived With the Wolves," Marpiyawin faces an internal conflict after the wolves take her back to her village. Explain the nature of this conflict.

_____

_____

9. Why does Marpiyawin continue to bring meat to the wolves in "The Old Woman Who Lived With the Wolves"? Use details from the story to support your answer.

_____

_____

_____

10. Describe Marpiyawin's relationship with the wolves at the end of "The Old Woman Who Lived With the Wolves." Support your description with details from the story.

_____

_____

_____

Essay

Write an extended response to the question of your choice or to the question or questions your teacher assigns you.

11. When Marpiyawin realizes her dog is missing in "The Old Woman Who Lived With the Wolves," she sets off to find him. The actions she takes tell us about her personality. What kind of person is she? In an essay, discuss what Marpiyawin does on her quest to find her dog and what these actions reveal about her. Use details from the story to support your description of her character.

12. In "The Old Woman Who Lived With the Wolves," the attitude that Marpiyawin and her people have toward wolves changes. In an essay, discuss this change. Consider the following: their attitude toward wolves at the beginning of the story, their attitude at the end of the story, and how and why their attitude changes. Use details from the story to support your ideas.

13. In "The Old Woman Who Lived With the Wolves," Marpiyawin realizes that "while man often considers the animal offensive, so do animals find man offensive." What lesson about humans and animals does the quotation illustrate? In an essay, explain how this lesson might make life better for both humans and animals.

14. **Thinking About the Big Question: Is conflict always bad?** In "The Old Woman Who Lived with the Wolves," Marpiyawin faces a conflict when she loses her dog. The journey she takes to find the animal opens a new world for her. In an essay, discuss how you think Marpiyawin would respond to the question "Is conflict always bad?" Use details from the story to support your point of view.

Oral Response

15. Go back to question 1, 5, 8, or 9 or to the question your teacher assigns to you. Take a few minutes to expand your answer and prepare an oral response. Find additional details in "The Old Woman Who Lived With the Wolves" that will support your points. If necessary, make notes to guide your response.

Name _____ Date _____

"The Old Woman Who Lived With the Wolves" by Chief Luther Standing Bear
Selection Test A

Critical Reading *Identify the letter of the choice that best answers the question.*

_____ 1. What is one reason that the Sioux move from place to place in "The Old Woman Who Lived With the Wolves"?
   A. to escape from their enemies
   B. to show their children new places
   C. to find grass for their ponies
   D. to be closer to their families

_____ 2. In "The Old Woman Who Lived With the Wolves," why do the Sioux feel that wherever they settle is home?
   A. because they have lived everywhere
   B. because they build houses wherever they go
   C. because they never stop anywhere for long
   D. because they move with their tipis and their families

_____ 3. How does the move in "The Old Woman Who Lived With the Wolves" cause conflict for young Marpiyawin?
   A. She has to leave a good friend.
   B. She loses her dog.
   C. She cannot keep up with her people.
   D. She doesn't like to move.

_____ 4. In "The Old Woman Who Lived With the Wolves," why can you infer that Marpiyawin is very independent?
   A. She helps her mother pack and unpack.
   B. She leaves the village without telling anyone.
   C. She carries her own tipi.
   D. She convinces her people to feed the wolves.

_____ 5. When does Marpiyawin come into conflict with nature?
   A. when she is trapped in a blizzard
   B. when she gets lost in the forest
   C. when she is attacked by wolves
   D. when she can't find enough food

_____ 6. In "The Old Woman Who Lived With the Wolves," which clue leads you to infer that Marpiyawin believes in her dreams?
  A. She is not afraid of the wolves when she wakes up.
  B. She finds her dog exactly where she dreamed he was.
  C. She follows the path she dreamed about.
  D. She dreams about food and finds food when she wakes up.

_____ 7. What does Marpiyawin smell when she comes back to her village?
  A. the odor of food cooking
  B. the odor of wolves
  C. the odor of fear
  D. the odor of humans

_____ 8. What do Marpiyawin's people think when they first see the wolves at the top of the hill?
  A. The wolves will soon attack.
  B. Marpiyawin has been living with the wolves.
  C. The wolves have suddenly become friendly.
  D. Marpiyawin has been in great danger.

_____ 9. Why does Marpiyawin give the wolves meat to eat?
  A. to keep them from attacking the village
  B. to thank them for helping her
  C. to trade with them for her dog
  D. to make sure they don't come back

_____ 10. Which phrase best describes Marpiyawin's relationship with the wolves at the end of the story?
  A. fearful and angry
  B. loving and playful
  C. fond and respectful
  D. suspicious and cautious

Vocabulary and Grammar

_____ 11. In which sentence is the word *coaxed* used correctly?
  A. Marpiyawin coaxed her dog to follow her.
  B. The wolves coaxed Marpiyawin with their fur.
  C. The villagers coaxed when they saw Marpiyawin return.
  D. Marpiyawin felt coaxed when she realized her dog was lost.

_____ 12. In which sentence is the word *conference* used correctly?

    A. Nobody knows which questions will be on the conference.

    B. The parent-teacher conference took place on Monday night.

    C. Kevin wanted to take home his conference after school.

    D. The bus driver forgot to conference before she began her route.

_____ 13. Which sentence contains the past tense form of *hope*?

    A. Marpiyawin hopes that someone is hiding her dog.

    B. Marpiyawin is hoping that someone is hiding her dog.

    C. Marpiyawin hoped that someone was hiding her dog.

    D. Marpiyawin had hoped that someone was hiding her dog.

_____ 14. Which of the following sentences contains the present participle form of *make*?

    A. The wolves make her their friend.

    B. The wolves are making her their friend.

    C. The wolves made her their friend.

    D. The wolves had made her their friend.

Essay

15. In "The Old Woman Who Lived With the Wolves," Marpiyawin realizes her dog is missing and she takes action. In an essay, tell what Marpiyawin did and what her actions tell us about her personality. What kind of person is she? Use information from the story to back up your analysis of her character.

16. In an essay, tell how Marpiyawin's life would have changed and how it would have stayed the same if she had remained with the wolves. Support your response with details from "The Old Woman Who Lived With the Wolves" and with your own prior knowledge about wolves and Native American life at the time of this story.

17. **Thinking About the Big Question: Is conflict always bad?** In "The Old Woman Who Lived with the Wolves," Marpiyawin faces a conflict when she loses her dog. As she searches for the dog, she gets lost in a storm and her life changes. In an essay, discuss how you think Marpiyawin would respond to the question "Is conflict always bad?" Use details from the story to support your point of view.

Name _____ Date _____

"The Old Woman Who Lived With the Wolves" by Chief Luther Standing Bear
Selection Test B

Critical Reading *Identify the letter of the choice that best completes the statement or answers the question.*

____ 1. In "The Old Woman Who Lived With the Wolves," the Sioux feel that wherever they settle is home because
   A. they have lived everywhere.
   B. they stay in the homes of their friends and relatives.
   C. all the land looks the same.
   D. they carry their tipis and their families with them.

____ 2. Why do the Sioux people travel in "The Old Woman Who Lived With the Wolves"?
   A. They must escape rising water in streams and rivers.
   B. They wish to find new puppies.
   C. They seek pure water, pure air, and a clean place for their tipis.
   D. They are at war and are escaping from their enemies.

____ 3. What can you infer from this passage in "The Old Woman Who Lived With the Wolves"?
   > She romped along with the pup, and the way seemed short because she played with it and with the young folks when not busy helping her mother with the packing and unpacking.

   A. Marpiyawin can be serious about life.
   B. Marpiyawin likes to have fun.
   C. Marpiyawin likes all animals.
   D. Marpiyawin wishes the journey were longer.

____ 4. How does moving to a new place cause a conflict for Marpiyawin?
   A. She has to leave a good friend.
   B. She loses her dog.
   C. She loves the place where they were living.
   D. She hates to move.

____ 5. What can you infer from this passage in "The Old Woman Who Lived With the Wolves"?
   > Without a word to anyone, she turned back, for she had no fear of becoming lost.

   A. Marpiyawin is very independent.
   B. Marpiyawin is very fearful.
   C. Marpiyawin does not love her people.
   D. Marpiyawin wants to meet wolves.

____ 6. Why does Marpiyawin have no fear when she leaves the camp to look for her dog?
   A. The young men of the village are escorting her.
   B. She has her mother's permission to leave camp to find her dog.
   C. Nothing bad has ever happened to her, so she does not expect problems.
   D. She knows that the wolves will watch over her.

___ 7. Marpiyawin encounters an external conflict when she
   A. is trapped in a blizzard.
   B. worries about her dog.
   C. is not allowed to leave her tipi.
   D. has a vision in a dream.

___ 8. What can you infer from this passage from "The Old Woman Who Lived With the Wolves"?

   As Marpiyawin neared the village, she smelled a very unpleasant odor. At first it mystified her, then she realized it was the smell of human beings.

   A. Marpiyawin has become a wolf.
   B. Marpiyawin no longer smells like a human.
   C. Marpiyawin is now afraid of humans.
   D. Marpiyawin cannot return to her people.

___ 9. What internal conflict does Marpiyawin face after the wolves lead her back to her people?
   A. She feels guilty for having left her people.
   B. She must decide whether to feed the wolves or feed her people.
   C. She is sad to say good-bye to the wolves, but she wants to rejoin her people.
   D. She is indecisive about whether or not to keep looking for her dog.

___ 10. When Marpiyawin's people see the wolves on the top of the hill, they think that
   A. Marpiyawin has been in great danger.
   B. Marpiyawin has been living with the wolves.
   C. the wolves have suddenly become friendly.
   D. the wolves are returning Marpiyawin's dog.

___ 11. How does Marpiyawin repay the wolves for their kindness?
   A. She sings to them.
   B. She brings them meat when food is scarce.
   C. She warns them when enemies are near.
   D. She teaches them her language.

___ 12. What information do the wolves share with Marpiyawin after she returns to her people?
   A. The wolves show the Sioux a new place to live.
   B. The wolves teach the Sioux how to hunt.
   C. The wolves advise the Sioux where to find food and water.
   D. The wolves warn Marpiyawin when bad weather and enemies are coming.

___ 13. Which statement can you infer from your knowledge about wolves and from information in "The Old Woman Who Lived With the Wolves"?
   A. Marpiyawin's people are probably uneasy having wolves near the village.
   B. Marpiyawin's people learned to get along well with wolves.
   C. Marpiyawin's people have never seen wolves before their arrival at the village.
   D. Marpiyawin's people will not be able to live in the same land as wolves.

Vocabulary and Grammar

___ 14. Marpiyawin *coaxed* her dog to come with her along the trail. This means that she
    A. forced him.
    B. ignored him.
    C. urged him gently.
    D. pulled him with a leash.

___ 15. In which sentence is the word *speculate* used correctly?
    A. The people tried to speculate about what the wolves wanted.
    B. Marpiyawin asked the wolves to speculate what gift they wanted from her.
    C. No one could speculate enough, because they were so happy to see Marpiyawin.
    D. The wolves were able to speculate in Marpiyawin's dream.

___ 16. Which principal part of the underlined verb is being used?
    Perhaps someone <u>liked</u> her playful pet and was keeping him concealed.

    A. past
    B. past participle
    C. present
    D. present participle

___ 17. Which principal part of the underlined verb is being used?
    Who <u>is calling</u> to Marpiyawin and what are they saying?

    A. present
    B. past
    C. present participle
    D. past participle

Essay

18. In "The Old Woman Who Lived With the Wolves," Marpiyawin learns that "while man often considers the animal offensive, so do animals find man offensive." In an essay, explain the lesson about humans and animals that the quotation illustrates. Use examples from the story to show how the idea it expresses might improve the lives of both humans and animals.

19. The Sioux people and Marpiyawin feel a certain way about wolves at the beginning of "The Old Woman Who Lived With the Wolves." Their feelings have changed by the end of the story. In an essay, describe the attitude of Marpiyawin and her people toward the wolves. Using details from the story, explain how and why those attitudes change.

20. **Thinking About the Big Question: Is conflict always bad?** In "The Old Woman Who Lived with the Wolves," Marpiyawin faces a conflict when she loses her dog. The journey she takes to find the animal opens a new world for her. In an essay, discuss how you think Marpiyawin would respond to the question "Is conflict always bad?" Use details from the story to support your point of view.

Vocabulary Warm-up Word Lists

Study these words from the selections. Then, complete the activities.

Word List A

average [AV uh rij] *n.* in sports, a measure of a player's skill on offense
Sandy's batting <u>average</u> was .357.

broad [BRAWD] *adj.* full or wide
The robbery occurred in the middle of the afternoon and in <u>broad</u> daylight.

crushed [KRUSHT] *v.* squashed
Andrew heard a crunching sound as he <u>crushed</u> the beetle with his foot.

envy [EN vee] *v.* feeling of jealousy
I <u>envy</u> my sister's skill in math.

interfere [in ter FEER] *v.* to involve yourself in a situation that has nothing to do with you
Rajiv tried not to <u>interfere</u> with his parents' plans to go on vacation.

quarrel [KWAWR rul] *v.* an argument
Manuel and Sam had a <u>quarrel</u> over who would play on first base.

sympathy [SIM puh thee] *n.* the understanding or sharing of other people's troubles
Annalisa felt <u>sympathy</u> for the wounded sparrow.

terrific [tuh RIF ik] *adj.* very good or excellent
Megan thinks that action-packed novels are a <u>terrific</u> read.

Word List B

ballplayer [BAWL play uhr] *n.* one who plays ball, especially baseball
Mickey Mantle was a great <u>ballplayer</u>.

barged [BARJD] *v.* entered loudly, rudely, and abruptly
The noisy group of students <u>barged</u> into the room.

outfield [OWT feeld] *n.* part of a baseball field between the infield and the foul lines
Derek's favorite baseball position was in the <u>outfield</u> behind second and third bases.

menace [MEN is] *n.* a threat or danger
Jonathan's ability to score made him a <u>menace</u> to other teams.

permanent [PUR muh nuhnt] *adj.* lasting or meant to last for a long time, or forever
After many changes, Lisa made a <u>permanent</u> move to the city.

trophy [TROH fee] *n.* a prize or award given to a winning team or athlete
The team's captain accepted the <u>trophy</u> after winning the big game.

uncertain [uhn SER tuhn] *adj.* not sure
I was <u>uncertain</u> about the umpire's decision to allow the player to remain on third base.

unreasonable [uhn REE zuhn uh buhl] *adj.* not showing good sense
She thought her parents' demand that she keep her room clean was <u>unreasonable</u>.

"Becky and the Wheels-and-Brake Boys" by James Berry
"The Southpaw" by Judith Viorst
Vocabulary Warm-up Exercises

Exercise A *Fill in each blank in the paragraph below with an appropriate word from Word List A. Use each word only once.*

Steve and Kelly had a big [1] _____ after school, right in

[2] _____ daylight. Kelly did not want Steve to [3] _____

with her plans for the day. She had a ticket to a [4] _____ action movie

that had gotten great reviews.

"You see too many movies," Steve protested. "Your [5] _____ is three

movies a week!" Secretly, he was hoping Kelly would give him her ticket.

Steve's hopes were quickly [6] _____, however. "You're just filled with

[7] _____ because I have a ticket and you don't," Kelly replied. She did

not have any [8] _____ for Steve's jealousy.

Exercise B *Answer the questions with complete explanations.*

Example: Would a bad driver be a <u>menace</u> on the road?
Yes, a bad driver would be a danger on the road because a bad driver is more likely to have an accident.

1. If someone <u>barged</u> into the room, would you notice immediately?
   _____

2. If your friend wins a <u>trophy</u>, should she be congratulated?
   _____

3. Are your plans for the future <u>uncertain</u>?
   _____

4. How long should a <u>permanent</u> change last? Explain.
   _____

5. Does winning a baseball game prove that someone is a good <u>ballplayer</u>? Explain.
   _____

6. If your coach asked you to practice for six hours a day, would that be <u>unreasonable</u>?
   _____

7. When someone is assigned to the <u>outfield</u>, can he or she also cover home plate?
   _____

"Becky and the Wheels-and-Brake Boys" by James Berry
"The Southpaw" by Judith Viorst
Reading Warm-up A

Read the following passage. Pay special attention to the underlined words. Then, read it again, and complete the activities. Use a separate sheet of paper for your written answers.

Alex saw her brother, Lucas, going out to play soccer with his friends. She felt a pang of <u>envy</u> every time she saw him playing with the boys who lived on their street. Alex was jealous that she wasn't allowed to play with them. Lucas didn't like it when she tried to <u>interfere</u> with his games. He thought playing soccer with his friends wasn't something she should get involved in.

As he stepped out the door, Alex ran after him. "Lucas," she said as she caught up with her brother, "wait for me. I want to play with you guys."

Lucas turned around and shook his head at his sister. "I'm sorry, but you just can't play with us today, and don't start a <u>quarrel</u> with me. You know Mom doesn't like it when we argue." Lucas was right. His mother no longer had any <u>sympathy</u> for either of them about this situation. She had stopped feeling sorry for Lucas, who wanted to avoid his sister, and for Alex, who felt left out.

For a second, Alex thought her hopes had been <u>crushed</u>, and she wouldn't be able to play. Then, she decided to stand up for herself.

"Why won't you let me play?" She protested. "You know I'm a <u>terrific</u> soccer player. My <u>average</u> was two goals a game last year."

Lucas knew his sister was right. It didn't matter that she was a girl. She could score more goals than anyone else Lucas knew.

Suddenly, Lucas realized how much he wanted to win that day. Alex had the skills to take his team to victory. If she scored the winning goal, the team would cheer Lucas on for having a great sister.

"All right," he said to Alex. "You can play today. Come with me."

Alex flashed a <u>broad</u> smile that filled her whole face. She knew she wouldn't let her brother down.

1. Underline the words that explain what it means to feel <u>envy</u>. Write a sentence about something that makes you feel *envy*.

2. Circle the words that tell you what it means to <u>interfere</u>. Use *interfere* in a sentence.

3. Underline the words that tell you what a <u>quarrel</u> is. Describe the last *quarrel* you had with someone.

4. Underline the name of the person who no longer had <u>sympathy</u> for Lucas and Alex. Use *sympathy* in a sentence.

5. Circle what has been <u>crushed</u>. Then tell what *crushed* means.

6. What does it mean when Alex says she's a <u>terrific</u> soccer player? What are you *terrific* at?

7. Circle Alex's soccer <u>average</u>. What is your *average* in your favorite sport?

8. Circle the words that tell you what <u>broad</u> means. Explain the word *broad* in your own words.

"Becky and the Wheels-and-Brake Boys" by James Berry
"The Southpaw" by Judith Viorst
Reading Warm-up B

Read the following passage. Pay special attention to the underlined words. Then, read it again, and complete the activities. Use a separate sheet of paper for your written answers.

In 1942, baseball was in a crisis. Many of the top players in America had gone off to fight in World War II. Baseball club owners like Philip K. Wrigley were looking for a new type of <u>ballplayer</u> to bring the crowds into their stadiums. Wrigley made a big decision that year. He was going to include women in minor league baseball.

Women had been playing semiprofessional sports since the 1870s. But in 1942, there was no professional baseball league for women. Many people found the idea of women playing pro baseball <u>unreasonable</u>. They thought the rules of the game made it too hard for women to play well. In 1942, however, four women's teams <u>barged</u> into the world of baseball. They were known as the All-American Girls Baseball League. At its height, the AAGBL had ten teams and drew thousands of eager fans.

With resolve, these women set out to prove that they could play baseball as well as anybody. Sophie Kurys of the Racine Bells was known for being a daring player. In 1946 alone, she stole 201 bases. That year, she led the Racine Bells to the AAGBL championship <u>trophy</u>. She still holds the record for the highest number of stolen bases in professional baseball.

Rose Gacioch of the Rockford Peaches started in the <u>outfield</u>. In 1946, she led the league in triples. Then she began pitching and became even more of a <u>menace</u> to other teams. In 1951, she won 20 games for her team.

Despite the league's success, the AAGBL did not become a <u>permanent</u> addition to baseball. In 1954, <u>uncertain</u> that women should play professional baseball, team owners decided to eliminate the league. Since the AAGBL was ended, opportunities for women in baseball have been limited. Still, the achievements of the AAGBL and its gutsy players have not been forgotten.

1. Circle the word that indicates where a <u>ballplayer</u> would play. Write a sentence with the word **ballplayer**.

2. Underline the sentence that tells you why people found the idea of women's baseball <u>unreasonable</u>. What is something you think is **unreasonable**?

3. Rewrite the sentence containing the word <u>barged</u>, using a synonym for **barged**. Then write what the word means.

4. Write a sentence describing how it might feel to win a <u>trophy</u> in your favorite sport.

5. In your own words, describe what the <u>outfield</u> is.

6. How did Rose Gacioch become a real <u>menace</u> to other teams? What would make an opposing player a **menace**?

7. What does it mean that the AAGBL was not <u>permanent</u>? Write a sentence using the word **permanent**.

8. What made the AAGBL team owners feel <u>uncertain</u>? Describe something about which you are **uncertain**.

Name _____ Date _____

"Becky and the Wheels-and-Brake Boys" by James Berry,
"The Southpaw" by Judith Viorst
Writing About the Big Question

Is conflict always bad?

Big Question Vocabulary

argue	battle	challenge	compete	conclude
convince	defend	game	issue	lose
negotiate	oppose	resolve	survival	win

A. *Use one or more words from the list above to complete each sentence.*

1. In a baseball _____, two teams play.

2. The two teams _____ each other, one on each side.

3. One team will _____, and the other will _____.

4. The losing team must _____ to do better next time.

B. *Respond to each item with a complete sentence.*

1. Describe a game you have played that was hard-fought.

   _____

   _____

2. Explain whether you won or lost, and why. Use at least two Big Question
   vocabulary words in your response.

   _____

   _____

   _____

C. *Complete this sentence. Then, write a brief paragraph in which you connect this
sentence to the Big Question.*

When a person uses force in a conflict to get what he or she wants, _____

   _____

   _____

   _____

   _____

   _____

   _____

   _____

Unit 2 Resources: Short Stories
© Pearson Education, Inc. All rights reserved.
105

"**Becky and the Wheels-and-Brake Boys**" by James Berry
"**The Southpaw**" by Judith Viorst

Literary Analysis: Comparing Characters' Traits and Motives

The qualities that make a character unique are called **character traits**. A **character's motives** are the reasons behind a character's thoughts, feelings, and actions. These motivations can be based on internal and external factors.

- *Internal factors* include thoughts and feelings, such as love, pride, or anger.
- *External factors* are events or actions, such as a natural disaster or winning a prize.

A. DIRECTIONS: *Read the following passage. Then, answer the questions.*

> Then, going home with the noisy flock of children from school, I had such a new, new idea. If Mum thought I was scruffy, Nat, Aldo, Jimmy, and Ben might think so, too. I didn't like that.
> After dinner I combed my hair in the bedroom.

1. What character traits does Becky reveal in this passage?

_____

2. What external factor motivates the narrator, Becky, to comb her hair?

_____

3. What internal factor motivates Becky to comb her hair?

_____

B. DIRECTIONS: *Read the following passages. Then, write a response.*

> Dear Richard,
>   I wasn't kicking exactly. I was kicking back.
>   Your former friend,
>   Janet
>
> P.S. In case you were wondering, my batting average is .345.

> Dear Janet,
>
>   Alfie is having his tonsils out tomorrow. We might be able to let you catch next week.
>   Richard

1. What character traits does Janet reveal in her note?

_____

2. What character traits does Richard reveal in his note?

_____

3. Alfie is mentioned in Richard's letter to Janet. Write a short letter from Alfie to Richard that explains the external motivation that will cause him to miss a baseball game.

_____

_____

_____

Name _____ Date _____

Word List

enviable	envied	envy	former	menace
reckless	recklessly	recklessness	unreasonable	

A. DIRECTIONS: *Write a sentence to answer each question. In your sentence, use a word from the Word List that has a similar meaning to the underlined word or words. The first one is done for you as an example.*

1. Who was your piano teacher in the past?

   My former piano teacher was Mr. Ruiz.

2. What habit is a danger to your health?

   _____

3. What rule might you find unfair?

   _____

4. What action might you expect from a careless truck driver?

   _____

5. When have you felt unhappiness because you wanted something that belonged to someone else?

   _____

   _____

B. DIRECTIONS: *Choose another form of the underlined word in each sentence. Use the new form in your answer.*

1. What might you envy about someone else's life?

   _____

2. What kind of reckless behavior have you seen?

   _____

3. What kind of talent have you envied?

   _____

4. Why do you think people sometimes act with recklessness?

   _____

"Becky and the Wheels-and-Brake Boys" by James Berry
"The Southpaw" by Judith Viorst

Integrated Language Skills: Support for Writing an Essay

Before you draft your essay comparing and contrasting the traits and motives of Becky and Janet, complete the graphic organizer below. In the first row, write what each girl wants. In the second row, tell what motivates each girl to try to get what she wants. Then, in the third row, tell whether their character traits help or hinder each girl as she strives to reach her goal.

	Becky	**Janet**
What She Wants		
What Motivates Her to Try to Get What She Wants?		
What Traits Help Her? What Traits Hinder Her?		

Now, use your notes to write a brief essay comparing and contrasting the motives and traits of Becky and Janet.

"Becky and the Wheels-and-Brake Boys" by James Berry
"The Southpaw" by Judith Viorst
Open-Book Test

Short Answer *Write your responses to the questions in this section on the lines provided.*

1. In "Becky and the Wheels-and-Brake Boys," Granny-Liz tells Becky, "A tomboy's like a whistling woman and a crowing hen, who can only come to a bad end." Explain what she means.

   _____

   _____

2. Describe the relationship between Becky and her mother in "Becky and the Wheels-and-Brake Boys." Use details from the story to support your description.

   _____

   _____

3. Near the end of "Becky and the Wheels-and-Brake Boys," Ben's eyes pop with envy when he sees Becky's bike. Explain why Becky feels envy at the beginning of the story.

   _____

   _____

4. In "The Southpaw," Janet and Richard refer to themselves as "former" friends. Explain what former action leads to the cockroach incident in "Becky and the Wheels-and-Brake Boys."

   _____

   _____

5. At the beginning of "The Southpaw," Richard and Janet are fighting. In his last letter, Richard asks Janet to at least call her goldfish "Richard" again. Explain what the last letter tells you about the relationship between Janet and Richard at the end of the story.

   _____

   _____

6. Both "Becky and the Wheels-and-Brake Boys" and "The Southpaw" tell about a fight between friends. How does Becky's motive, or reason, for fighting with Shirnette differ from Janet's motive for fighting with Richard? Include details from the stories in your answer.

   _____

   _____

   _____

7. Think about how the main characters in "Becky and the Wheels-and-Brake Boys" and "The Southpaw" are able to get what they want. What is a main idea shared by both stories? Use examples from the stories to support your answer.

_____

_____

_____

8. The main characters of "Becky and the Wheels-and-Brake Boys" and "The Southpaw" share some of the same motivations. What is one internal motivation that Becky and Janet share? Use examples from the stories to support your answer.

_____

_____

9. External factors motivate other characters in both "Becky and the Wheels-and-Brake Boys" and "The Southpaw." On the chart, write the external factor that motivates the character and what happens because of that factor. Then tell how the actions of these characters influence the outcome of both stories.

Character	External Factor	What Happens
Becky's mother		
Richard		

_____

10. The main characters from "Becky and the Wheels-and-Brake Boys" and "The Southpaw" both get what they want by the end of the stories. Do you think the two girls are more motivated by internal or external factors? Use details to explain.

_____

_____

_____

Essay

Write an extended response to the question of your choice or to the question or questions your teacher assigns you.

11. Both Becky in "Becky and the Wheels-and-Brake Boys" and Janet in "The Southpaw" have strong ideas about what girls can do. Consider what each character believes about girls and their abilities. Then in an essay, explain how these ideas either create or solve problems for the two characters. Use details from the stories to support your ideas.

12. The main characters of both "Becky and the Wheels-and-Brake Boys" and "The Southpaw" are girls. Suppose the main characters had been boys instead. In an essay, discuss how this would change the stories. Consider the conflict of each story and how or if the story would change. Use details from the stories to support your ideas.

13. The main characters of "Becky and the Wheels-and-Brake Boys" and "The Southpaw" have motives behind their actions. In an essay, discuss the reasons behind one important action that Becky and Janet take. Focus on the internal and external factors that motivate the character to take that action. Include details from the stories in your answer.

14. **Thinking About the Big Question: Is conflict always bad?** Both Becky in "Becky and the Wheels-and-Brake Boys" and Janet in "The Southpaw" face conflicts when something gets in the way of their goals. In an essay, discuss if the conflicts the girls face are bad or good for them. Use details from the stories to support your ideas.

Oral Response

15. Go back to question 2, 6, 7, or 8 or to the question your teacher assigns to you. Take a few minutes to expand your answer and prepare an oral response. Find additional details in "Becky and the Wheels-and-Brake Boys" and "The Southpaw" that will support your points. If necessary, make notes to guide your response.

"Becky and the Wheels-and-Brake Boys" by James Berry
"The Southpaw" by Judith Viorst
Selection Test A

Critical Reading *Identify the letter of the choice that best answers the question.*

____ 1. What is Becky's problem in "Becky and the Wheels-and-Brake Boys"?
   A. Becky wants to learn to ride a bike, but the boys will not teach her.
   B. Becky wants a bike, but her grandmother will not let her have one.
   C. Becky wants to be friends with Shirnette, but Shirnette will not speak to her.
   D. Becky wants a bike, but her mother cannot afford one.

____ 2. Which sentence best describes Becky's relationship with her mother?
   A. They love each other, but they don't always agree.
   B. They barely speak to each other.
   C. Becky's mother loves her, but Becky doesn't love her mother.
   D. Neither has any feelings for the other.

____ 3. Why does Becky want her own bike?
   A. so she won't have to help out at home
   B. so the boys will be jealous of her
   C. so she can ride with the boys
   D. so she can get away from Shirnette

____ 4. In "Becky and the Wheels-and-Brake Boys," what is Becky's motive when she tries to sell her father's helmet?
   A. The boys dare her to do it.
   B. She is angry with her grandmother.
   C. She feels sorry for her mother.
   D. The helmet reminds her of her father.

____ 5. Janet writes this to Richard in the first letter in "The Southpaw":

   If I'm not good enough to play on your team, I'm not good enough to be friends with.

   What motivates Janet to write this letter?
   A. Janet enjoys having a good argument with her friend Richard.
   B. Richard hurt Janet's feelings when he did not invite her to play baseball.
   C. Janet thinks she is not skilled enough to play baseball.
   D. Richard does not want any friends.

_____ 6. In "The Southpaw," why do Richard and Janet disagree?

　　A. Richard says he is a good baseball player and Janet disagrees.

　　B. Janet wants to be invited to Richard's birthday party and he disagrees.

　　C. Janet wants to be the captain of the baseball team and Richard disagrees.

　　D. Janet thinks girls should play on Richard's baseball team and he disagrees.

_____ 7. In "The Southpaw," what motivates Richard to let Janet play on the team?

　　A. He is tired of arguing with Janet.

　　B. Janet does not invite him to get a sundae.

　　C. Janet is good at knitting.

　　D. His team is having a losing streak.

_____ 8. In the last letter in "The Southpaw," Richard writes the following:

　　At least could you call your goldfish Richard again?

　　What does this sentence tell you about Janet and Richard's relationship at the end of "The Southpaw"?

　　A. They are friends again.

　　B. Richard is angry with Janet, but she wants to be friends again.

　　C. They have agreed to be teammates but not friends.

　　D. They are angry with each other.

_____ 9. What character trait is shared by both Becky in "Becky and the Wheels-and-Brake Boys" and Janet in "The Southpaw"?

　　A. Both are determined.

　　B. Both are fearful.

　　C. Both are good sports.

　　D. Both want to be popular.

_____ 10. Why are the main characters of Becky in "Becky and the Wheels-and-Brake Boys" and Janet in "The Southpaw" left out of a group?

　　A. The two characters do poorly in sports.

　　B. The two characters are left out of boys-only groups.

　　C. The two characters have no sports equipment.

　　D. The two characters do not tell anyone they want to be in the group.

_____ 11. Which opinion would most likely be shared by Becky and Janet?

　　A. Boys and girls should stay in separate groups.

　　B. Boys can do most things better than girls.

　　C. Girls can do anything that boys can do.

　　D. Girls can do most things better than boys.

Unit 2 Resources: Short Stories
113

___ 12. Which of the following best states the theme in both "Becky and the Wheels-and-Brake Boys" and "The Southpaw"?

A. It pays to be selfish.

B. It pays to be determined.

C. It never pays to speak your mind.

D. It never pays to invite yourself into a group.

Vocabulary

___ 13. What does the word *envy* mean in this sentence?

Seeing my bike much, much newer than his, my cousin Ben's eyes popped with envy.

A. pain

B. danger

C. carelessness

D. jealousy

___ 14. In "The Southpaw," Janet signs her letter "Your former friend." What is a *former* friend?

A. someone who used to be a friend

B. someone who will always be a friend

C. someone who will never be a friend

D. a future friend

Essay

15. Both Becky in "Becky and the Wheels-and-Brake Boys" and Janet in "The Southpaw" have strong ideas about girls and their abilities. In an essay, explain how these ideas create or overcome problems for the two characters. Use examples from the stories to support your ideas.

16. Both Becky in "Becky and the Wheels-and-Brake Boys" and Janet in "The Southpaw" have motives, or reasons, for their actions. In an essay, tell about an important action each character takes and identify the character's motives for that action. End your essay by discussing one motive that both girls share.

17. **Thinking About the Big Question: Is conflict always bad?** Becky faces a conflict that gets in the way of what she wants in "Becky and the Wheels-and-Brake Boys." Janet faces a similar conflict in "The Southpaw." In an essay, tell whether you think the conflicts are bad or good for the girls. Use details about the conflicts to support your ideas.

"Becky and the Wheels-and-Brake Boys" by James Berry

"The Southpaw" by Judith Viorst

Selection Test B

Critical Reading *Identify the letter of the choice that best completes the statement or answers the question.*

____ 1. In "Becky and the Wheels-and-Brake Boys," Becky thinks that if she had a bike of her own,
    A. she would be able to ride faster than the boys.
    B. the boys would want her to ride with them.
    C. the boys would envy her new bike.
    D. she wouldn't have to stay home and help her mother.

____ 2. In "Becky and the Wheels-and-Brake Boys," which external factor motivates Becky to ask for a bike?
    A. Her mother doesn't have enough money.
    B. The boys ride away from her every time she comes near.
    C. Janice Gordon has a bike.
    D. She knows that her father would have bought her a bike.

____ 3. Which of the following best describes Becky's problem?
    A. Becky wants to learn how to ride a bike, but the boys will not teach her.
    B. Becky wants a bike, but her mother does not want her to have one.
    C. Becky wants to make up with Shirnette, but Shirnette will not speak to her.
    D. Becky wants a bike, but her mother cannot afford one.

____ 4. What does Granny-Liz mean when she tells Becky, "A tomboy's like a whistling woman and a crowing hen, who can only come to a bad end."
    A. Only men can whistle and only roosters can crow.
    B. If Becky had a bike, she would probably fall down and hurt herself.
    C. Some things are just for boys, and girls should not try to do them.
    D. It is bad luck for a woman to whistle.

____ 5. What is one of Becky's motives for trying to sell her father's helmet?
    A. She feels sorry for her mother.
    B. The boys dare her to do it.
    C. She is angry with her grandmother.
    D. The helmet reminds her of her father.

____ 6. Which sentence best describes the relationship between Becky and her mother in "Becky and the Wheels-and-Brake Boys"?
    A. They love each other, but they don't always agree.
    B. They barely speak to each other.
    C. Becky's mother loves her, but doesn't care if Becky is happy.
    D. Becky is so selfish that she won't consider how her mother feels.

____ 7. In "The Southpaw," what internal factor motivates Janet to write Richard the first letter?
A. She feels sorry that she has been rude to Richard.
B. She wants her sweatshirt back.
C. Her feelings are hurt because he won't let her play baseball.
D. Richard did not invite her to his birthday party.

____ 8. Which of the following cause Richard and Janet to disagree in "The Southpaw"?
I. whether Richard is a good baseball player
II. whether Janet should be allowed to play on the Mapes Street baseball team
III. whether girls should be allowed to play on the Mapes Street baseball team
IV. whether Janet should replace Richard as the captain of the Mapes Street baseball team
A. II only   B. I and IV   C. II and III   D. IV only

____ 9. Which of Richard's statements in "The Southpaw" reveals his motive for quarreling with Janet?
A. "Ronnie caught the chicken pox and Leo broke his toe and Elwood has these stupid violin lessons."
B. "I want my comic books now—finished or not."
C. "No girl has ever played on the Mapes Street baseball team, and as long as I'm captain, no girl ever will."
D. "I hope when you go for your checkup you need a tetanus shot."

____ 10. In "The Southpaw," what external factor motivates Richard to invite Janet to play on the team?
A. He feels guilty about the way he has treated Janet.
B. Janet did not come to his birthday party.
C. Janet does not want to learn to knit.
D. His team has a 12-game losing streak.

____ 11. Which best describes the relationship between Janet and Richard at the end of "The Southpaw"?
A. They are still angry with each other.
B. Richard is angry with Janet, but she wants to be friends again.
C. They have reached an agreement but are not friends.
D. They are friends again.

____ 12. Both Becky in "Becky and the Wheels-and-Brake Boys" and Janet in "The Southpaw" want
A. to learn a sport.
B. to be given a chance.
C. to teach someone a lesson.
D. to buy something new.

____ 13. Becky and Janet would most likely agree that
A. girls can do most things better than boys.
B. boys should do their own things, and girls should do their own things.
C. girls can do anything that boys can do.
D. boys can do most things better than girls.

___ **14.** Which character trait is shared by both Becky and Janet?
   A. determination
   B. a dislike of sports
   C. the desire to be popular
   D. jealousy

___ **15.** Both Becky in "Becky and the Wheels-and-Brake Boys" and Janet in "The Southpaw" have been left out of a group because
   A. they are too pushy.
   B. they are not good athletes.
   C. they are girls.
   D. they do not own sports equipment.

Vocabulary

___ **16.** Which of the phrases below best defines the word *reckless* in the following sentence?
   Next, most reckless and fierce, all the boys raced against each other.

   A. not caring about winning   C. not caring about danger
   B. unskilled and clumsy   D. brave and daring

___ **17.** In "Becky and the Wheels-and-Brake Boys," what is the object of Becky's *envy*?
   A. her mother's kitchen   C. Shirnette's blouse
   B. the boys' bikes   D. her father's sun helmet

___ **18.** When Janet signs a letter to Richard "Your *former* friend," what does she mean?
   A. that they are friends once again   C. that they will always be friends
   B. that they were never friends   D. that they used to be friends

Essay

19. Both Becky in "Becky and the Wheels-and-Brake Boys" and Janet in "The Southpaw" have ideas about what girls can do. In an essay, explain what these ideas are and how they differ from the ideas of the other people in the stories. In your opinion, do Becky's and Janet's ideas create problems for them or help them solve problems? How? Use examples from the stories to support your ideas.

20. In both "Becky and the Wheels-and-Brake Boys" and "The Southpaw," characters undergo a change in perspective—the way a character views something. In an essay, describe how the perspective of a character from each story changes. Once that character's perspective changes, what else changes as a result? Use details from the stories to support your points.

21. Both Becky in "Becky and the Wheels-and-Brake Boys" and Janet in "The Southpaw" have motives for their actions. In an essay, discuss one important action each character takes. Describe the internal and external factors that motivate the character to take that action and how the action reflects the character's traits.

22. Thinking About the Big Question: Is conflict always bad? Both Becky in "Becky and the Wheels-and-Brake Boys" and Janet in "The Southpaw" face conflicts when something gets in the way of their goals. In an essay, discuss whether the conflicts the girls face are bad or good for them. Use details from the stories to support your ideas.

Writing Workshop—Unit 2, Part 1
Response to Literature: Review

Prewriting: Gathering Details

For the literary work you choose, think about the point you will discuss. To help you do this, answer the questions in the chart provided. Then, list details from the work that support your answers.

Questions:	Yes / No	Details from the work that support your answer:
Was the plot believable?		
Could you relate to the characters?		
Did you agree with the message?		

Drafting: Organizing Your Response

Organize your draft by using the following graphic organizer. In the boxes on the right, list the parts of your essay in order.

Introduction
Include a brief summary that describes the central problem.

Body
Offer evidence to support your idea, including quotations and examples.

Conclusion
Restate your interpretation and perhaps include feelings or opinions about what you have read.

Writing Workshop—Unit 2, Part 1
Review: Integrating Grammar Skills

Correcting Errors in the Use of Troublesome Irregular Verbs

In irregular verbs, the past and past participle are not formed by adding -ed or -d to the present tense.

Present	Present Participle	Past	Past Participle
drink	(am) drinking	drank	(have) drunk
do	(am) doing	did	(have) done
bring	(am) bringing	brought	(have) brought

Troublesome verbs are verb pairs that are easily confused.

Troublesome Verb Pairs (lay/lie, raise/rise/, set/sit)	Example
Lay means "to put or place something." *Lie* means "to be situated."	Tom *laid* the pen on the table. Barb *is lying* in the hammock.
Raise means "to lift up." It takes a direct object. *Rise* means "to get up." It does not take a direct object.	The wind *has raised* some dust. My neighbors *rise* very early.
Set means "to put something in a certain place." It is followed by a direct object. *Sit* means "to rest." It does not take a direct object.	Ms. Wendt *set* the vase near the window. Jamie *is sitting* near the pool.

Using Irregular Verbs and Troublesome Verbs

A. DIRECTIONS: *On the line, write the letter of the correct verb for the sentence.*

1. The game _____ five minutes ago.
   A. begin   B. began   C. begun

2. The Wildcats have already _____ up two goals.
   A. give   B. gave   C. given

3. We're waiting for LaRue to _____ one in for our team.
   A. lay   B. lie   C. laid

4. The crowd will _____ to cheer if we score a point now.
   A. raise   B. rise   C. risen

Fixing Incorrect Forms of Irregular Verbs and Troublesome Verbs

B. DIRECTIONS: *On the lines, rewrite the italicized words using the correct verb forms.*

1. The bell *rung* to signal the end of the quarter. _____

2. We're behind, but the team is *striven* to win. _____

3. We won't take a loss *laying* down. _____

4. Look! They have *drove* the ball down the court. _____

Unit 2: Short Stories
Benchmark Test 3

MULTIPLE CHOICE

Reading Skill: Making Inferences

1. What is an inference?
   A. a logical assumption about something not in the text
   B. a reader's appreciation of an author's skills or techniques
   C. a conversation in which characters have to read between the lines
   D. the central idea or insight expressed in a literary work

2. Which of these steps is basic to making inferences?
   A. focusing on the main ideas
   B. using details that the text provides
   C. separating fact from opinion
   D. restating in simpler words

Read this selection from a story. Then, answer the questions that follow.

It was Act 1, Scene 1. As soon as Rafe got on stage, his whole body tensed. When he tried to deliver his lines, he stammered. Finally, he took a deep breath and was able to speak.

3. From the details in the selection and your own prior knowledge, what inference can you make about Rafe's situation?
   A. He is performing with a band.
   B. He is giving an oral report in English class.
   C. He is performing in a play.
   D. He is delivering a political speech in front of his school.

4. From the details in the selection, what can you infer about Rafe's feelings or attitude?
   A. He feels calm and well prepared.
   B. He is not concerned with the impression he makes.
   C. He loves being the center of attention.
   D. He is very nervous about performing well.

Read the selection. Then, answer the questions that follow.

Meghan was practically the first one out of school when the bell rang. Now, she walked down the street with a smile on her face and a spring in her step. Finally, her mom had agreed that they could afford the dance classes. Meghan couldn't wait to put on her ballet slippers and begin learning the steps and positions. Glancing at the clock in front of the bank, she began walking even more rapidly. She wished she had taken the bus, but she always walked when she could save on bus fares. Still, it wouldn't do to be late to her first dance class.

5. Using your prior knowledge and the details in the selection, what can you infer about the time this selection takes place?
   A. It is probably a weekday in early morning.
   B. It is probably a weekday in late afternoon.
   C. It is probably a weekend in early morning.
   D. It is probably a weekend in late afternoon.

Reading Skill: Using Text Aids and Features

6. In textbooks, what is the main purpose of the text aids and text features?
   A. to preview the information in each chapter
   B. to organize details and highlight important information
   C. to entertain readers and keep them from getting bored
   D. to test the information in each chapter

7. Which of these most often provide examples or illustrations of information in textbooks?
   A. headings
   B. subheadings
   C. charts
   D. pictures

8. Which of the following text features might explain a picture or a chart?
   A. a subheading
   B. a caption
   C. a heading
   D. a graphic organizer

Literary Analysis: Characterization and Conflict

9. What is characterization?
   A. the people who appear in a story or another work
   B. the relationships between characters in a work
   C. the way writers develop and reveal characters
   D. the reasons behind characters' thoughts and actions

10. Which of these is an example of direct characterization?
    A. Jerry was angry and upset.
    B. Jerry clenched his fists.
    C. "How dare you!" Jerry shrieked.
    D. "I'm going to scream," Jerry thought.

11. What do you call the part of a story in which the conflict is settled?
    A. the exposition
    B. the rising action
    C. the climax
    D. the resolution

12. Which of these is an internal conflict?
    A. A sailor struggles to survive a shipwreck.
    B. A child struggles to make the right decision.
    C. An athlete struggles to defeat her competition.
    D. Two men in love with the same woman struggle to win her regard.

Read this selection. Then, answer the questions that follow.

Today was the day, Heather decided. She would row that boat across the river in less than half an hour, beating her brother's record. Of course, even on a sunny, windless day like today, she knew the task would be difficult. No matter the weather, the river currents were always strong. Still, Heather was strong too. She was a very competitive person. She had been practicing rowing for months. She knew all the tips for using the oars to achieve speed and smoothness in the water. She had built up her upper-arm strength and mastered her rhythm and breathing. "I'll show you," she told her father. "Girls can be as good athletes as boys are."

13. Which of these details from the selection is an example of direct characterization of Heather?
    A. She was a very competitive person.
    B. She had built up her upper-arm strength and mastered her rhythm and breathing.
    C. She had been practicing rowing for months.
    D. "I'll show you," she told her father. "Girls can be as good athletes as boys are."

14. What can you conclude about Heather from the examples of indirect characterization?
    A. She is talented but lazy.
    B. She is nervous and shy.
    C. She is hard working and determined.
    D. She is jealous and cruel.

15. Which of these is most clearly an internal conflict that Heather faces?
    A. her struggle to win her father's approval
    B. her struggle with the river currents
    C. her struggle to achieve personal excellence
    D. her competition with her brother

16. What seems to be the two main motives for Heather's efforts to row across the river?
    A. She loves to spend time in the great outdoors and wants to outperform her brother.
    B. She wants her father's approval and needs an inexpensive way to reach the other side.
    C. She wants to outperform her brother and prove to her father that females can be good athletes.
    D. She loves the river, and she wants to prove to her father that females are good athletes.

17. Which statement about characters' motives is the most accurate?
    A. Motives often lead characters to act in certain ways.
    B. Motives are based mainly on internal factors.
    C. Motives are based mainly on external factors.
    D. A character usually has just one motive for his or her behavior.

18. Which of these is an internal factor that could explain a character's motives?
    A. the character's actions
    B. the character's thoughts
    C. the events surrounding the character
    D. the times in which the character lives

Vocabulary: Prefixes

19. Using your knowledge of the prefix *re-*, what is the meaning of *revive* in the following sentence?

Can we ever revive the lost art of letter writing?
    A. make corrections
    B. decide on
    C. make popular
    D. bring back into use

20. Using your knowledge of the prefix *dis-*, which definition best fits the word *dislodge* in the following sentence?

The workers had to dislodge the big rock.
    A. put back into place
    B. force out of position
    C. fix the position of again
    D. cover in order to hide

21. What is one meaning of the prefix *ex-*?
    A. out
    B. into
    C. through
    D. between

22. Using your knowledge of the prefix *in-*, what is the meaning of *intrude* in the following sentence?

Jane decided not to intrude when she saw her friends arguing.
    A. keep oneself out
    B. force oneself in
    C. get involved again
    D. leave

23. Using your knowledge of the prefix *re-*, what is the meaning of *refund* in the following sentence?

    The producers will refund our money for the canceled concert.

    A. add to
    B. take away
    C. give back
    D. save for later

24. Using your knowledge of the prefix *ex-*, what is the meaning of *excel* in the following sentence?

    Jova wished to excel in science.

    A. work hard
    B. be average
    C. stand out
    D. get extra help

Grammar: Verbs

25. Which sentence uses an action verb?
    A. The test was finally over.
    B. Joanne felt relieved.
    C. She answered all the questions.
    D. The answers seemed right to her.

26. What do you call a verb that connects a noun or a pronoun to a word that identifies or describes it?
    A. an action verb
    B. a linking verb
    C. a regular verb
    D. an irregular verb

27. Identify the linking verb in this sentence.

    When the librarian misses her bus and the volunteers are sick, the library opens late.

    A. misses
    B. volunteers
    C. are
    D. opens

28. What are the principal parts of verbs?
    A. the roots of verbs without any prefixes or suffixes
    B. the four main forms of verbs
    C. the most common forms of the most common verbs
    D. action, linking, regular, irregular

29. How do you form the past tense and past participle of regular verbs?
   A. Use the helping verb *will* and the base form of the verb.
   B. Add *-s* or *-es* to the base form of the verb.
   C. Add *-ed* or *-d* to the base form of the verb.
   D. Add *-en* or *-ed* to the base form of the verb.

30. Which sentence uses the present participle of the verb *march*?
   A. Juanita marched in the parade.
   B. Juanita is marching in the parade.
   C. Juanita will march in the parade.
   D. Juanita has marched in the parade.

31. Which sentence uses verbs correctly?
   A. I have done all my homework.
   B. Please raise up from your seats.
   C. Shelley has drank all the milk.
   D. Tom brung raisins with his lunch.

32. Which sentence uses verbs correctly?
   A. Sophia is laying on the beach.
   B. Lily lay her towel on the sand.
   C. Do not lay directly in the sun.
   D. You can lie in the shade instead.

ESSAY

Writing

33. Imagine that you are looking for someone to help you with school work or chores around the home. On your paper or a separate sheet, write a help wanted ad that might appear in your school newspaper.

34. On your paper or a separate sheet, jot down ideas for a persuasive speech in which you convince others to donate money or time to a worthy charity.

35. Think of a movie or TV show that made a strong positive or negative impression on you. On your paper or a separate sheet, write a review of that film or TV show.

Unit 2 Resources: Short Stories
125

Name _____ Starting Date _____ Ending Date _____

Unit 2: Short Stories Skills Concept Map—2
Is conflict always bad?

Reading Skills and Strategies: Draw Conclusions

You can draw conclusions about details in a literary work → by → (asking questions)

and by → (using your own prior knowledge)

(demonstrated in this selection)
Selection name: _____

(demonstrated in this selection)
Selection name: _____

Informational Text: Article

You can examine similarities and differences → by → (analyzing compare-and-contrast organization)

(demonstrated in this selection)
Selection name: _____

Literary Analysis: Short Story

[A Short Story] — has → (a theme) — and → (a setting)

Basic Elements of Short Stories

- Characters
- Setting
- Plot
- Theme
- Conflict

Comparing Literary Works: Theme

is developed through → (the characters' thoughts and feelings)
→ (events in the story)

(demonstrated in these selections)
Selection names:
1.
2.

Words you can use to discuss the Big Question

_____
_____
_____
_____
_____

Student Log

Complete this chart to track your assignments.

Writing	Extend Your Learning	Writing Workshop	Other Assignments

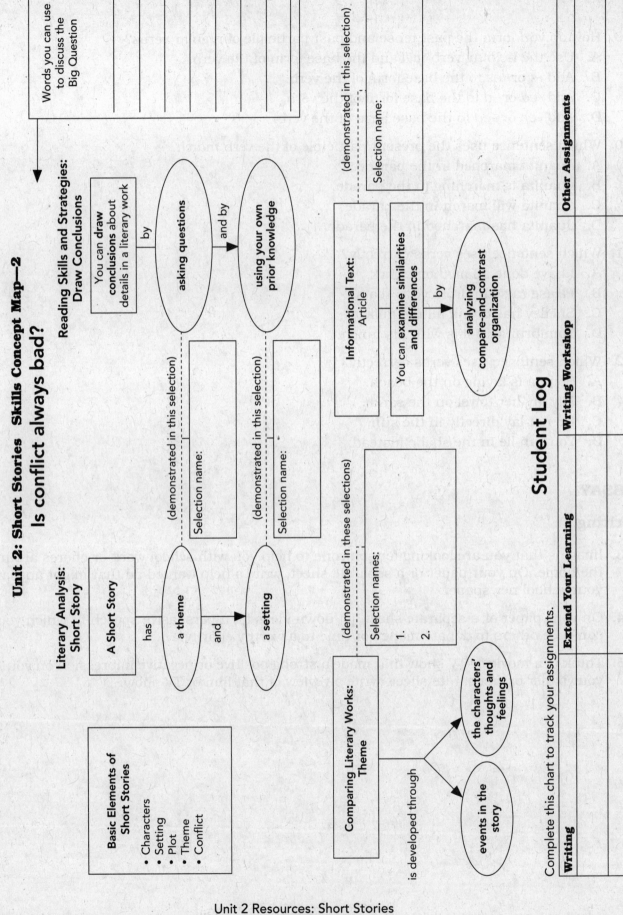

Vocabulary Warm-up Word Lists

Study these words from "The Circuit." Then, complete the activities that follow.

Word List A

accompanied [uh KUHM puh need] *v.* went along with
Mike <u>accompanied</u> Tim to the store to help him choose new sneakers.

dizzy [DIZ ee] *adj.* confused and unsteady
Riding around and around on the tire swing had made him <u>dizzy</u>.

hesitantly [HEZ uh tuhnt lee] *adv.* with pauses, not steadily
He wasn't sure he wanted to play, so he joined the game <u>hesitantly</u>.

original [uh RIJ uh nuhl] *adj.* first or earliest
There were no lenses in the earliest, or <u>original</u>, cameras.

peak [PEEK] *n.* the best time for something
I try to eat strawberries at their <u>peak</u>, because that's when they are the sweetest.

signaling [SIG nuh ling] *v.* making an action to call attention to
The catcher was <u>signaling</u> the pitcher to throw a fast ball.

stained [STAYND] *v.* marked or colored
The chairs were <u>stained</u> blue to match the sofa.

sunset [SUHN set] *n.* the time in the evening when the sun goes down
Ervin loved to watch the <u>sunset</u> at the beach every evening.

Word List B

acquired [uh KWY erd] *v.* got; gained possession of
I <u>acquired</u> my sister's bicycle after she left for college.

clasped [KLASPT] *v.* held tightly and firmly
As we jumped, I <u>clasped</u> my brother's hand and would not let go.

detect [di TEKT] *v.* discover; sense
The police officer at the scene did not <u>detect</u> anything out of place.

drone [DROHN] *n.* a dull humming sound that goes on and on
We heard the <u>drone</u> of the air conditioners all summer long.

foreman [FAWR muhn] *n.* one who supervises a group of workers
The <u>foreman</u> told the diggers to take a break.

husky [HUHS kee] *adj.* big and strong
Two <u>husky</u> movers carried the piano up the stairs.

instinct [IN stingkt] *n.* behavior that is natural rather than thought out
The dog found its way home through <u>instinct</u>.

thoroughly [THUHR uh lee] *adv.* in a careful and complete way
I checked the grocery list <u>thoroughly</u> to make sure I hadn't forgotten something.

"The Circuit" by Francisco Jiménez
Vocabulary Warm-up Exercises

Exercise A *Fill in each blank in the paragraph below with an appropriate word from Word List A. Use each word only once.*

Mary was waving her arms and [1] _____ to James to come over. James

[2] _____ walked over to meet her because he knew that she was

[3] _____ by her cousin Lynn. Lynn was the [4] _____

love of James's life. Seeing her made him feel slightly [5] _____. Still, he

decided to be bold. He asked her to go see the [6] _____ with him at the

beach. He said that at its [7] _____, it looked incredible, like a piece of

[8] _____ glass. To his surprise and delight, Lynn said yes.

Exercise B *Answer the questions with complete explanations.*

Example: Would a story told with a <u>drone</u> probably be interesting to listen to? Why or why not?
    It would probably be boring because a <u>drone</u> is a dull sound.

1. What kind of help might you expect to get from a <u>husky</u> man?
_____

2. If you have your hands <u>clasped</u>, could you be typing? Explain.
_____

3. If a friend <u>acquired</u> a box of old comic books, would he have more or less storage space? Explain.
_____

4. Is reading a book something that comes by <u>instinct</u> to people? Explain.
_____

5. If you <u>detect</u> a strange smell in your house, would you want to look around <u>thoroughly</u>? Why or why not?
_____

6. Would you expect to see the <u>foreman</u> of a farm picking cotton? Explain.
_____

"The Circuit" by Francisco Jiménez
Reading Warm-up A

Read the following passage. Pay special attention to the underlined words. Then, read it again, and complete the activities. Use a separate sheet of paper for your written answers.

These days, America's supermarkets sell farm-fresh produce in every season. In many megastores, the variety of fruits and vegetables for sale is enough to make you <u>dizzy</u>. When your world stops spinning, however, you would probably admit that you like it that way. Americans are used to buying what we want when we want it. In fact, most of us would be surprised if stores ran out of lettuce in December.

It wasn't always that way, however. Before the 1940s, different fruits and vegetables appeared in different seasons. People tended to eat produce when it was at its <u>peak</u>, or perfect ripeness. Fresh lettuce hit the stores early in the year, <u>signaling</u> the arrival of spring. Fresh corn was a sure sign of summer. Fresh squash meant fall had arrived. In fact, you could guess the season by the fruits and vegetables your mom wrote down on her weekly grocery list. Sure, some vegetables you could buy at any time. Still, no one insisted on having fresh peaches in January. Ripe peaches—<u>stained</u> the yellow and red of <u>sunset</u>—were a summer treat.

All of that began to change in the mid-1940s. Better farming methods, <u>accompanied</u> by new technologies, began to change agriculture. Advances on the <u>original</u>, or earliest, ideas began to produce hardier plants. These plants could grow in more extreme temperatures. They had a longer growing season. Many did not have as much flavor as less hardy plants. Still, they stayed fresh longer.

At first <u>hesitantly</u>, but then regularly, fruits and vegetables became available all year. Farmers began to deliver them all across the country. Now everyone can buy everything from bananas to green beans, all year long.

1. Underline the words that help you know what <u>dizzy</u> means. Write a sentence about a time when you might get *dizzy*.

2. Circle the phrase that describes fruit at its <u>peak</u>. Which fruit or vegetable do you like to eat at its *peak*?

3. Underline the words that tell what the lettuce was <u>signaling</u>. Then, write what *signaling* means.

4. In this passage, which fruits are <u>stained</u>? Write a sentence explaining what *stained* means.

5. Circle the colors that are in a <u>sunset</u>. Then describe a *sunset* you have enjoyed.

6. Circle the words that tell what new technologies <u>accompanied</u>. What might *accompany* a cookie?

7. Write a sentence about what new farming methods produced that the <u>original</u> methods did not.

8. What was done <u>hesitantly</u> at first? Describe something you might do *hesitantly*.

"The Circuit" by Francisco Jiménez

Reading Warm-up B

Read the following passage. Pay special attention to the underlined words. Then, read it again, and complete the activities. Use a separate sheet of paper for your written answers.

It seemed as if every time Dawn began to feel at home in a new place, it was time to pick up and move again.

"Do we really have to move?" she asked, fearful that the question might upset her father.

"We can't stay here without a job," her father replied with a shrug of his broad shoulders. He was a <u>husky</u> man, but he looked weak now as he slouched sadly in his favorite chair.

Dawn <u>clasped</u> her hands tightly together and held them under her chin, thinking. She was not looking forward to the prospect of starting over again as the new kid in some unfamiliar city. She decided to explore her options <u>thoroughly</u>. She felt she needed to try everything.

"Couldn't you find a job around here?" she asked hesitantly. "My friend's dad is a <u>foreman</u> at the mill . . ."

"He's not hiring at the mill right now," her father interrupted, and Dawn could <u>detect</u> the frustration in his voice. "Anyway, you know I can't stand the <u>drone</u> of machinery. The endless noise gives me a headache."

That settled it, then—they would be moving. Without thinking, as if by <u>instinct</u> Dawn smiled and leaned over to kiss her father's cheek. She knew this move was important to him.

"So where are we going this time?" she asked.

"Back to California," said her father. "Actually, our new place isn't far from where we used to live."

"Really?" said Dawn. Suddenly the future was beginning to look a whole lot brighter as she imagined them loading up the car her father had recently <u>acquired</u> and setting out for sunny California. As much as she liked it here, Dawn had to admit that she loved California's sun and surf even more. And it *would* be awfully nice to hang out with her old friends again.

Maybe this move wasn't going to be so bad after all!

1. Circle the word that means the opposite of <u>husky</u>, and then write a sentence describing a *husky* person.

2. Underline the words that help you know what Dawn did when she <u>clasped</u> her hands. Then, describe a time when you *clasped* your hands.

3. Underline the sentence that tells you what <u>thoroughly</u> means. Why is it important to do a job *thoroughly*?

4. Write a sentence listing two things from the passage that describe this <u>foreman</u>'s job.

5. In your own words, rewrite the sentence containing the word <u>detect</u>. Then, write what *detect* means.

6. Write a sentence describing how the <u>drone</u> of machinery probably sounds.

7. Dawn kissed her father's cheek by <u>instinct</u>. Does that mean she thought about it? Explain.

8. What had Dawn's father just <u>acquired</u>? Write about something that you have *acquired*.

"The Circuit" by Francisco Jiménez
Writing About the Big Question

Is conflict always bad?

Big Question Vocabulary

argue	battle	challenge	compete	conclude
convince	defend	game	issue	lose
negotiate	oppose	resolve	survival	win

A. *Use one or more words from the list above to complete each sentence.*

1. When you are the new kid at school, the first day is a real _____.

2. You have to _____ to try to fit in and make friends.

3. You can _____ other kids that you are interesting and fun.

4. They will _____ that you would make a good friend.

B. *Respond to each item with a complete sentence.*

1. Describe an experience you have had being a new kid at school, or imagine what it would be like.

   _____

   _____

2. Tell what you did or would do at a new school to make friends. Use at least two Big Question vocabulary words in your response.

   _____

   _____

C. *Complete this sentence. Then, write a brief paragraph in which you connect this experience to the Big Question.*

   When I talk through conflicts with my family, _____.

   _____

   _____

   _____

   _____

   _____

   _____

"The Circuit" by Francisco Jiménez

Reading: Draw Conclusions

A conclusion is a decision or opinion based on details in a literary work. To **identify the details** that will help you draw conclusions, **ask questions,** such as

- Why is this detail included in the story?
- Does this information help me understand the story better?

Example from "The Circuit":

The thought of having to move to Fresno and knowing what was in store for me there brought tears to my eyes.

You might ask what the narrator expects to happen in Fresno. The thought brings tears to his eyes. You can draw the conclusion that something in Fresno makes him sad.

A. DIRECTIONS: *The following passages from "The Circuit" are told from Panchito's point of view. Use details from each passage to draw a conclusion to answer the question.*

1. Suddenly I noticed Papa's face turn pale as he looked down the road. "Here comes the school bus," he whispered loudly in alarm. Instinctively, Roberto and I ran and hid in the vineyards.
   Does Papa want Roberto and Panchito to go to school? How do you know? _____
   _____

2. He walked up to me, handed me an English book, and asked me to read. "We are on page 125," he said politely. When I heard this, I felt my blood rush to my head; I felt dizzy.
   What makes Panchito feel dizzy? _____
   _____

3. Mr. Lema was sitting at his desk correcting papers. When I entered he looked up at me and smiled. I felt better. I walked up to him and asked if he could help me with the new words.
   How does Panchito feel about asking the teacher for help? _____
   _____

B. DIRECTIONS: *Underline details in this passage from "The Circuit" that help you draw the conclusion that the family is preparing to move. Then tell why these details help you draw this conclusion.*

I thought they were happy to see me, but when I opened the door to our shack, I saw that everything we owned was neatly packed in cardboard boxes.

Conclusion:

_____

_____

"The Circuit" by Francisco Jiménez
Literary Analysis: Theme

The **theme,** or central idea of a story, is a thought about life that the story conveys. Sometimes the theme is stated directly. Other times you must figure it out by considering events in the story, characters' thoughts and feelings, and the story's title.

A. DIRECTIONS: *Write a statement about the theme of "The Circuit."*

Theme: _____

_____

B. DIRECTIONS: *In the chart below, write the details from each passage that tell about or support the theme of "The Circuit." The first one is started for you as an example.*

Passage From "The Circuit"	What the Details Tell About Theme
1. Yes, it was that time of year. When I opened the front door to the shack, I stopped. Everything we owned was neatly packed in cardboard boxes. Suddenly I felt even more the weight of hours, days, weeks, and months of work.	The word *shack* indicates that the family is poor. Packed boxes indicate a change or move.
2. He was not going to school today. He was not going tomorrow, or next week, or next month. He would not go until the cotton season was over, . . .	
3. I thought they were happy to see me, but when I opened the door to our shack, I saw that everything we owned was neatly packed in cardboard boxes.	

"The Circuit" by Francisco Jiménez
Vocabulary Builder

Word List

accompanied   drone   enroll   instinctively   savoring   surplus

A. DIRECTIONS: *Each sentence below features a word from the list. For each sentence, explain why the underlined word does or does not make sense in the sentence.*

1. There was a <u>surplus</u> of food for the party, so everyone was still hungry.

   _____

2. The <u>drone</u> of the television made it hard to concentrate.

   _____

3. Megan went home after school so she could <u>enroll</u> in a school club.

   _____

4. Carlos <u>instinctively</u> ducked when the ball came toward his face.

   _____

5. Jaime ate so fast he almost choked, <u>savoring</u> every bite.

   _____

6. Maria <u>accompanied</u> her sister to the fair.

   _____

B. WORD STUDY: *The Latin root -com- means "to move or to wander." Answer each question by paying attention to each of the underlined words with the root -com-. Then, explain your answer.*

1. Could you <u>combine</u> peanut butter and jelly to make a sandwich?

   _____

2. Could a pet ever be a good <u>companion</u> for a lonely person?

   _____

3. If you <u>compress</u> the items in a suitcase, is it harder to close it?

   _____

"The Circuit" by Francisco Jiménez
Enrichment: César Chávez and Migrant Workers

Panchito and his family came to California to work as migrant workers in the late 1940s. At about the same time, César Chávez, a young Mexican American, was also working in the orchards of San Jose, California. Chávez had to quit school in the eighth grade to help support his family. When a man named Fred Ross encouraged him to join the Community Service Organization, a group that helped migrant workers and their families, Chávez did so. He helped the organization to grow and then decided to devote himself to creating a labor union for farm workers. Chávez organized the UFW, the United Farm Workers, and the group worked to raise wages for migrant workers. Because of Chávez, farm workers in California are now able to make better wages, allowing their children to attend school.

A. DIRECTIONS: *Look in a biography about César Chávez or on the Internet to find out what happened in Chávez's life on the dates below. Write the events on the lines.*

March 31, 1927:

_____

September 30, 1962:

_____

March–April 1966:

_____

December, 1970:

_____

April 23, 1993:

_____

August 8, 1994:

_____

B. DIRECTIONS: *Write a paragraph explaining how Panchito's life in the story "The Circuit" might have been different if César Chávez had completed his work before the family came to California.*

_____

_____

_____

_____

_____

Name _____ Date _____

"The Circuit" by Francisco Jiménez
Open-Book Test

Short Answer *Write your responses to the questions in this section on the lines provided.*

1. Why is Panchito upset about the move to Fresno in "The Circuit"? Include details from the story in your answer.

   _____

   _____

2. What conclusion can you draw about Papá from this passage from "The Circuit"? Explain your answer.

   When he finally chose the "Carcanchita," he checked it thoroughly before driving it out of the car lot. He examined every inch of the car.

   _____

   _____

   _____

3. In "The Circuit," Panchito works in the field along with his father and brother. In each oval of the diagram, write a word or phrase from the story that tells why Panchito does not like field work. Then, on the lines below, describe the work in your own words.

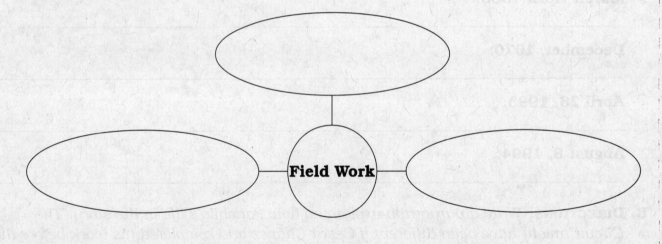

   _____

   _____

4. In "The Circuit," Panchito and Roberto instinctively run and hide when the school bus approaches. What does this tell you about how often the boys have been doing this? Explain.

   _____

   _____

5. In "The Circuit," Panchito is savoring the thought of starting the sixth grade. What is one other thing that he savors in the story? Explain your answer.

_____

_____

6. In "The Circuit," Panchito keeps his head down so he does not have to face Roberto on the first day of school. Think about what Roberto has to do instead of going to school. Explain why Panchito is unable to face his brother.

_____

_____

7. Think about what happens to Panchito's life when the family moves in "The Circuit." How does the boy feel about moving? Explain your answer.

_____

_____

_____

8. Think about how Panchito feels about school and learning in "The Circuit." Explain why he asks for help with his English.

_____

_____

9. Near the end of "The Circuit," Panchito becomes excited when Mr. Lema offers to teach him how to play the trumpet. Explain how this event highlights the theme of the story.

_____

_____

_____

10. Cardboard boxes appear at the beginning of "The Circuit" and again at the end. Explain how these boxes support the theme of the story.

_____

_____

Essay

Write an extended response to the question of your choice or to the question or questions your teacher assigns you.

11. In "The Circuit," Panchito's family is constantly moving from place to place. Panchito must work, so he cannot always go to school. When he does go to school, he never is able to stay for any length of time. In an essay, discuss how Panchito's life as a migrant worker affects his attitude toward school. Use details from the story to support your ideas.

12. The author of "The Circuit" makes the harshness of Panchito's life very real. In an essay, analyze how Jiménez vividly expresses the cold reality of the boy's childhood. Include sensory images, descriptions of the narrator's emotions, and any other details that help the reader understand the migrant worker's difficult life.

13. The word *circuit* means "a path or route that brings you back to its starting point." This relates to Panchito's childhood in "The Circuit." In an essay, explain how his life is like a circuit and how the title expresses the theme of the story. Use details from the story to support your ideas.

14. **Thinking About the Big Question: Is conflict always bad?** In "The Circuit," Panchito is in conflict with his way of life, wanting an education that seems always out of his grasp. Like his character Panchito, Francisco Jiménez was a migrant worker as a child. The respect he gained for education led him to become a teacher, a college official, and an award-winning author. In an essay, discuss whether Panchito's conflict is bad. Use details from the story as well as information about the author to support your ideas.

Oral Response

15. Go back to question 1, 2, 7, or 10 or to the question your teacher assigns to you. Take a few minutes to expand your answer and prepare an oral response. Find additional details in "The Circuit" that will support your points. If necessary, make notes to guide your response.

"The Circuit" by Francisco Jiménez
Selection Test A

Critical Reading *Identify the letter of the choice that best answers the question.*

____ 1. In "The Circuit," how does Panchito feel about moving?
   A. He dislikes constantly moving from place to place.
   B. He thinks living in one place would be boring.
   C. He enjoys moving around but dislikes the work.
   D. He does not mind moving from place to place.

____ 2. Why does the iron pot mean so much to Panchito's mother?
   A. She believes it makes food taste better.
   B. She can use it to carry goods as well as for cooking.
   C. It remains the same no matter where the family goes.
   D. Her mother gave the iron pot to her.

____ 3. How would you describe the work Panchito does in the fields?
   A. interesting
   B. scary
   C. easy
   D. exhausting

____ 4. When the school bus arrives the first time, what do Panchito and Roberto do?
   A. They climb on board.
   B. They run and hide.
   C. They watch it wistfully.
   D. They shout and make faces.

____ 5. Read the passage from "The Circuit." Which question could you ask to help you conclude that Panchito feels guilty about going to school?

   I sat at the table across from Roberto, but I kept my head down. I did not want to look up and face him.

   A. Why does Panchito do poorly in school?
   B. Why does Panchito not look at Roberto on the first day of school?
   C. Why does Panchito teach Roberto what he learns each night?
   D. Why does Panchito ask Roberto to forgive him?

____ 6. Who is Mr. Lema in "The Circuit"?
   A. He is a sharecropper.
   B. He is a *bracero.*
   C. He is a school bus driver.
   D. He is a teacher.

Name _____ Date _____

____ 7. In "The Circuit," why does Panchito ask for help with his English?
   A. He wants the other students to like him.
   B. He wants to do his best in school.
   C. He wants to get a job.
   D. He wants to be smarter than his brother.

____ 8. Which detail helps you conclude that Panchito likes to learn?
   A. He is afraid of reading in front of the class.
   B. He does not want to move to Fresno.
   C. He asks Mr. Lema for extra help.
   D. His father sends him to school instead of sending Roberto.

____ 9. At the end of "The Circuit," what do the cardboard boxes mean to Panchito?
   A. He will have to stop going to school and move again.
   B. He has not been working hard enough in the fields.
   C. It is Roberto's turn to go to school.
   D. The officials have found out that Roberto does not go to school.

____ 10. What is one thing in Panchito's family life that does not change when the family moves?
   A. their home
   B. Papa's "Carcanchita"
   C. the crops that they pick
   D. their teachers

____ 11. Which word best describes the ending of "The Circuit"?
   A. discouraging
   B. hopeful
   C. satisfying
   D. startling

Vocabulary and Grammar

____ 12. Which definition best fits the word *drone* in this sentence?
   All I could hear was the drone of insects.
   A. loud wailing
   B. huge wing
   C. continuous humming
   D. shiny rock

____ 13. Which word or phrase is closest in meaning to *happily*?
   A. full of happiness
   B. happy
   C. in a happy manner
   D. without happiness

____ 14. Which of these sentences contains a verb in the past tense?
   A. Panchito worked in the fields.
   B. Panchito is so hot he feels sick.
   C. Mr. Lema seems very nice.
   D. Papa is afraid of the school bus.

____ 15. Which of these sentences contains a verb in the future tense?
   A. Papa checks the car carefully.
   B. Roberto urges Panchito to drink slowly.
   C. Panchito wants to play the trumpet.
   D. Panchito will become a better reader.

Essay

16. In an essay, analyze how the author of "The Circuit" makes the harshness of Panchito's life especially vivid. In your essay, mention sensory images, descriptions of the narrator's emotions, and any other details that effectively convey an impression of the farm worker's difficult day-to-day life.

17. How does constantly moving affect Panchito's attitude toward school? In an essay, discuss Panchito's attitude. Use details from the story to support your conclusions.

18. **Thinking About the Big Question: Is conflict always bad?** In "The Circuit" Panchito is in conflict with his way of life. He wants a chance to get an education, but his life as a migrant worker keeps that from happening. Like Panchito, Francisco Jiménez was a migrant worker as a child. His respect for education led him to become a teacher, a college official, and an award-winning author. In an essay, discuss whether Panchito's conflict is bad. Use details from the story as well as information about the author to support your ideas.

"The Circuit" by Francisco Jiménez
Selection Test B

Critical Reading *Identify the letter of the choice that best completes the statement or answers the question.*

____ 1. In "The Circuit," the narrator doesn't want to move to Fresno because
A. he does not like the city.
B. he does not know if the family will find a place to live there.
C. he is moving once again and will be doing more hard work.
D. he dislikes traveling by car.

____ 2. What conclusion can you draw about Papa from this passage in "The Circuit"?
When he finally chose the "Carcanchita," he checked it thoroughly before driving it out of the car lot. He examined every inch of the car.

A. He used to be a car salesman.
B. He knows a lot about cars.
C. He is a very careful man.
D. He loves cars of all kinds.

____ 3. Which word best describes the field work in "The Circuit"?
A. interesting
B. frightening
C. satisfying
D. exhausting

____ 4. In "The Circuit," the brothers hide from the school bus because
A. they don't want to go to school.
B. they have to work instead of going to school.
C. their parents don't think education is important.
D. they think the other students will laugh at them.

____ 5. In "The Circuit," Panchito
A. is glad that he doesn't have to go to school.
B. is determined to grow strong enough to work hard.
C. longs to go to school and learn as much as he can.
D. is furious with his father for making him work.

____ 6. In "The Circuit," what does it show about Panchito's character that he asks Mr. Lema to help him with his English?
A. He likes to make a good impression on people.
B. He wants to do his best in school.
C. He wants Mr. Lema to feel useful.
D. He wants to appear smarter than his brother.

_____ 7. Why does the author include this passage about a trumpet in "The Circuit"?

"How would you like to learn to play it?" he asked. He must have read my face because before I could answer, he added: "I'll teach you to play it during our lunch hours."

    A. It shows that Panchito has great musical talent.
    B. It shows how much Panchito wants to learn.
    C. It shows that Mr. Lema is really a music teacher.
    D. It shows that musical education is very important.

_____ 8. At the end of "The Circuit," the packed cardboard boxes tell Panchito that
    A. the family is moving again.
    B. Roberto is going to school.
    C. he must work in the fields.
    D. his mother is sick.

_____ 9. What is the one sure and constant thing in Panchito's life?
    A. the family's home
    B. Papa's black Plymouth
    C. the school bus
    D. his teachers

_____ 10. "The Circuit" describes
    A. the narrator's first experience as a farm worker.
    B. the narrator's worst experience as a farm worker.
    C. the narrator's most memorable experience as a farm worker.
    D. one of the narrator's typical experiences as a farm worker.

_____ 11. What theme is supported by this passage about Roberto from "The Circuit"?

He was not going to school today. He was not going tomorrow, or next week, or next month.

    A. The family cannot get the education needed to break the cycle of poverty.
    B. Roberto doesn't like school, so he will not get an education.
    C. The family believes only in work.
    D. The family members are better workers because they are not distracted by school.

_____ 12. How does Mr. Lema's offer to teach Panchito the trumpet highlight the theme of "The Circuit"?
    A. It reveals the effect of kindness on Panchito and his family.
    B. It shows Panchito's need for a stable adult figure in his life.
    C. It shows the contrast between what Panchito wants and what he gets.
    D. It shows the result of a lack of music in Panchito's life.

_____ 13. How do cardboard boxes support the theme of "The Circuit"?
    A. The boxes represent the family's constant moving.
    B. The boxes are the only toys the children have.
    C. The boxes can be gotten for free from a grocery store.
    D. The boxes hold all the wonderful things in the family's life.

Vocabulary and Grammar

____ 14. To do something *instinctively* is to do it
A. carefully.
B. easily.
C. thoughtfully.
D. automatically.

____ 15. Three of these words have similar meanings. Which word does not have a similar meaning?
A. buzz
B. hum
C. drone
D. drowse

____ 16. In which sentence is the underlined verb in the past tense?
A. Roberto <u>feels</u> sad when he cannot go to school.
B. Panchito <u>becomes</u> a better reader.
C. Papa <u>seems</u> to pale when he sees the school bus.
D. Panchito <u>drank</u> too much water and felt sick.

____ 17. In which sentence is the underlined verb in the future tense?
A. Panchito <u>will be</u> glad when he can go to school.
B. Roberto and Panchito <u>work</u> very hard.
C. The sun <u>beats</u> down on the workers.
D. Mr. Lema <u>helps</u> Panchito with his reading.

Essay

18. In an essay, discuss the cycle or cycles in which Panchito's family is caught in "The Circuit." Describe the cycle and tell how it affects the migrant family.

19. Decide on one word you could use to describe the story "The Circuit." Then, in an essay, use examples from the selection to support your choice of word.

20. A *circuit* is a path or route that brings you back to its starting point. In a way, this characterizes Panchito's life as a growing child in "The Circuit." In an essay, explain why the title is appropriate for this story and tell how the title expresses the theme of the story. Use examples from the selection to support your explanation.

21. **Thinking About the Big Question: Is conflict always bad?** In "The Circuit," Panchito is in conflict with his way of life, wanting an education that seems always out of his grasp. Like his character Panchito, Francisco Jiménez was a migrant worker as a child. The respect he gained for education led him to become a teacher, a college official, and an award-winning author. In an essay, discuss whether Panchito's conflict is bad. Use details from the story as well as information about the author to support your ideas.

Vocabulary Warm-up Word Lists

Study these words from "The All-American Slurp." Then, complete the activities.

Word List A

constantly [KAHN stuhnt lee] *adv.* always, continually
Leia is <u>constantly</u> arriving late to school, blaming her alarm clock.

dictionary [DIK shuh ner ee] *n.* a book that explains the meanings of words
Look in a <u>dictionary</u> if you don't know what that word means.

dumping [DUHMP ing] *v.* tossing or emptying something in a careless way
Tim made a mess on the floor while <u>dumping</u> the leftovers into the garbage.

local [LOH kuhl] *adj.* nearby, from the area around where you live
Since we don't like to travel far, we vacation in <u>local</u> areas.

peculiar [puh KYOOL yer] *adj.* strange, weird
Chicken-flavored ice cream? That's pretty <u>peculiar</u>!

raw [RAW] *adj.* uncooked
I don't like <u>raw</u> carrots; they are too hard and not as sweet as cooked ones.

shreds [SHREDZ] *n.* long, thin strips that have been torn off something
The holiday wrapping paper was in <u>shreds</u> all over the floor.

western [WES tern] *adj.* having to do with countries in the Western Hemisphere
The U.S. and Canada are <u>western</u> countries; China and India are eastern countries.

Word List B

menu [MEN yoo] *n.* a list showing foods or dishes that can be bought
The snack bar has a small <u>menu</u>; you can only buy hamburgers, hot dogs, and soft drinks.

murky [MER kee] *adj.* dark, hard to see through
The lake water was so <u>murky</u> that I couldn't see my feet.

permanent [PER muh nint] *adj.* meant to last a very long time
A tattoo is <u>permanent</u>; it stays on your skin forever.

platters [PLA terz] *n.* large trays used to hold or carry food and dishes
We used <u>platters</u> to carry the food out to the back yard.

promotion [pruh MOH shun] *n.* a move to a better job with more important duties
Before the <u>promotion</u> she just swept floors; now she's in charge of everything.

reference [REHF er ens] *n.* mention of a thing or person
I didn't make a <u>reference</u> to Tony; I never said his name.

resolved [ri ZOLVD] *v.* decided to try hard to do something
Nancy <u>resolved</u> to do better in math and studied hard for her next test.

waiter [WAY ter] *n.* a person who delivers food to tables in a restaurant
We were still hungry since the <u>waiter</u> hadn't come with our food.

"The All-American Slurp" by Lensey Namioka
Vocabulary Warm-up Exercises

Exercise A *Fill in each blank in the paragraph below with an appropriate word from Word List A. Use each word only once.*

How was school? Well, these days we are [1] _____ looking at maps. Ms. Aiken showed us maps of the [2] _____ Hemisphere. We also looked at [3] _____ maps showing nearby places. In English class, we used a [4] _____ to find word meanings. At lunch, the school always serves [5] _____ dishes, but today we had the weirdest dish ever: a bowl filled with [6] _____ of mystery meat and pieces of [7] _____ vegetables. My friends and I ended up [8] _____ the whole thing in the trash.

Exercise B *Revise each sentence so that the underlined vocabulary word is used in a logical way. Be sure to keep the vocabulary word in your revision.*

Example: There are so few choices on this <u>menu</u>, it's hard to decide what to eat.
There are so many choices on this <u>menu</u>, it's hard to decide what to eat.

1. Diane <u>resolved</u> to eat more healthfully, so she started eating candy and soda.

   _____

2. You can draw on your face with this marker; it uses <u>permanent</u> ink.

   _____

3. I don't want a <u>promotion</u>; I need a better job.

   _____

4. There is a lot of food to carry, so we may not need to use the <u>platters</u>.

   _____

5. Since Barry is the <u>waiter</u>, his job is to cook the food.

   _____

6. Turn off the lights! It's too <u>murky</u> in here.

   _____

7. I guess you don't think about Jack a lot because that's the third <u>reference</u> you've made to him.

   _____

Name _____ Date _____

"The All-American Slurp" by Lensey Namioka
Reading Warm-up A

Read the following passage. Pay special attention to the underlined words. Then, read it again, and complete the activities. Use a separate sheet of paper for your written answers.

Soup is a popular dish all around the world. It has been for a long time. The Ancient Greeks loved soup. So did the Ancient Romans. Yet, the same soups aren't eaten everywhere. Often, places have their own <u>local</u> favorites, soups that are made from ingredients gathered nearby.

In <u>western</u> countries, soup is normally eaten for lunch or dinner. Eating soup for breakfast seems <u>peculiar</u>, or strange. However, in many Asian countries, that is not the case. Soup is often eaten for breakfast. Vietnam is one example. The Vietnamese eat a delicious soup called *pho*. Pho is a noodle soup made with boiled beef. <u>Raw</u> herbs and vegetables, such as basil, cilantro, and bean sprouts, are added to the soup at the table. They cook a little bit in the hot soup. The Japanese also love breakfast soup. They eat miso soup, a broth made out of soybeans. In China, too, it's normal to start the day with *congee*. Congee is thick soup, almost like porridge. It's not served sweet like oatmeal or other breakfast porridges. Instead, it's filled with long tasty <u>shreds</u> of pork or other meats to give it a delicious savory taste.

Who invented soup? No one knows for sure. Still, we do know where the word comes from. If you look in a <u>dictionary</u>, you'll see that it came from the word "sop." Sop was a piece of bread dipped in hot liquid. Eventually, the bread disappeared, the liquid stayed, and the word *soup* was born.

Cooks love serving soup because it's easy to make. You gather together a bunch of ingredients. Then you begin <u>dumping</u> them into a pot with water and letting the whole thing simmer. People love eating soup because it's nutritious *and* great tasting. Most people are <u>constantly</u> looking for food that offers this combination.

1. Underline the words that tell what <u>local</u> favorites are. Then tell what *local* means.

2. Circle the words that tell when soup is eaten in <u>western</u> countries. Then name three foods people often eat for breakfast in our *western* country.

3. Circle the nearby word that has the same meaning as <u>peculiar</u>. Then describe something you'd find *peculiar*.

4. Underline the words that tell what <u>raw</u> ingredients are added to *pho*. Then tell what *raw* means.

5. Underline the words that tell what kind of <u>shreds</u> you will find in *congee*. Then tell what *shreds* means.

6. Write a sentence telling what a <u>dictionary</u> is used for.

7. Circle the words that tell you what to do after <u>dumping</u> the ingredients into a pot. Then tell what *dumping* means.

8. Circle the words that tell what people are <u>constantly</u> looking for. Then tell what *constantly* means.

"The All-American Slurp" by Lensey Namioka
Reading Warm-up B

Read the following passage. Pay special attention to the underlined words. Then, read it again, and complete the activities. Use a separate sheet of paper for your written answers.

Richard was excited. He had just gotten his first summer job ever! He had been looking for weeks, but the task was extremely difficult. Most businesses were only offering <u>permanent</u> jobs. Richard only wanted to work for two months, however; when school started again, he would have to leave.

While Richard was having dinner at a restaurant with his parents and grandparents, he overheard the manager make a <u>reference</u> to a shortage of employees. "In summer, we get a lot busier, but it's hard to find employees," the manager was saying. Richard stopped browsing through the food choices on the <u>menu</u> and jumped out of his chair. He <u>resolved</u> to get the job.

"I'm searching for a job, just during the summer, and I'm very hard working," Richard nearly shouted.

The manager hired him immediately, telling Richard to come back the following morning. Richard started out working in the back room. He folded napkins, sorted silverware, set the tables, and did anything that needed to be done before the restaurant opened each day. After a single week, he received a <u>promotion</u> to a position with more responsibility.

"I'm going to make you a <u>waiter</u>," said the manager. "The job is more difficult—you will have to take orders from the customers, deliver food, and figure out the checks. I'm sure you'll be able to handle it."

The manager was right—the job wasn't easy. At first, Richard had the most trouble delivering <u>platters</u> covered with plates of food. The platters were heavy and difficult to handle. There weren't many lights in the main dining room, so in the corners it could be <u>murky</u>. Once Richard didn't see the leg of a customer sticking out from beneath a table. He tripped, almost dropping the platter of dishes he was carrying!

1. Underline the words that tell why Richard can't take a <u>permanent</u> job. Then tell what *permanent* means.

2. Circle the words that explain what the manager makes a <u>reference</u> to. Then tell what *reference* means.

3. Underline the words that tell what you do while reading a <u>menu</u>. Then tell what *menu* means.

4. Underline the words that show how <u>resolved</u> Richard was to get the job. Write a sentence about something you recently *resolved* to do.

5. Circle the words that explain what you get when you get a <u>promotion</u>. Then tell what *promotion* means.

6. Underline the words that tell what duties Richard will have as a <u>waiter</u>. Then write a sentence using the word *waiter*.

7. Underline the words that tell what <u>platters</u> are used to carry. Then tell what *platters* means.

8. Circle the words that explain why it was <u>murky</u> in the corners. Then tell what *murky* means.

Name _____ Date _____

Is conflict always bad?

Big Question Vocabulary

argue	battle	challenge	compete	conclude
convince	defend	game	issue	lose
negotiate	oppose	resolve	survival	win

A. *Use one or more words from the list above to complete each sentence.*

1. The family dinner table is often the site of a _____ over food.

2. What to eat is often an _____ that family members fight about.

3. Parents try to _____ children that they should eat healthful food.

4. Children try to _____ with their parents so they can have something sweet to eat.

B. *Respond to each item with a complete sentence.*

1. Describe an issue involving food that your family has faced or that you have noticed in someone else's home.

   _____

   _____

2. Explain how the food issue was resolved. Use at least two of the Big Question vocabulary words.

   _____

   _____

C. *Complete this sentence. Then, write a brief paragraph in which you explain how differences in a new country can lead to a conflict.*

   Getting used to differences in a new country _____

   _____

   _____

   _____

   _____

   _____

   _____

   _____

"The All-American Slurp" by Lensey Namioka
Reading: Draw Conclusions

A conclusion is a decision or opinion based on details in a literary work. To **identify the details** that will help you draw conclusions, **ask questions,** such as

- Why is this detail included in the story?
- Does this information help me understand the story better?

Example from "The All-American Slurp":

> After arriving at the house, we shook hands with our hosts and packed ourselves into a sofa. As our family of four sat stiffly in a row, my younger brother and I stole glances at our parents for a clue as to what to do next.

You might ask what the visiting family is feeling in this scene. They are sitting stiffly and unsure of what to do. You can draw the conclusion that they are nervous and feel out of place.

A. DIRECTIONS: *The following passages from "The All-American Slurp" are told from the point of view of the narrator. Use details from each passage to draw a conclusion to answer the question.*

1. To my left, my parents were taking care of their own stalks. *Z-z-zip, z-z-zip, z-z-zip.* Suddenly I realized that there was dead silence except for our zipping.
   Why is the dinner party suddenly quiet? _____

   _____

2. The Gleasons' dinner party wasn't so different from a Chinese meal after all. My mother also puts everything on the table and hopes for the best.
   What does the narrator realize about Chinese and American cultures? _____

   _____

3. In this perfumed ladies' room, with its pink-and-silver wallpaper and marbled sinks, I looked completely out of place. What was I doing here? What was our family doing in the Lakeview Restaurant? In America?
   What emotions is the narrator feeling? _____

   _____

B. DIRECTIONS: *Underline details in this passage from "The All-American Slurp" that help you draw the conclusion that the family is adjusting to American life. Then tell why these details help you draw this conclusion.*

> Next day we took the bus downtown and she bought me a pair of jeans. In the same week, my brother made the baseball team of his junior high school. Father started taking driving lessons, and Mother discovered rummage sales.

Conclusion:

_____

_____

"The All-American Slurp" by Lensey Namioka
Literary Analysis: Theme

The **theme,** or central idea of a story, is a thought about life that the story conveys. Sometimes the theme is stated directly. Other times you must figure it out by considering events in the story, characters' thoughts and feelings, and the story's title.

A. DIRECTIONS: *Write a statement about the theme of "The All-American Slurp."*

Theme: _____

_____

B. DIRECTIONS: *In the chart below, write the details from each passage that tell about or support the theme of "The All-American Slurp." The first one is started for you as an example.*

Passage	What Details Tell About Theme
1. But I had another worry, and that was my appearance. My brother didn't have to worry, since Mother bought him blue jeans for school, and he dressed like all the other boys. But she insisted that girls had to wear skirts.	The narrator is worried about her appearance.
2. Of course Chinese etiquette forced Father to say that I was a very stupid girl and Mother to protest that the teacher was showing favoritism toward me. But I could tell they were both very proud.	
3. "Do you always slurp when you eat a milkshake?" I asked, before I could stop myself. Meg grinned. "Sure. All Americans slurp."	

"The All-American Slurp" by Lensey Namioka
Vocabulary Builder

Word List

acquainted   consumption   emigrated   etiquette   smugly   systematic

A. DIRECTIONS: *Each sentence below features a word from the list. For each sentence, explain why the underlined word does or does not make sense in the sentence.*

1. Proper <u>etiquette</u> says you will thank your host after a party.

   _____

2. Charley had a <u>consumption</u> after he ate too many candies.

   _____

3. Luis's <u>systematic</u> method of studying resulted in his failing the test.

   _____

4. The girls glanced at Rachel and smiled <u>smugly</u>, causing Rachel to feel grateful for their kind thoughts.

   _____

5. Margarita's family <u>emigrated</u> from Chile to America.

   _____

6. Marly and June got <u>acquainted</u> on their first day of school.

   _____

B. WORD STUDY: *The Latin root -migr- means "to move or to wander." Answer each question by paying attention to each of the underlined words with the root -migr-. Then, explain your answer.*

1. Could an <u>emigrant</u> move to a place where he or she would have to speak a new language?

   _____

2. When scientists study bird <u>migration</u>, are they looking at the birds' nests?

   _____

3. Did <u>immigrants</u> settle in North America in the 1600s and 1700s?

   _____

"The All-American Slurp" by Lensey Namioka
Enrichment: Community Diversity

Many communities in the United States have diverse populations, with people from different countries and cultures living near each other. People from diverse backgrounds share different cultures and traditions, as the narrator's family and the Gleasons do in "The All-American Slurp." These differences sometimes cause conflict when people from different national or cultural backgrounds don't understand each other. But more often diversity enriches a community and makes it more interesting by contributing arts, crafts, music, language, literature, food, fashions, and traditions from more than one background.

A. DIRECTIONS: *With a partner, look around your community to find restaurants, food or clothing stores, schools, or other businesses that reflect the influence of at least two countries or cultures in your community. List them on the chart below. Here is an example of how you might fill in your chart.*

Name of Business	Type of Business	Country or Culture
Example: Riu Renshi Dan	Karate school	Japan

B. DIRECTIONS: *Write a short paragraph explaining how diversity enriches a community or makes some aspect of it more interesting.*

_____

_____

_____

_____

_____

_____

_____

_____

_____

_____

"The Circuit" by Francisco Jiménez
"The All-American Slurp" by Lensey Namioka
Integrated Language Skills: Grammar

Simple Verb Tenses

A **verb** is a word that expresses an action or a state of being. A **verb tense** shows the time of the action or state of being. The **simple verb tenses** show present, past, and future time. Form the past tense of regular verbs with *-ed* or *-d*. Memorize the past tense of irregular verbs. Form the future tense of all verbs with the helping verb *will*.

Tenses	Regular Verb: Ask	Irregular Verb: Eat	Irregular Verb: Be
Present	I ask.	I eat.	I am.
Past	I asked.	I ate.	I was.
Future	I will ask.	I will eat.	I will be.

A. PRACTICE: *Underline the verb in each sentence. Then, on the line before the sentence, write whether the verb is in the* present, past, *or* future *tense.*

_____ 1. We grow corn, carrots, tomatoes, and beans on our farm.

_____ 2. We will pick the vegetables in late summer and fall.

_____ 3. We always display the vegetables on a small farm stand.

_____ 4. The tomatoes sell better than the other crops.

_____ 5. Next year, we will grow more tomatoes.

_____ 6. Last year, we also planted parsnips.

_____ 7. It was a bumper year for parsnips.

_____ 8. We ate parsnips in our soup all winter long.

B. Writing Application: *Write a sentence about a sports event using verbs in the past tense. Then, rewrite the sentence using verbs in the present tense. Finally, rewrite the sentence using verbs in the future tense. Study these examples:*

PAST TENSE: Rodrigo <u>pitched</u> the ball to the second batter.

PRESENT TENSE: Rodrigo <u>pitches</u> the ball to the second batter.

FUTURE: Rodrigo <u>will pitch</u> the ball to the second batter.

_____

_____

_____

Unit 2 Resources: Short Stories
154

Name _____ Date _____

"**The Circuit**" by Francisco Jiménez
"**The All-American Slurp**" by Lensey Namioka

Integrated Language Skills: Support for Writing a Character Description

Choose a character from "The Circuit" or "The All-American Slurp." Then, use the chart below to list details that describe that character. Include information from the story that illustrates the details used.

Name of Character: _____

Details That Describe the Character	Examples From the Story

Use the details that describe the character and examples from the story to write your character description.

"**The Circuit**" by Francisco Jiménez
"**The All-American Slurp**" by Lensey Namioka
Integrated Language Skills: Support for Extend Your Learning

Listening and Speaking: "The Circuit"

With your partner, prepare for an interview with the narrator of "The Circuit." Write questions and answers that you can use in your interview.

1. Questions about the narrator's age and family:

   Questions: _____

   Answers: _____

   _____

2. Questions about the narrator's observations on American life:

   Questions: _____

   Answers: _____

   _____

3. Questions about the narrator's favorite things:

   Questions: _____

   Answers: _____

   _____

Listening and Speaking: "The All-American Slurp"

With your partner, prepare for an interview with the narrator of "The All-American Slurp." Write questions and answers that you can use in your interview.

1. Questions about the narrator's age and family:

   Questions: _____

   Answers: _____

   _____

2. Questions about the narrator's observations on American life:

   Questions: _____

   Answers: _____

   _____

3. Questions about the narrator's favorite things:

   Questions: _____

   Answers: _____

   _____

Name _____ Date _____

Short Answer *Write your responses to the questions in this section on the lines provided.*

1. Complete the chart to draw a conclusion about the Lin family in "The All-American Slurp."

Question	Details That Answer Question	Conclusion
At the Gleasons' dinner party, how do the Lins sit on the sofa?		

2. Think about what happens when the narrator's family eats raw celery for the first time in "The All-American Slurp." How does the narrator feel about the situation? Use details from the story to support your answer.

   _____

   _____

3. In "The All-American Slurp," Meg says that her mother just hopes for the best when having a dinner party. The narrator's mother does the same. Explain what Meg's statement helps the narrator realize about Americans and Chinese.

   _____

   _____

4. In "The All-American Slurp," what does the way in which the narrator's father learns English reveal about him? Explain your answer.

   _____

   _____

5. In "The All-American Slurp," the narrator's father smugly gives an example of difficult verb tenses. Explain what the word *smugly* tells you about how he feels about mastering these tenses.

   _____

   _____

   _____

6. In "The All-American Slurp," the narrator's parents studied books on western etiquette before coming to America. What etiquette does the narrator exhibit at her family's dinner party? Explain your answer.

   _____

   _____

   _____

7. In "The All-American Slurp," the Lins are startled when the Gleasons mix together different foods. Explain what their reaction suggests about how the Lins usually eat.

_____

_____

_____

8. In "The All-American Slurp," how does the behavior of the Lins and Gleasons at each other's dinner party highlight the theme? Support your answer with details from the story.

_____

_____

_____

9. Think about what members of the Lin family do in "The All-American Slurp" to be more like Americans. Based on what they do, you can conclude that they want to fit in to American society. Give two details from the story that would help you draw this conclusion.

_____

_____

_____

10. At the end of "The All-American Slurp," Meg says that all Americans slurp when drinking a milkshake. Explain how this statement relates to the story's theme.

_____

_____

_____

_____

Essay

Write an extended response to the question of your choice or to the question or questions your teacher assigns you.

11. Think about how well the title of "The All-American Slurp" fits the story. How does it relate to the story's theme, or central idea? In an essay, evaluate the title, focusing on how well it reflects the theme. Use details from the story to support your ideas.

12. In an essay, explain how the narrator of "The All-American Slurp" deals with change. Focus on the kind of problems she faces and how the problems are solved. Use details from the story to support your ideas.

13. The characters in "The All-American Slurp" are different in the way they adjust to a new culture. Choose two members of the Lin family. In an essay, compare and contrast how well they adjust to living in America based on their personalities. Include details from the story in your answer.

14. **Thinking About the Big Question: Is conflict always bad?** In "The All-American Slurp," the narrator faces a conflict as she struggles to adapt to a new culture. In an essay, discuss whether this conflict is a bad thing. Use details from the story to support your point of view.

Oral Response

15. Go back to question 4, 5, 9, or 10 or to the question your teacher assigns to you. Take a few minutes to expand your answer and prepare an oral response. Find additional details in "The All-American Slurp" that will support your points. If necessary, make notes to guide your response.

Name _____ Date _____

"The All-American Slurp" by Lensey Namioka
Selection Test A

Critical Reading *Identify the letter of the choice that best answers the question.*

____ 1. In "The All-American Slurp," how does the narrator feel the first time her family eats raw celery?
A. amused
B. embarrassed
C. sad
D. angry

____ 2. Which of the following is a detail in "The All-American Slurp" that helps you conclude that Chinese people eat celery differently from Americans?
A. The Lins give the Gleasons instructions on how to eat celery.
B. The Gleasons laugh when the Lins eat celery.
C. Everyone stares as the Lins eat celery.
D. The Lins are the only ones who cut their celery into little pieces.

____ 3. How does Meg make the narrator feel better after the dinner party in "The All-American Slurp"?
A. Meg teases the narrator about the party until they both start to laugh.
B. Meg mentions that her mother doesn't plan for parties and just hopes for the best.
C. Meg doesn't mention the party.
D. Meg tells the narrator that her mother and the other guests liked the Lins.

____ 4. Why does the narrator of "The All-American Slurp" think her brother is adjusting better to American life than she is?
A. He is making friends easily.
B. He is better at riding a bicycle.
C. He gets better grades in school.
D. He knows how to eat American food.

____ 5. In "The All-American Slurp," why does the narrator explain how each person in the Lin family approaches English?
A. to show how Chinese people learn English
B. to prove that children learn new languages more easily than adults
C. to show the personality of each family member
D. to point out that English is a difficult language to learn

_____ 6. How does comparing the problems the Lins and the Gleasons experienced at each others' homes help reveal the theme of "The All-American Slurp"?

A. The comparison points out the vast differences between two cultures.

B. The comparison shows that the two cultures do not understand each other.

C. The comparison shows that the families will never get along.

D. The comparison shows that the families have certain similarities.

_____ 7. In "The All-American Slurp," which of the Lins is the first to fit in with American culture?

A. the narrator

B. the narrator's mother

C. the narrator's father

D. the narrator's brother

_____ 8. What can you conclude about the Lin family based on details in "The All-American Slurp"?

A. They all want to go back to China.

B. They all want to fit in to American society.

C. They do not like Americans very much.

D. They will never be comfortable in America.

_____ 9. Which of the following details from "The All-American Slurp" best expresses the theme of fitting in?

A. The mother buys blue jeans for the narrator.

B. The Lins immigrated to America.

C. Chinese dumplings are called pot-stickers.

D. The correct way to eat soup is to slurp it.

_____ 10. Which pair of words best describes the relationship between the narrator and her friend Meg in "The All-American Slurp"?

A. tense and angry

B. easy and relaxed

C. cautious and half-hearted

D. stiff and restrained

_____ 11. In "The All-American Slurp," what does the narrator discover when she drinks a milkshake with Meg?

A. Chinese people do not like milkshakes.

B. Americans do not know how to drink milkshakes.

C. Americans slurp when drinking milkshakes.

D. American milkshakes are different from Chinese milkshakes.

___ 12. What does the narrator learn about slurping in "The All-American Slurp"?

A. Slurping is considered bad manners everywhere.

B. Slurping is considered normal behavior in most restaurants.

C. Americans and Chinese both slurp in some situations.

D. Slurping is only considered acceptable in America.

Vocabulary and Grammar

___ 13. Which of the following is closest in meaning to the word *etiquette* as used in the following sentence?

Read a book on etiquette before you dine at the White House.

A. good manners

B. equestrian rules and horsemanship

C. restaurant food

D. history

___ 14. Which of these sentences contains an action verb?

A. The narrator feels embarrassed at the dinner party.

B. Meg seems unaware of any social problem.

C. The Lins all slurp their soup.

D. The family becomes more American every day.

___ 15. Which of these sentences contains a linking verb?

A. The Gleasons try to eat with chopsticks.

B. Meg loves Chinese food and waits eagerly for the dinner party.

C. American and Chinese people possess different eating habits.

D. The Lins are amused when they see the Gleasons eating Chinese food.

Essay

16. The narrator in "The All-American Slurp" learns an important lesson about life. In an essay, explain what you think she learns. Support your ideas with details and examples from the story.

17. In an essay, evaluate the title of "The All-American Slurp." Do you think this title reflects the theme of this story? Explain your answer using details from the story.

18. **Thinking About the Big Question: Is conflict always bad?** In "The All-American Slurp," the narrator struggles to get used to a new culture and new ways of doing things. In an essay, discuss whether this conflict is a bad thing for the narrator. Use details from the story to support your point of view.

"The All-American Slurp" by Lensey Namioka
Selection Test B

Critical Reading *Identify the letter of the choice that best completes the statement or answers the question.*

____ 1. What conclusion can you draw about the Lins from this passage in "The All-American Slurp"?

> As our family of four sat stiffly in a row, my younger brother and I stole glances at our parents for a clue as to what to do next.

    A. The Lins are not welcome at the party.
    B. The Lins feel anxious and unsure.
    C. The Lins are having a terrible time.
    D. The Lins are eager to fit in.

____ 2. How does Meg help the narrator of "The All-American Slurp" see that Americans and Chinese are not so different?
    A. Meg says her mother just hopes for the best when having a dinner party.
    B. Meg says Americans eat exactly the same way as Chinese.
    C. Meg says that Americans and Chinese eat celery the same way.
    D. Meg gives her clothes to the narrator so they will look alike.

____ 3. In "The All-American Slurp," the manner in which the narrator's father learns English characterizes him as
    A. easygoing and amusing.
    B. tense and irritable.
    C. emotional and unpredictable.
    D. organized and precise.

____ 4. In "The All-American Slurp," why does the narrator go to the ladies' room at the French restaurant?
    A. She doesn't feel well.
    B. She is embarrassed by her family.
    C. She wants to spit out the food she has eaten.
    D. She is afraid to eat the food that has been served.

____ 5. The Lins are startled when the Gleasons mix together different dishes. How do you think the Lins usually eat?
    A. They never eat rice with other food.
    B. They mix all their food together.
    C. They eat one type of food at a time.
    D. They never eat together.

____ 6. What do the Gleasons have trouble with when they eat Chinese-style in "The All-American Slurp"?
    A. unfamiliar etiquette
    B. American food
    C. sitting on the floor
    D. Chinese language

____ 7. What can you conclude about the narrator from this passage in "The All-American Slurp"?

> . . . I understood the message: the Gleasons were not used to Chinese ways and they were just coping the best they could. For some reason I thought of celery strings.

    A. She believes that the Gleasons are ignorant and foolish.
    B. She feels that Chinese food and customs are superior to those of America.
    C. She realizes that the Gleasons will never understand Chinese traditions and customs.
    D. She understands that her family and the Gleasons are similar in some ways.

____ 8. By the end of "The All-American Slurp," the narrator discovers that
    A. slurping is considered bad etiquette throughout the world.
    B. slurping is considered normal behavior in most restaurants.
    C. Americans and Chinese both slurp, but they find it acceptable at different times.
    D. slurping is considered acceptable only in America.

____ 9. At the conclusion of "The All-American Slurp," how have the Lins adjusted to life in America?
    A. They give up Chinese customs for American ways.
    B. They are comfortable with American ways but still keep many Chinese customs.
    C. They do not know which Chinese customs to follow and which to give up.
    D. They do not adjust to American life and are returning to China.

____ 10. Which of the following best summarizes "The All-American Slurp"?
    A. The narrator makes a new best friend.
    B. The narrator's parents have trouble adjusting to change in a new country.
    C. The Lin family encounters challenges as they adapt to their new country.
    D. The Gleason family discovers that they have new Chinese neighbors.

____ 11. The theme of "The All-American Slurp" can best be found by comparing
    A. the way Mr. and Mrs. Lin learn to speak English.
    B. Chinese clothing to American clothing.
    C. the brother and sister in the Lin family.
    D. the problems the Lins and Gleasons have during dinner at each others' homes.

____ 12. Which of the following best states the theme of "The All-American Slurp"?
    A. It is not wise to move to a strange land.
    B. Cultures and customs may be different, but people are not so different.
    C. No matter where a person travels, good manners are important.
    D. Change is an important part of growing up.

Vocabulary and Grammar

____ 13. To do something *eventually*, such as to eventually clean out a closet, is to do it
    A. right away.
    B. after a while.
    C. correctly.
    D. reluctantly.

____ 14. Which of the following phrases best defines the word *emigrated* in this sentence?
We had emigrated to this country from China, and during our early days here we had a
hard time with American table manners.

    A. traveled a long distance
    B. come from one country to another
    C. crossed an ocean
    D. carried many belongings

____ 15. In which sentence is an action verb underlined?
    A. The Lins <u>are</u> unsure of what to do at the Gleasons' house.
    B. Celery <u>is</u> good with sour cream dip.
    C. Mrs. Gleason <u>offers</u> celery sticks to the Lins.
    D. The guests <u>seem</u> amused by the Lins' actions.

____ 16. In which sentence is the underlined word a linking verb?
    A. The narrator <u>works</u> hard to learn English.
    B. The narrator's brother <u>seems</u> very comfortable speaking English.
    C. The narrator's mother <u>memorizes</u> many English words.
    D. The narrator's father <u>tries</u> a scientific approach to learning English.

____ 17. Which sentence contains both an action verb and a linking verb?
    A. Meg helps the narrator, and soon she feels more comfortable with American
habits.
    B. The narrator and Meg try on each others' clothes and laugh about it.
    C. Meg and the narrator drink milkshakes, and Meg makes loud slurping noises.
    D. Meg likes Chinese food, but she eats it in an American way.

Essay

18. Write an essay explaining how the narrator in "The All-American Slurp" deals with
change. What kind of problems does she face? How are these problems solved? Use
details and examples from the story to support your ideas.

19. In an essay, discuss the similarities between the Lins' dinner party in "The All-American
Slurp" and the Gleasons' dinner party. Tell how these two story events support the
theme of the story.

20. **Thinking About the Big Question: Is conflict always bad?** In "The All-American
Slurp," the narrator faces a conflict as she struggles to adapt to a new culture. In an
essay, discuss whether this conflict is a bad thing. Use details from the story to support
your point of view.

Vocabulary Warm-up Word Lists

Study these words from "The King of Mazy May." Then, complete the activities.

Word List A

delayed [dee LAYD] *v.* waited; took a lot of time
   I couldn't make up my mind so I <u>delayed</u> before deciding.

glimpses [GLIMP siz] *n.* quick looks; glances
   We only caught <u>glimpses</u> of the robber because he ran away quickly.

increase [in CREES] *v.* make larger
   If you <u>increase</u> the amount of sugar in the cookies, they will taste sweeter.

labor [LAY buhr] *n.* hard work
   Charlie put in more <u>labor</u> so he could finish the job in one day.

objected [uhb JEKT id] *v.* disagreed with; spoke against
   When Camille <u>objected</u> to our first plan, we came up with a new one.

proceeded [pruh SEED id] *v.* went ahead with doing something
   After finishing the meatballs, he <u>proceeded</u> to eat the spaghetti.

slackened [SLAK ind] *v.* weakened, died down
   Our excitement <u>slackened</u> when we found out that we weren't getting the reward.

streak [STREEK] *n.* a mark, line, or strip
   Using chalk, she made a blue <u>streak</u> on the concrete to divide the playground in two.

Word List B

haste [HAYST] *n.* speed in doing something
   If you work the test questions in <u>haste</u>, you might make silly mistakes.

manliness [MAN lee nes] *n.* qualities (like strength or courage) people associate with men
   I don't think picking up a hot coal shows <u>manliness</u>, just foolishness.

newcomers [NOO kuhm erz] *n.* people who just arrived; first-timers
   The <u>newcomers</u> don't know the game; you'll have to tell them the rules.

overtake [oh ver TAYK] *v.* to catch up with and pass by
   The first-place runner sped up so no one could <u>overtake</u> her.

perilously [PER i luhs lee] *adv.* dangerously
   The car drove <u>perilously</u> close to the edge of the cliff.

prospectors [PRAH spek terz] *n.* people who make money finding gold
   During the great Gold Rush, many <u>prospectors</u> headed to California.

suspense [suh SPENS] *n.* feeling of not knowing what is going to happen next
   Nilda couldn't take the <u>suspense</u>, so she skipped to the end of the book.

thermometer [ther MAHM uh ter] *n.* instrument used to measure hot and cold
   Put on a warm coat; the <u>thermometer</u> shows that it's freezing outside.

Name _____ Date _____

Vocabulary Warm-up Exercises

Exercise A *Fill in each blank in the paragraph below with an appropriate word from Word List A. Use each word only once.*

I guess you could call me lazy. [1] _____ isn't my favorite thing. So I [2] _____ in joining the rest of the family as they got the house ready for Halloween. From the couch, I caught [3] _____ of them working. Aiden poured a [4] _____ of fake blood onto the steps. Kelly pumped up the pumpkin balloons, trying to [5] _____ their size. When one popped, she [6] _____ to blow up another. No one [7] _____ to my lack of activity. When the family's energy [8] _____, I finally got up to do the work they couldn't finish.

Exercise B *Write a complete sentence to answer each question. For each item, use a word from Word List B to replace the underlined word or group of words without changing its meaning.*

1. What is a quality you think people often connect with <u>being a man</u>?
   _____

2. Would people on a plane be scared if it flew <u>dangerously</u> close to a mountain?
   _____

3. When can too much <u>speed</u> be dangerous?
   _____

4. Have you ever read about <u>people looking for gold</u>?
   _____

5. Do <u>people who haven't done something before</u> usually do well right away?
   _____

6. What kind of movies often leave you with a feeling of <u>not knowing what is going to happen</u>?
   _____

7. Are you leading in a race if a few people <u>pass you by</u>?
   _____

8. What good is <u>an instrument that is used to measure hot and cold</u>?
   _____

Name _____ Date _____

Reading Warm-up A

Read the following passage. Pay special attention to the underlined words. Then, read it again, and complete the activities. Use a separate sheet of paper for your written answers.

"We're off to find some gold," said Uncle Richard. "I'm ready to get rich." Uncle Richard ran his hands through the <u>streak</u> of gray in the middle of his black beard. He always did this when he got excited about something. None of us <u>objected</u> to Uncle Richard's idea. Why should we disagree with it? Sometimes his ideas don't work out, but we always have a good time.

Uncle Richard <u>proceeded</u> to write down a list of items he thought we would need. Then, we all jumped in the car and headed off to the hardware store. We waited outside while he did the shopping. Through the window, I caught a few <u>glimpses</u> of a black-bearded man running from aisle to aisle with his arms full of tools. A few minutes later, Uncle Richard came back out with shovel, pans, and who knew what else.

From there, it was a two-hour drive to a state park, followed by a half-hour walk to a small, muddy creek. "Let's get going," my uncle said as he handed out the tools.

Now, none of us really knew what we were doing. I dug around in the mud looking for shiny stuff. After an hour or two, I got tired and stopped to take a rest. "What's wrong?" said my uncle. "Can't you handle a little bit of <u>labor</u>? Hard work will <u>increase</u> the size of your muscles. And if we find gold, it will increase the size of your wallet, too."

"Won't find any gold around here," came a voice from behind us. It was the park ranger. "You <u>delayed</u> too long in coming. The last discoveries of gold in this area were made about two hundred years ago. Feel free to dig around and have a good time, though."

After the park ranger spoke, Uncle Richard's desire to look for gold suddenly <u>slackened</u>. We packed up, drove home, and made burgers in the backyard.

1. Underline the words that tell you where the <u>streak</u> is. Then tell what a *streak* is.

2. Underline the nearby words that have a similar meaning to <u>objected</u>. Then write a sentence about something you *objected* to.

3. Circle the words that tell what Uncle Richard <u>proceeded</u> to do. Then tell what *proceeded* means.

4. Underline the words that tell what the narrator caught <u>glimpses</u> of. Then write a sentence using the word *glimpses*.

5. Circle the nearby word that has the same meaning as <u>labor</u>. Then write a sentence about a time when you did some *labor*.

6. Circle the words that tell what Uncle Richard says hard work will <u>increase</u>. Then tell what *increase* means.

7. Underline the sentence that explains why Uncle Richard <u>delayed</u> too long. Then tell what *delayed* means.

8. Circle the words that tell what <u>slackened</u>. Then tell what *slackened* means.

Name _____   Date _____

"The King of Mazy May" by Jack London
Reading Warm-up B

Read the following passage. Pay special attention to the underlined words. Then, read it again, and complete the activities. Use a separate sheet of paper for your written answers.

Some call it "the last great race on Earth." The race they are talking about is the Iditarod Trail Sled Dog Race, a competition for sled dogs and their drivers. The race is held every year in Alaska. The dog teams and their drivers, called mushers, start out in Anchorage. Then, they race across a thousand miles of the Iditarod Trail to Nome.

The trail used to supply <u>prospectors</u> who were looking for gold in the Alaskan interior. It passes through some of the roughest, toughest wilderness there is. The dogs must race through mountains, forests, frozen rivers, and vast stretches of icy tundra. Since the race is held at the end of winter, the numbers on the <u>thermometer</u> can get pretty scary, and blizzards aren't uncommon.

In the old days, most of the teams used to come from Alaska. Now the race is an international event. Each year brings many <u>newcomers</u>. These first-time racers come from states across the country and countries around the world. The race also draws lots of tourists, drawn by the <u>suspense</u> of watching to see who will win.

For years, people considered Iditarod a test of <u>manliness</u>. Few women entered the race. Then, Susan Butcher came along and changed everyone's ideas about what manliness means. Yes, the Iditarod takes strength and courage, but you don't need to be a man to win. Butcher is the only person, male or female, to win the race three times in a row.

Racers need to make <u>haste</u>, but they also need to be careful. As mushers try to <u>overtake</u> the leading team, they also need to watch the trail and the weather. It's <u>perilously</u> easy to get lost in the fierce snowstorms that spring up out of nowhere.

1. Underline the words that tell what <u>prospectors</u> did. Then write a sentence using the word.

2. Why do you think the numbers on a <u>thermometer</u> get pretty scary?

3. Circle the nearby words that tell what kind of racers <u>newcomers</u> are. Then tell what *newcomers* means.

4. Underline the words that tell what kind of <u>suspense</u> draws tourists. Then tell about a time you felt *suspense*.

5. Circle the thing that people considered a test of <u>manliness</u>. Then tell how Butcher changed people's ideas about *manliness*.

6. Rewrite the first sentence of the last paragraph, changing the phrase "to make <u>haste</u>" to another word or phrase that has the same meaning.

7. Underline the words that tell who mushers try to <u>overtake</u>. Then tell what *overtake* means.

8. Circle the words that tell what is <u>perilously</u> easy to do. Then tell what *perilously* means.

"The King of Mazy May" by Jack London
Writing About the Big Question

Is conflict always bad?

Big Question Vocabulary

argue	battle	challenge	compete	conclude
convince	defend	game	issue	lose
negotiate	oppose	resolve	survival	win

A. *Use one or more words from the list above to complete each sentence.*

1. Sometimes on the playground, bigger kids will _____ little kids and try to take something away from them.

2. The little kids are not able to _____ themselves.

3. It is very difficult for someone small to _____ someone bigger.

4. A small child cannot _____ with a bigger child physically.

B. *Answer each question with a complete sentence.*

1. Describe a time when you were challenged by someone bigger or stronger. What were you battling over?

_____

_____

2. Explain the outcome of the incident. Who won? Who lost? Why? Use at least two Big Question vocabulary words in your response.

_____

_____

C. *Complete this sentence. Then, write a brief paragraph in which you write about how stealing can lead to conflict.*

If someone tried to steal my friend's property, I would _____

_____

_____

_____

_____

_____

_____

Name _____ Date _____

"The King of Mazy May" by Jack London
Reading: Use Prior Knowledge to Draw Conclusions

Drawing conclusions means making decisions or forming opinions about what has happened in a literary work. You make your conclusions using details from the text and your own **prior knowledge**—what you know from your own experience. You bring prior knowledge with you whenever you read a story.

Example from "The King of Mazy May":

> He has never seen a train of cars nor an elevator in his life, and for that matter he has never once looked upon a cornfield, a plow, a cow, or even a chicken. He has never had a pair of shoes on his feet, nor gone to a picnic or a party, nor talked to a girl.

Details from the passage tell you what Walt Masters has never done or seen. Your own prior knowledge about what the author describes tells you that Walt does not live in a city or on a farm. You can conclude that Walt lives somewhere very isolated from civilization.

A. DIRECTIONS: *Fill in this chart with your own prior knowledge and the conclusions you can draw. The first one has been done for you as an example.*

Story Details	Prior Knowledge	Conclusion
1. The Mazy May creek is beginning to reward the prospectors for their hard work.	Prospectors came to the Yukon to find gold.	The prospectors are beginning to find gold.
2. Walt is able to stay by himself, cook his own meals, and look after the claim.		
3. The days are short and the nights are long when the story takes place.		
4. The stampeders try to kill Walt to keep him from reaching Dawson.		

B. DIRECTIONS: *Write about another conclusion that you can make on your own from "The King of Mazy May." Explain your conclusion by telling the details and the prior knowledge you used.*

_____

_____

_____

_____

"The King of Mazy May" by Jack London
Literary Analysis: Setting

The **setting** of a literary work is the time and place of the action. The time may be established as a historical era, the present or future, the season of the year, or the hour of the day. The place can be as general as planet Earth or as specific as a room in a house. As you read, notice how characters and events in a story are affected by the setting of the story.

Example from "The King of Mazy May":

> But he has seen the sun at midnight, watched the ice jams on one of the mightiest of rivers, and played beneath the northern lights . . .

This passage tells you that the story takes place in the far north, which is where you can see the sun at midnight and the northern lights.

A. DIRECTIONS: *Use the chart to tell about the setting of "The King of Mazy May." In column two, record your answer and the details from the story that help you answer each question.*

Questions About the Setting of the Story	Answer and Story Details
1. Where does the first part of "The King of Mazy May" take place?	
2. When does the first part of "The King of Mazy May" take place?	
3. Where does the chase take place?	
4. When does the chase take place?	

B. DIRECTIONS: *Use the information in your chart to help you answer the following questions.*

How important is the setting in this story? Why is it important?

_____

_____

_____

_____

_____

_____

_____

"The King of Mazy May" by Jack London
Vocabulary Builder

Word List

abruptly   declined   endured   liable   pursuing   summit

A. DIRECTIONS: *Provide an answer and an explanation for each question.*

1. If you have *endured* the experience of watching a movie, did you enjoy the film?
   _____

2. If a friend *declined* an invitation to a party, would he or she be going to it?
   _____

3. If a teacher is *liable* to spring a pop quiz on your class, should you expect a quiz?
   _____

4. If a hiker reached the *summit* of a mountain, how much farther is it to the top?
   _____

5. If you left a party *abruptly*, would you be in a hurry?
   _____

6. If someone was *pursuing* you, would you feel nervous?
   _____

B. WORD STUDY: *The Latin root -clin- means "lean." Think about the meaning of the root -clin- in each underlined word. Then, write two reasons for each statement.*

1. You are going up a steep incline. Why?
   _____

   _____

2. You have declined a piece of cake. Why?
   _____

   _____

3. You have reclined on the couch. Why?
   _____

   _____

"The King of Mazy May" by Jack London
Enrichment: The Iditarod

Walt Masters and the other prospectors in the story are looking for gold in Canada's Yukon Territory. Over one hundred years ago, gold was found in Alaska and many people rushed there, hoping to get rich. Gold-rush towns sprang up everywhere. In 1925, people in one of those towns, Nome, became ill from a disease called diphtheria. The medicine they needed was in Anchorage, more than 1,000 miles away. A train carried the medicine from Anchorage to its last stop, Nenana. From there, sled-dog teams and their mushers, or drivers, raced the medicine 674 miles to Nome, along a mining route called the Iditarod Trail.

In 1967, in memory of that journey, the first Iditarod Sled Dog Race was organized, with mushers and their dog teams racing along 56 miles of the trail.

A. DIRECTIONS: *Look in reference books or on the Internet to find information to answer these questions.*

1. How long is today's Iditarod? _____

2. Where does the race begin and end? _____

   _____

3. How many dogs can be on each team? What kinds of dogs are used?

   _____

   _____

B. DIRECTIONS: *Write a description of the character traits a musher in the Iditarod would need to complete the race. Explain why each trait would be necessary.*

_____

_____

_____

_____

_____

_____

_____

_____

_____

_____

_____

_____

Name _____   Date _____

"The King of Mazy May" by Jack London
Open-Book Test

Short Answer *Write your responses to the questions in this section on the lines provided.*

1. Jack London begins "The King of Mazy May" by describing Walt Masters as "not a very large boy, but there is manliness in his make-up." Considering what Walt does later in the story, explain what the author means by "manliness."

   _____

   _____

2. "The King of Mazy May" takes place in a frozen wilderness. Think about how well Walt Masters has adapted to the Yukon. What effect has this setting had on Walt? Use details from the story to support your answer.

   _____

   _____

3. The author of "The King of Mazy May" says that the prospectors endured great hardships the previous year. What did Loren Hall endure on his way to Dawson?

   _____

   _____

4. Think about what claim jumpers do to the hard-working prospectors in "The King of Mazy May." Explain why Walt dislikes the claim jumpers so much.

   _____

   _____

   _____

5. In "The King of Mazy May," Walt's father leaves him alone to take care of himself and Loren Hall's claim. Explain what this reveals about Mr. Masters's opinion of his son.

   _____

   _____

   _____

6. The creek is part of the setting in "The King of Mazy May." In what ways does the creek affect events in the story? Use two details from the story to explain your answer.

   _____

   _____

7. Think about the problems Walt has with the cold as he races on the sled in "The King of Mazy May." Which of his actions helps you conclude that the low temperatures are dangerous?

   _____

   _____

Name _____ Date _____

8. In "The King of Mazy May," Walt stretches flat on the sled as he clears the summit of each ice jam to avoid the claim jumpers' bullets. Explain why this is the time when the claim jumpers would have the best chance of hitting him.

_____

_____

_____

9. In "The King of Mazy May," what aspects of the setting make Walt's race to Dawson challenging? Use details from the story in your answer.

_____

_____

_____

10. In "The King of Mazy May," Walt keeps going on the sled even though he faces mortal danger. List two details from the story that tell what happened to Walt as he raced to Dawson. Then add what you know about people like Walt to draw a conclusion about the boy.

Details		Prior Knowledge		Conclusion
	+		→	

Essay

Write an extended response to the question of your choice or to the question or questions your teacher assigns you.

11. The conflict in "The King of Mazy May" is between a boy and a group of men. Walt stands for good, and the claim jumpers stand for evil. In an essay, describe Walt's good qualities and the claim jumpers' bad qualities. Use examples from the story to support your ideas.

12. The setting of "The King of Mazy May" is a frozen wilderness far from the comforts of civilization. The details of the setting are very important to the plot of the story. In an essay, explain the effect of this setting on the story. Describe the setting, using details from the story. Then, explain how the setting significantly affects the story events.

13. In "The King of Mazy May," we learn about Walt from what the narrator tells us, what others say about him, and his own thoughts and actions. In an essay, analyze Walt's character traits. State which of his qualities you think are part of his nature and which might result from how and where he grew up. Use examples from the story to support your ideas.

14. **Thinking About the Big Question: Is conflict always bad?** In "The King of Mazy May," Walt faces some very dangerous claim jumpers. In an essay, first discuss in what ways this conflict is bad for Walt. Then discuss what positive results come out of the conflict. Last, explain whether you think Walt would undertake such a conflict again. Use details from the story to support your ideas.

Oral Response

15. Go back to question 1, 2, 9, or 10 or to the question your teacher assigns to you. Take a few minutes to expand your answer and prepare an oral response. Find additional details in "The King of Mazy May" that will support your points. If necessary, make notes to guide your response.

"The King of Mazy May" by Jack London
Selection Test A

Critical Reading *Identify the letter of the choice that best answers the question.*

____ 1. In "The King of Mazy May," why hasn't Walt ever seen a train or an elevator?
A. These machines have not been invented yet.
B. He prefers to stay away from cities.
C. He does not want anything to do with machines.
D. He lives in an area where these things have not yet come into use.

____ 2. Where does the story of "The King of Mazy May" take place?
A. in the Yukon
B. in California
C. in Europe
D. in South America

____ 3. When does "The King of Mazy May" take place?
A. during the California Gold Rush
B. during the gold rush in the Yukon
C. during the Civil War
D. after World War II

____ 4. Why doesn't Walt like claim-jumpers?
A. They think about nothing but getting rich.
B. They steal what others have worked hard to get.
C. They have bad tempers.
D. They treat their dogs very badly.

____ 5. Why do the claim-jumpers chase Walt?
A. They are angry that he has been spying on them.
B. They want to find out what he knows.
C. They want to make sure he doesn't get to Dawson first.
D. They want their dogs and sled back.

____ 6. Why can you conclude that the low temperatures Walt faces are dangerous?
A. He has to stop to build a fire.
B. He has to run beside the sled to keep warm.
C. He has to stop to pick up a warmer coat.
D. His dogs begin to freeze to death.

_____ 7. Why do the claim-jumpers keep shooting at Walt?

    A. He is so brave and smart they can't stop him any other way.

    B. They are trying to defend themselves against Walt's whip attacks.

    C. They think he is carrying gold.

    D. Walt challenged them to a win-or-die race.

_____ 8. Why can you conclude that Walt is determined to get to Dawson before the stampeders?

    A. He tells a friend about his determination.

    B. He says as much to the head stampeder.

    C. He faces mortal danger but keeps going.

    D. He is desperate to keep the gold himself.

_____ 9. Which word best describes Walt's character in "The King of Mazy May"?

    A. angry

    B. timid

    C. stubborn

    D. self-reliant

_____ 10. Which word does not describe Walt?

    A. brave

    B. honest

    C. hot-tempered

    D. quick-witted

_____ 11. How does the creek in the setting of "The King of Mazy May" contribute to the story?

    A. Gold is found there, and Walt follows the creek on his journey.

    B. The stampeders finally drown in the creek.

    C. Walt paddles down the creek to get to Dawson.

    D. The creek floods, putting the prospectors in danger.

Vocabulary and Grammar

_____ 12. Which word is closest in meaning to the word *declined* as used in this sentence?

    The proud and independent miner declined the help offered by the other miners.

    A. threw

    B. answered

    C. lowered

    D. refused

____ 13. Which word is closest in meaning to the word *lovable* as used in this sentence?
He was a crusty old miner, but underneath his tough exterior he was a lovable guy.

    A. lovely

    B. admirable

    C. desirable

    D. able to be loved

____ 14. Which sentence contains the past tense of *follow*?

    A. Walt follows the creek to the Yukon River.

    B. Walt followed the creek to the Yukon River.

    C. Walt is following the creek to the Yukon River.

    D. Walt has followed the creek to the Yukon River.

____ 15. Which sentence contains the present tense of *yell*?

    A. The stampeders yell at their dogs to make them run faster.

    B. The stampeders yelled at their dogs to make them run faster.

    C. The stampeders are yelling at their dogs to make them run faster.

    D. The stampeders have yelled at their dogs to make them run faster.

Essay

16. In outrunning the claim-jumpers and their bullets in "The King of Mazy May," Walt Masters overcomes many obstacles and faces many dangers. What makes him persist? In an essay, describe the challenges Walt faces and the character traits that enable him to go on. Use examples from the story to support your statements.

17. "The King of Mazy May" is about a conflict between a boy and a group of men. It is also a story of conflict between good and bad. In an essay, describe Walt's good qualities and the claim-jumpers' bad qualities. Cite examples from the story to support your description.

18. **Thinking About the Big Question: Is conflict always bad?** In "The King of Mazy May," Walt faces some very dangerous claim-jumpers. The conflict could easily have resulted in Walt's being hurt or killed. In an essay, discuss whether the conflict is all bad or if some good comes from it. Explain whether you think Walt would behave in the same way again. Use details from the story to support your ideas.

"The King of Mazy May" by Jack London
Selection Test B

Critical Reading *Identify the letter of the choice that best completes the statement or answers the question.*

_____ 1. "The King of Mazy May" begins with "Walt Masters is not a very large boy, but there is manliness in his make-up." Judging from Walt's later actions in the story, what does the author mean by "manliness"?
A. physical strength and athletic skill
B. intelligence, cleverness, and creativity
C. physical strength and persistence
D. courage and confidence

_____ 2. The setting of "The King of Mazy May" is
A. the Yukon gold rush.
B. the California gold rush.
C. the Colorado gold rush.
D. an imaginary gold rush.

_____ 3. Based on what you know about gold prospectors, what can you conclude from this passage from "The King of Mazy May"?

. . . the creek, in turn, was just beginning to show up its richness and to reward them for their heavy labor.

A. The creek water is good to drink.
B. Prospectors carry heavy loads.
C. The prospectors have built a dam.
D. The prospectors are finding gold.

_____ 4. What time of year is indicated in this passage from "The King of Mazy May"?

But with the news of their discoveries, strange men began to come and go through the short days and long nights. . . .

A. spring
B. summer
C. fall
D. winter

_____ 5. Walt's father leaves Walt to take care of himself. This shows that the father
A. has confidence in Walt.
B. is desperate to find gold.
C. is careless.
D. wants to test Walt's courage.

_____ 6. Why do you think the Klondike attracted dishonest outlaws as well as honest, hardworking prospectors?
A. The Klondike offered the opportunity to make a new start in life.
B. The promise of easily gained riches often attracts dishonest people.
C. Harsh living conditions often attract dishonest people.
D. Criminals could hide out there without fear of being caught.

___ 7. Why is the water temperature in the creek an important part of "The King of Mazy May"?
  A. The cold water is more likely to produce gold.
  B. The claim-jumpers fall in the water and have to stop their pursuit.
  C. The water freezes Loren Hall's feet so he can't guard his claim.
  D. The frozen creek makes it easier for the claim-jumpers to chase Walt.

___ 8. Why does Walt not like the claim-jumpers?
  A. They think only about getting rich.
  B. They steal what others have worked hard to get.
  C. They have bad tempers.
  D. They mistreat their dogs.

___ 9. Why does Walt sometimes run beside the sled when he is chased by the claim-jumpers?
  A. to lighten the load the dogs must pull
  B. to show the lead dog where to go
  C. to warm himself up
  D. to get a better view of the trail

___ 10. When Walt leaves the dying lead dog behind, he shows that he
  A. is insensitive to suffering.
  B. uses good judgment.
  C. loves animals.
  D. acts selfishly.

___ 11. Walt finally begins to pull ahead of the claim-jumpers when he
  A. shoots the lead claim-jumper.
  B. tangles the claim-jumpers' dog team.
  C. crosses the river.
  D. uses his whip on his dogs.

___ 12. The story of "The King of Mazy May" shows that
  A. everyone should fight like Walt.
  B. the other men respected Walt for his efforts.
  C. life in the wilderness is better than other places.
  D. young people used to be stronger than they are now.

Vocabulary and Grammar

___ 13. Which word is most nearly opposite to identifiable?
  A. identify
  B. impossible
  C. anonymous
  D. known

_____ **14.** Which word correctly completes the following sentence?
   If you have *endured* hardship, you have _____.
   A. triumphed
   B. lost
   C. won
   D. suffered

_____ **15.** In which sentence is the verb *run* a past participle?
   A. The dogs run as fast as they can.
   B. The dogs ran as fast as they can.
   C. The dogs are running as fast as they can.
   D. The dogs have run as fast as they can.

_____ **16.** In which sentence is the verb *pursue* a present participle?
   A. The claim-jumpers pursue Walt and shoot at him.
   B. The claim-jumpers pursued Walt and shot at him.
   C. The claim-jumpers are pursuing Walt and shooting at him.
   D. The claim-jumpers have pursued Walt and shot at him.

_____ **17.** In which sentence is the verb *speed* in the past tense?
   A. The sled speeds along the hard-packed snow.
   B. The sled sped along the hard-packed snow.
   C. The sled is speeding along the hard-packed snow.
   D. The sled has sped along the hard-packed snow.

Essay

18. In an essay, analyze Walt's character in "The King of Mazy May." Using details from the text to support your analysis, state which of his qualities you think are part of his nature and which might result from how and where he grew up.

19. "The King of Mazy May" is set in a rugged wilderness with few comforts of civilization. Write an essay in which you explain the effect of this setting on the story. Begin your essay by describing the setting, using details from the text. Continue by explaining how the setting, including climate and terrain, has a significant effect on the events of the story.

20. Thinking About the Big Question: Is conflict always bad? In "The King of Mazy May," Walt faces some very dangerous claim-jumpers. In an essay, first, discuss in what ways this conflict is bad for Walt. Then, discuss the positive results that come out of the conflict. Last, explain whether you think Walt would undertake such a conflict again. Use details from the story to support your ideas.

Vocabulary Warm-up Word Lists

Study these words from "Aaron's Gift." Then, complete the activities that follow.

Word List A

genius [JEEN yuhs] *n.* an unusually smart or talented person
    Mozart was a musical <u>genius</u> who contributed many great works of art to civilization.

heal [HEEL] *v.* cure or recover from an injury or wound
    When I broke my arm it took six weeks to <u>heal</u>.

miserable [MIZ er uh buhl] *adj.* feeling great sadness or discomfort
    Tim was a big Yankee fan and felt <u>miserable</u> when the team lost.

properly [PRAHP er lee] *adv.* in a correct or appropriate way
    When I use a hammer <u>properly</u> I rarely bend a nail.

series [SEER eez] *n.* a group of related things that happen one after the other
    A <u>series</u> of mistakes by the driver led to the accident.

shack [SHAK] *n.* small, poorly built hut or house
    We use the old <u>shack</u> in the backyard as a clubhouse.

soothe [SOO*TH*] *v.* to make someone feel calmer and less worried, angry, or upset
    The baby was upset, but her mother was able to <u>soothe</u> her with a bottle.

thrashing [THRASH ing] *v.* moving in a wild or uncontrolled way
    The fish was <u>thrashing</u> about after the fisherman dropped him in the pail.

Word List B

aviator [AY vee ay ter] *n.* someone who flies a plane
    Only a trained <u>aviator</u> can pilot a plane.

cooing [KOO ing] *v.* making soft, birdlike sounds
    The baby birds were <u>cooing</u> softly in their nest.

fantastic [fan TAS tik] *adj.* incredible or amazing
    Fourth of July fireworks are a <u>fantastic</u> thing to see.

frenzied [FREN zeed] *adj.* wild; frantic
    The hungry dogs made a <u>frenzied</u> run for the pile of biscuits.

pavement [PAYV ment] *n.* hard material, like cement, used to cover roads and sidewalks
    The taxicab driver slowed down because of the broken <u>pavement</u>.

remarkably [ree MAHRK uh blee] *adv.* unusually; notably
    Howard was <u>remarkably</u> tall for a five-year-old; he looked at least nine.

sparrows [SPA rohs] *n.* small brown and white birds often found in cities
    You won't find eagles in town, but you'll see plenty of <u>sparrows</u>.

temporarily [tem puh RAIR uh lee] *adv.* for a short time; not permanently
    She was mad at me <u>temporarily</u>; five minutes later she had forgotten our fight.

Name _____ Date _____

"**Aaron's Gift**" by Myron Levoy
Vocabulary Warm-up Exercises

Exercise A *Fill in each blank in the paragraph below with an appropriate word from Word List A. Use each word only once.*

Because the old [1] _____ in the backyard was not built

[2] _____ , it was no surprise when it fell down. After a

[3] _____ of crashes, we heard a scream and the sound of someone

[4] _____ about. "Mike, is that you?" I called out.

   "Who else would it be, [5] _____! Get me out of here," came the

reply in a [6] _____ sounding voice. We pulled Mike out from beneath

the boards. He was shaken up, but my older brother and I were able to

[7] _____ him. Mike was lucky. There were no broken bones, just a

bruised shoulder that took a week or two to [8] _____ .

Exercise B *Decide whether each statement below is true or false. Circle T or F. Then, explain your answers.*

1. German Shepherds usually make <u>cooing</u> sounds.
   T / F _____

2. A few spoons of rice will only make hunger go away <u>temporarily</u>.
   T / F _____

3. An <u>aviator</u> never leaves the ground.
   T / F _____

4. A person acting in a <u>frenzied</u> way is very calm and peaceful.
   T / F _____

5. It is easier to skate on <u>pavement</u> than in mud.
   T / F _____

6. If your jokes are <u>remarkably</u> funny, people will laugh.
   T / F _____

7. <u>Sparrows</u> would enjoy eating bird food.
   T / F _____

8. Watching someone park a car is a <u>fantastic</u> thing to see.
   T / F _____

Name _____ Date _____

Read the following passage. Pay special attention to the underlined words. Then, read it again, and complete the activities. Use a separate sheet of paper for your written answers.

Veterinarians are doctors who practice medicine on animals. Most vets are people who want to help animals. It's not easy to become one, however. You don't have to be a genius, though being smart helps. You do have to put in some really hard work. Normally, it takes four years of college followed by ten or more years of veterinary study. Getting into a veterinary school is tough. Many people say that it is harder to get into vet school than medical school.

In fact, being a vet may be tougher than being a doctor. Why? Think about this: Doctors only have to practice medicine properly on one type of animal, humans. Vets may have to treat a series of different animals, from dogs to chickens to monkeys, all in the same day.

While many doctors focus on one thing—surgery or children's medicine, for example—vets can have many responsibilities. They may be both surgeons and dentists to the animals they treat. Vets also need good communication skills. Trying to soothe a human patient is easy. You use words. Yet, how do you calm down a hurt and angry horse? How do you calm down a cat that's thrashing about? Vets learn how.

Also, vets don't always do their work in beautiful well-equipped hospitals. Sometimes, they may be called on to deliver a baby animal in a shack on the edge of a field.

Many vets do have specialties. Some focus on animals that live in the sea and go to work for marine parks. Others specialize in treating farm animals or common household pets.

There is one thing most vets have in common: a desire to help animals heal. Nothing makes a vet feel better than helping a sick and miserable animal feel happier.

1. Underline the nearby words that help you know what genius means. Then tell what *genius* means.

2. Circle the words that explain what doctors have to do properly. Then tell what *properly* means.

3. Underline the words that tell what may be included in this series. Then tell what *series* means.

4. Circle the nearby words that have the same meaning as soothe. Then tell who can *soothe* a hurt and angry horse.

5. Circle the words that tell what is thrashing about. Then tell what *thrashing* means.

6. Underline the words that tell where you might find a shack. Then tell what *shack* means.

7. Circle the words that tell what vets have a desire to heal. Then tell what *heal* means.

8. Underline the nearby word that means the opposite of miserable. Then tell what *miserable* means.

"Aaron's Gift" by Myron Levoy
Reading Warm-up B

Read the following passage. Pay special attention to the underlined words. Then, read it again, and complete the activities. Use a separate sheet of paper for your written answers.

When you go to the park, someone is always there feeding crumbs to the pigeons. The pigeons hop around on the <u>pavement</u>. The bird feeder watches the <u>frenzied</u> fight for food. Indeed, pigeons are probably the most common type of bird found on the streets of America's cities and towns. If you think that pigeons are the only birds that people can see in the city, however, think again! Many different bird species fly through urban skies.

Some birds show up <u>temporarily</u>, not on a permanent basis. These are migratory birds. Migratory birds are ones that fly from north to south during the winter. A flock of migratory birds flying overhead is a <u>fantastic</u> sight. Don't close your eyes, though, or you'll miss it. These birds are just passing through on their way to warmer winter homes.

Other birds are full-time residents of the city. The soft sound of baby crows, <u>sparrows</u>, and blackbirds <u>cooing</u> is commonly heard on city blocks. Increasingly, so are the screeches of larger birds like hawks. Scientists are trying to bring big birds like hawks and falcons into the cities. They're doing it because these species are endangered. Their populations have been shrinking for a long time. Scientists are finding new ways to help them. In the cities, scientists believe, these big birds face fewer threats than they do in the country. Many are doing <u>remarkably</u> well. It turns out that the ledges of city buildings provide homes that are just as good as the cliffs that these birds normally live in.

While the birdwatcher is thrilled by the number of birds that live in urban areas, the <u>aviator</u> is not. Birds can cause big problems for airplanes. When birds collide with powerful jet engines, engines have been known to fail.

1. Underline the words that tell what is happening on the <u>pavement</u>. Then write a sentence using the word *pavement*.

2. Circle the words that <u>frenzied</u> describes. Then describe something else that might be *frenzied*.

3. Circle the nearby word that means the opposite of <u>temporarily</u>. Then tell what *temporarily* means.

4. Underline the <u>fantastic</u> sight you will miss if you close your eyes. Then describe a sight you would find *fantastic*.

5. Underline the nearby words that tell you where <u>sparrows</u> can be found. Then tell what *sparrows* are.

6. Underline the animals that are commonly <u>cooing</u>. Name two other animals you might hear *cooing*.

7. Underline the sentence that tells why big birds are doing <u>remarkably</u> well in the city.

8. Underline the sentence that tells why an <u>aviator</u> might be unhappy about birds. Then tell what an *aviator* is.

"Aaron's Gift" by Myron Levoy

Writing About the Big Question

Is conflict always bad?

Big Question Vocabulary

argue	battle	challenge	compete	conclude
convince	defend	game	issue	lose
negotiate	oppose	resolve	survival	win

A. *Use one or more words from the list above to complete each sentence.*

1. A parent and child may _____ about the child's choices.

2. A friend who gets into trouble may be an _____ that causes an argument.

3. It can be hard to _____ your choice of a friend.

4. You must try to _____ your parent that your choice is a good one.

B. *Answer each question with a complete sentence.*

1. Why do you think a parent might disapprove of a child's friend?

_____

_____

2. Imagine you had to defend your choice of a friend to a parent. What would you say? Use at least two Big Question vocabulary words in your response.

_____

_____

C. *Complete this sentence. Then, write a brief paragraph about how children and parents can resolve conflicts.*

Children may not always agree with their parents, but _____

_____

_____

_____

_____

_____

_____

_____

"Aaron's Gift" by Myron Levoy

Reading: Use Prior Knowledge to Draw Conclusions

Drawing conclusions means making decisions or forming opinions about what has happened in a literary work. You make your conclusions using details from the text and your own **prior knowledge**—what you know from your own experience. You bring prior knowledge with you whenever you read a story.

Example from "Aaron's Gift":

Aaron skated back and forth on the wide walkway of the park, pretending he was an aviator in an air race zooming around pylons, which were actually two lamp posts.

Details from the passage tell you that Aaron invents stories when he plays. Your own prior knowledge about inventing stories might tell you that a person who invents stories has a good imagination. You can conclude that Aaron has a good imagination.

A. DIRECTIONS: *Fill in this chart with your own prior knowledge and the conclusions you can draw. The first one has been done for you as an example.*

Story Details	Prior Knowledge	Conclusion
1. Aaron treats the wounded pigeon very gently.	People who like animals are gentle with them.	Aaron likes animals.
2. Aaron's father is amazed at how he set the pigeon's wing and calls him a genius.		
3. Aaron's mother wants him to stay away from the gang of older boys.		
4. Aaron wants to give his grandmother a wonderful present.		

B. DIRECTIONS: *Write about another conclusion that you can make on your own from "Aaron's Gift." Explain your conclusion by telling the details and the prior knowledge you used.*

_____

_____

_____

_____

Name _____ Date _____

"Aaron's Gift" by Myron Levoy
Literary Analysis: Setting

The **setting** of a literary work is the time and place of the action. The time may be established as a historical era, the present or future, the season of the year, or the hour of the day. The place can be as general as planet Earth or as specific as a room in a house. As you read, notice how characters and events in a story are affected by the setting of the story.

Example from "Aaron's Gift":

Aaron Kandel had come to Tompkins Square Park to roller-skate, for the streets near Second Avenue were always too crowded with children and peddlers and old ladies and baby buggies.

This passage tells you that the story takes place in New York City (where Tompkins Square Park and Second Avenue are). It hints that the time is in the past because it refers to "peddlers."

A. DIRECTIONS: *Use the chart to tell about the setting of "Aaron's Gift." In column two, record your answer and the details from the story that help you answer each question.*

Questions About the Setting of the Story	Answer and Story Details
1. Where does the main story of "Aaron's Gift" take place?	
2. When does the main story of "Aaron's Gift" take place?	
3. Where does the story of the pogrom take place?	
4. When does the story of the pogrom take place?	

B. DIRECTIONS: *Use the information in your chart to help you answer the following questions.*

How important is the setting in this story? Why is it important? _____

_____

_____

_____

_____

_____

Name _____ Date _____

"Aaron's Gift" by Myron Levoy
Vocabulary Builder

Word List

coaxed   consoled   hesitated   pleaded   temporarily   thrashing

A. DIRECTIONS: *Provide an answer and an explanation for each question.*

1. If a small animal is *thrashing* in your hands, how does it probably feel?

_____

2. If a boy *hesitated* before climbing a tree, do you think he enjoyed heights?

_____

3. If a friend needs to be *consoled* after running a race, did she win the race?

_____

4. If a girl *pleaded* to be allowed to go to a party, how much did she want to go?

_____

5. If you *coaxed* a dog out of its hiding place, how would you act toward it?

_____

6. If your phone is *temporarily* out of order, when would you expect it to work again?

_____

B. WORD STUDY: *The Latin root -tempor- means "time." Think about the meaning of the root -tempor- in each underlined word. Then, write two reasons for each statement.*

1. This detour is <u>temporary</u>. Why?

_____

_____

2. It is hard to give an <u>extemporaneous</u> speech. Why?

_____

_____

3. Fashion magazines show <u>contemporary</u> clothes. Why?

_____

_____

"Aaron's Gift" by Myron Levoy

Enrichment: Becoming a Veterinarian

The main character in "Aaron's Gift" has a love for animals and a talent for taking care of them. Aaron knew how to bandage Pidge's wing and how to take care of the bird until it got well. A possible career choice for someone like Aaron is to become a veterinarian, a doctor who cares for animals.

To become a veterinarian, you must attend a four-year veterinary school. All veterinary students have strong backgrounds in science. While in college, they complete a curriculum that includes courses in biology, zoology, and chemistry. There is a great deal of competition for admittance into veterinary schools, so it helps to have experience in an animal-related job. Many applicants have worked on farms, in animal shelters, or in veterinary offices.

A. DIRECTIONS: *Answer the following questions about preparing to become a veterinarian. Circle the letter of the best answer.*

1. For how many years do students attend veterinary school?
   A. one year   C. four years
   B. two years   D. six years

2. Which of the following courses is most likely to be a required part of a preveterinary curriculum?
   A. American history   C. chemistry
   B. astronomy   D. geology

B. DIRECTIONS: *Imagine that you are interviewing students for admission to veterinary school. Write three questions that you would ask to find out if they are suited for careers as veterinarians. After you complete your questions, exchange papers with a classmate and respond to each other's questions. Then discuss the responses to see if each of you would make a good candidate for veterinary training.*

1. Question: _____
   Answer: _____
   _____

2. Question: _____
   Answer: _____
   _____

3. Question: _____
   Answer: _____
   _____

"The King of Mazy May" by Jack London
"Aaron's Gift" by Myron Levoy
Integrated Language Skills: Grammar

Perfect Tenses

The **perfect tenses** of verbs combine a form of the helping verb *have* with the past participle of the main verb. The past participle usually ends in *-ed* or *-d*.

- The **present perfect tense** shows an action that began in the past and continues into the present.
- The **past perfect tense** shows a past action or condition that ended before another past action began.
- The **future perfect tense** shows a future action or condition that will have ended before another begins.

Present Perfect	Past Perfect	Future Perfect
have, has + past participle	had + past participle	will have + past participle
They *have arrived.*	They *had arrived* before we came.	They *will have arrived* before the show starts.

A. PRACTICE: *Complete each sentence by using the form of the verb requested in parentheses. Write the verb on the line provided.*

(travel-past perfect) **1.** Joe _____ to Alaska after gold was discovered there.

(remain-present perfect) **2.** He _____ in Alaska ever since.

(reside-future perfect) **3.** By this May, he _____ here for ten years.

(live-present perfect) **4.** His wife _____ in Alaska all her life.

(propose-past perfect) **5.** They wed after he _____ to her for the fifth time.

(finish-future perfect) **6.** Next month, they _____ work on their new igloo.

B. Writing Application: *Write a paragraph about a valuable object or experience. Use verbs in the present perfect, past perfect, and future perfect tenses. Use each of the three perfect tenses at least once.*

_____

_____

_____

_____

_____

Unit 2 Resources: Short Stories
193

Name _____ Date _____

Integrated Language Skills:
Support for Writing a Personal Narrative

Use a timeline to help you list the events you will describe in your personal narrative. Write your events on the left-hand side of the write-on line. Write details that describe the events on the right-hand side. Be sure to place the events in correct time order.

First Event

1.

Events   **Details**

2. _____

3. _____

4. _____

5. _____

6. _____

Final Event

7.

Now use the details from your timeline to write your personal narrative.

"The King of Mazy May" by Jack London
"Aaron's Gift" by Myron Levoy

Integrated Language Skills: Support for Extend Your Learning

Research and Technology: "Aaron's Gift"

Use this chart or make a chart on a separate sheet of paper to list the information you find about carrier pigeons.

What Carrier Pigeons Look Like	What Carrier Pigeons Eat	What Carrier Pigeons Can Do	How Carrier Pigeons Are Trained

Research and Technology: "The King of Mazy May"

Use this chart or make a chart on a separate sheet of paper to list the information you find about gold mining and the life of a gold miner.

Where and When Gold Was Found in Canada	Who Mined the Gold	What Miners' Lives Were Like	What Miners Found

"Aaron's Gift" by Myron Levoy
Open-Book Test

Short Answer *Write your responses to the questions in this section on the lines provided.*

1. The setting is the time and place of the action of a story. "Aaron's Gift" takes place in New York City. What does the fact that "few children had bicycles in those days" tell you about when the story takes place? Explain your answer.

   _____

   _____

2. In "Aaron's Gift," Aaron takes Pidge home and mends its wing. Think about the way he treats the injured pigeon. Describe what type of person Aaron is. Support your description with another example from the story.

   _____

   _____

   _____

3. Describe Aaron's feelings for his grandmother in "Aaron's Gift." Use details from the story to support your description.

   _____

   _____

   _____

4. In "Aaron's Gift," Aaron waits for "the expected storm" as his father stares at the pigeon. Based on what Aaron's father says next, what can you conclude about why Mr. Kandal does not get angry? Explain.

   _____

   _____

5. In "Aaron's Gift," Aaron's mother does not let him do something even though he pleads with her. Think about what it is that she will not let him do. Explain what she refuses to let him do and why you can conclude that she is a protective mother.

   _____

   _____

6. The narrator of "Aaron's Gift" says that Aaron's grandmother could not be consoled at the loss of her pet goat. Explain how she consoled Aaron after his fight with Carl.

   _____

   _____

7. In each oval of the word web, write a phrase from "Aaron's Gift" that describes a detail of the Ukraine setting as Aaron's grandmother remembers it. Then, on the line below, describe the feeling conveyed by this setting.

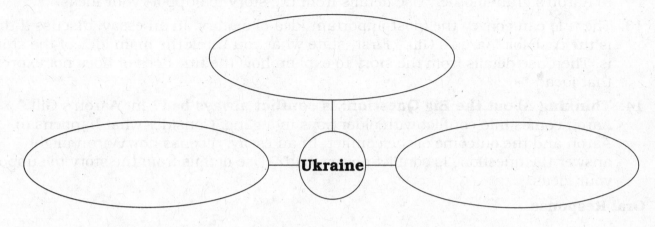

_____

8. In "Aaron's Gift," Aaron's grandmother remembers a time in the Ukraine. How is this change of setting important to the story? Use details from the story to support your answer.

_____

_____

_____

9. In "Aaron's Gift," Aaron hesitated after walking up to the shack in the empty lot. Explain what the word *hesitated* tells you about his state of mind.

_____

_____

10. Near the end of "Aaron's Gift," Aaron's grandmother has him look in her mirror. Explain why she does this.

_____

Essay

Write an extended response to the question of your choice or to the question or questions your teacher assigns you.

11. In "Aaron's Gift," both Aaron and his grandmother are the victims of cruelty. In an essay, compare Aaron's experience with the gang to his grandmother's experience with the Cossacks. Be sure to include what each character learns from the experience. Use details from the story to support your ideas.

12. At the end of "Aaron's Gift," Aaron smiles when he thinks that his grandmother's goat "has escaped from the Cossacks at last." In an essay, explain what Aaron means. In your explanation, be sure to tell what the goat and the pigeon represent to Aaron's grandmother. Use details from the story to support your ideas.

13. The title can convey the most important idea of a story. In an essay, discuss if this is the case for "Aaron's Gift." First, state what you think the main idea of the story is. Then use details from the story to explain how the title does or does not express that idea.

14. **Thinking About the Big Question: Is conflict always bad?** In "Aaron's Gift," Aaron comes into conflict with older boys in a gang. Consider what happens to Aaron and the outcome of the conflict. In an essay, discuss how Aaron might answer the question "Is conflict always bad?" Use details from the story to support your ideas.

Oral Response

15. Go back to question 2, 4, 8, or 10 or to the question your teacher assigns to you. Take a few minutes to expand your answer and prepare an oral response. Find additional details in "Aaron's Gift" that will support your points. If necessary, make notes to guide your response.

"Aaron's Gift" by Myron Levoy
Selection Test A

Critical Reading *Identify the letter of the choice that best answers the question.*

_____ 1. In "Aaron's Gift," what do we learn about Aaron's character when he takes Pidge home to mend his wing?
A. Aaron wants to be a doctor someday.
B. Aaron has always wanted a pet.
C. Aaron is a quick thinker.
D. Aaron is a kind, gentle person.

_____ 2. Why can you conclude that Aaron is good with animals?
A. He is gentle and thoughtful with the pigeon.
B. He thinks it is funny that his grandmother feeds the birds.
C. He is always helping injured or sick animals.
D. He has worked in a pet store.

_____ 3. In "Aaron's Gift," why does Aaron's mother tell him to stay away from Carl and the older boys?
A. She thinks he should play with children his own age.
B. She worries that they will keep Aaron out late at night.
C. She worries that they are involved in dangerous or violent activities.
D. She knows they don't like animals.

_____ 4. Why can you conclude that Aaron's mother is very protective of him?
A. She refuses to let him have any friends.
B. She lets him keep the pigeon.
C. She is firm about his choice of friends.
D. She gets very angry if he is late.

_____ 5. Why does the narrator of "Aaron's Gift" say that Aaron's grandmother's family was lucky?
A. The Cossacks didn't burn down their house or kill the family.
B. The Cossacks didn't kill all their sheep and goats.
C. The Cossacks didn't hear the goat in the cellar.
D. The Cossacks didn't find their house at all.

_____ 6. Where was the pogrom that Aaron's grandmother experienced?
A. in New York City
B. in Germany
C. in Poland
D. in the Ukraine

___ 7. How does Aaron feel when he calls the boys in the gang "Cossacks"?
A. hopeless
B. terrified
C. helpless
D. angry

___ 8. How are Carl and his friends like the Cossacks in "Aaron's Gift"?
A. They are mean and violent to innocent people.
B. They enjoy burning people's homes.
C. They kill people for no reason.
D. Everyone hates them.

___ 9. Why can you conclude that Aaron's grandmother loves birds?
A. She bandages the pigeon's wing.
B. She feeds birds.
C. She always has a bird for a pet.
D. She once had a pet bird.

___ 10. How does Aaron's grandmother react when Aaron tells her the pigeon flew away?
A. She is very disappointed.
B. She is pleased and happy.
C. She is angry at Aaron.
D. She is terribly sad.

___ 11. Where does the main story of "Aaron's Gift" take place?
A. on a farm
B. in New York City
C. in the Ukraine
D. in a small town

___ 12. When in time does the main story of "Aaron's Gift" take place?
A. in the present
B. in the future
C. in the past
D. at no particular time in history

Vocabulary and Grammar

_____ 13. Which word is closest in meaning to *believable* as used in the following sentence?

Your promise is believable when you back up your words with action.

A. trustworthy

B. incredible

C. unreal

D. impossible

_____ 14. Which word is closest in meaning to *pleaded* as used in the following sentence?

The youngest child pleaded to hear just one more story.

A. demanded

B. begged

C. requested

D. said

_____ 15. Which of the following sentences contains the past perfect tense of *talk*?

A. Aaron talks to his pigeon.

B. Aaron had talked to his pigeon before he fed it.

C. Aaron will have talked to his pigeon before giving it to his grandmother.

D. Aaron has talked to his pigeon.

Essay

16. In "Aaron's Gift," the story about Aaron's grandmother is within the main story. In an essay, describe the setting of the story of the Cossacks and the pogrom. Explain why this story is important. Use details from the selection to illustrate your explanation.

17. Think about the title of "Aaron's Gift." In an essay, explain two or more meanings of the word *gift* in the story. Use details from the selection to support your explanations.

18. **Thinking About the Big Question: Is conflict always bad?** In "Aaron's Gift," Aaron comes into conflict with older boys in a gang. Think about what happens at the clubhouse shack and then afterward at Aaron's home. In an essay, discuss how Aaron might answer the question "Is conflict always bad?" Use details from the story to support your ideas.

Name _____ Date _____

"Aaron's Gift" by Myron Levoy
Selection Test B

Critical Reading *Identify the letter of the choice that best completes the statement or answers the question.*

____ 1. "Aaron's Gift" takes place in
   A. a farm community.
   B. New York City.
   C. the Ukraine.
   D. a small town.

____ 2. In "Aaron's Gift," the presence of street peddlers and Aaron's roller skates hint that
   A. the story could happen anywhere.
   B. the story takes place in the present.
   C. the story takes place in the past.
   D. the story takes place in the future.

____ 3. What can you conclude about Aaron's grandmother from this passage in "Aaron's Gift"?

   And she fed the sparrows and jays and crows and robins on the back fire escape with every spare crumb she could find.

   A. She loves birds.
   B. She does not love other animals.
   C. She is a little crazy.
   D. She wants Aaron to have a pet.

____ 4. What kind of relationship does Aaron have with his grandmother?
   A. a tense relationship
   B. a loving relationship
   C. a distant relationship
   D. an angry relationship

____ 5. What happens when Aaron tells everyone about the pigeon?
   A. Hearing about the pigeon gives Carl and his friends ideas.
   B. Aaron's father finds out about the pigeon and gets angry.
   C. Hearing about the pigeon makes people think Aaron is strange.
   D. Everyone wants a pigeon of their own.

____ 6. What does your prior knowledge lead you to conclude about why Aaron wants to be a friend of the boys in the gang?
   A. He wants to make trouble.
   B. He wants to defy his mother.
   C. He is lonely and wants to fit in.
   D. He wants to be the leader of the gang.

____ 7. What can you conclude about Aaron's mother from this passage in "Aaron's Gift"?
   But his mother told Aaron to stay away from those boys, or else. And Aaron, miserable, argued with his mother and pleaded and cried and coaxed. It was no use.

   A. She is very mean.
   B. She wants Aaron to have friends.
   C. She is protective of Aaron.
   D. She doesn't understand Aaron.

____ 8. Aaron's grandmother experienced a pogrom when she was a child in
   A. New York City.
   B. Germany.
   C. Poland.
   D. the Ukraine.

____ 9. The narrator of "Aaron's Gift" says that Aaron's grandmother's family was lucky because the Cossacks did not
   A. kill the family.
   B. kill all their sheep and goats.
   C. hear the goat in the cellar.
   D. bash in any walls in their house.

____ 10. In "Aaron's Gift," Carl and his friends are like the Cossacks because
   A. they are cruel and hateful to innocent people.
   B. they enjoy destroying people's homes and families.
   C. they kill people for no reason.
   D. everyone hates and fears them.

____ 11. At the end of "Aaron's Gift," why does Aaron's grandmother ask him to look in her mirror?
   A. She wants him to see his bruised face.
   B. She wants him to wash the dirt off his face.
   C. She wants him to see how beautiful he is.
   D. She wants to give him the mirror.

____ 12. At the end of "Aaron's Gift," what does Aaron mean when he says his grandmother's goat "had escaped from the Cossacks at last"?
   A. Pidge's escape has helped Aaron's grandmother get over her goat's death.
   B. Aaron's grandmother finds out that her goat wasn't killed after all.
   C. Aaron's grandmother imagines that her goat escaped from the Cossacks.
   D. Aaron's grandmother can now get another goat.

Vocabulary and Grammar

____ 13. Aaron *pleaded* with his mother to let him play with the gang. The *best* meaning for the word *pleaded* in this sentence is
   A. yelled.
   B. wept.
   C. demanded.
   D. begged.

___ 14. Aaron's grandmother *consoled* him after Pidge flew away. In other words, she
   A. comforted him.
   B. teased him.
   C. criticized him.
   D. laughed at him.

___ 15. Which of the following phrases best defines the word *lovable* in this sentence?
   Aaron found the wounded pigeon *lovable* and cherished him as he got better.

   A. full of love
   B. able to be loved
   C. with love
   D. in love

___ 16. In which of the following sentences is the word *survive* in the past perfect tense?
   A. Aaron's grandmother survives a pogrom.
   B. Aaron's grandmother survived a pogrom.
   C. Aaron's grandmother is surviving a pogrom.
   D. Aaron's grandmother had survived a pogrom.

___ 17. In which of the following sentences is the verb *tell* in the present perfect tense?
   A. Aaron tells his grandmother that Pidge flew away.
   B. Aaron told his grandmother that Pidge flew away.
   C. Aaron has told his grandmother that Pidge flew away.
   D. Aaron will have told his grandmother that Pidge flew away.

Essay

18. At the end of "Aaron's Gift," Aaron thinks about his grandmother: "Her goat has escaped from the Cossacks at last." In an essay, explain the meaning of Aaron's thought. Then, tell what the goat and the pigeon represent to Aaron's grandmother. Support your analysis with examples from the story.

19. The title of a story often expresses the most important idea in the story. In an essay, evaluate the title of "Aaron's Gift." State what you think is the main idea of the story. Then, using examples from the story, tell how the title does or does not express that idea.

20. **Thinking About the Big Question: Is conflict always bad?** In "Aaron's Gift," Aaron comes into conflict with older boys in a gang. Consider what happens to Aaron and the outcome of the conflict. In an essay, discuss how Aaron might answer the question "Is conflict always bad?" Use details from the story to support your ideas.

Vocabulary Warm-up Word Lists

Study these words from the selection. Then, complete the activities.

Word List A

absence [AB suhns] *n.* a lack of; the fact of missing something
The <u>absence</u> of air on the moon makes it impossible to breathe.

geography [jee AH gruh fee] *n.* the study of the surface of the land
We will learn about the rivers of the United States in our unit on <u>geography</u>.

inspector [in SPEK ter] *n.* a person whose job is to examine something or someone
The <u>inspector</u> will make sure the building is safe to use.

obvious [AHB vee uhs] *adj.* easy to see; not hard to realize
It's <u>obvious</u> that he is excited about today's game.

permanent [PER muh nuhnt] *adj.* lasting forever or for a very long time
That blueberry juice will leave a <u>permanent</u> stain on the napkin.

progress [PRAHG res] *n.* advancement; improvement
She learns quickly, so her <u>progress</u> in Spanish has been fast.

scornful [SKORN fuhl] *adj.* showing disgust and disrespect
He gave his enemy a <u>scornful</u> glance.

sensible [SEN suh buhl] *adj.* reasonable; showing good judgment
A bathing suit is not a <u>sensible</u> clothing choice for school.

Word List B

concealing [kuhn SEEL ing] *v.* hiding; covering up
I know that the magician is <u>concealing</u> the rabbit inside that hat.

detect [dee TEKT] *v.* to notice; to discover
Mia listened at the door, but she couldn't <u>detect</u> any sound.

dispute [dis PYOOT] *v.* to argue; to express opposition to
Jen believed the election results were wrong, so she decided to <u>dispute</u> them.

insert [in SERT] *v.* to put one thing inside another thing
Please <u>insert</u> your letter into the envelope.

mechanical [mi KAN i kuhl] *adj.* operated by a machine
My <u>mechanical</u> pencil sharpener turns on by itself.

remainder [ri MAYN der] *n.* others; rest of
Half the team went into the gym; the <u>remainder</u> stayed on the bus.

satisfactory [sat is FAK tuh ree] *adj.* good enough; acceptable
Your work on the first lesson was <u>satisfactory</u>, so you may move on.

vacant [VAY kuhnt] *adj.* empty
All people and furniture were gone; the room was completely <u>vacant</u>.

Name _____ Date _____

"The Fun They Had" by Isaac Asimov
"Feathered Friend" by Arthur C. Clarke
Vocabulary Warm-up Exercises

Exercise A *Fill in the blanks, using each word from Word List A only once.*

I stood in the storage room at the back of the jewelry store. The [1] _____

stood beside me. He gave me a [2] _____ frown. It was [3]

_____ that he doubted I could help him solve this puzzling case. It was

my first day at work as a junior detective. It might be my last. My boss was a [4]

_____ man, but he could sometimes be impatient. He had searched this

storage room and turned up nothing; the [5] _____ of clues was striking.

I looked more closely. In the corner, something caught my eye. It was a map showing

the [6] _____ of Mexico. We knew the thieves had fled there. My boss

patted my back and said we were finally making [7] _____. I decided that

my chances of being offered a [8] _____ job had just improved.

Exercise B *Answer the questions with complete explanations.*

Example: If a seat is not <u>vacant</u>, can you sit in it?
No; vacant means "empty," so if a seat is not <u>vacant</u>, someone else is already sitting in the seat.

1. What would you do if you <u>detect</u> the smell of smoke in your house?

   _____

2. What is a mask usually <u>concealing</u>?

   _____

3. You ate half the chocolate bar. Would you put the <u>remainder</u> in your back pocket?

   _____

4. If you were charged too much at a store, would you <u>dispute</u> the bill?

   _____

5. What must you <u>insert</u> into a locked door in order to open it?

   _____

6. If your work is <u>satisfactory</u>, is it the best you can do?

   _____

7. Would you like to have a <u>mechanical</u> pet?

   _____

Unit 2 Resources: Short Stories

"The Fun They Had" by Issac Asimov
"Feathered Friend" by Arthur C. Clarke
Reading Warm-up A

Read the following passage. Pay special attention to the underlined words. Then, read it again, and complete the activities. Use a separate sheet of paper for your written answers.

Have you ever considered a career as a building inspector? A person who examines buildings needs to know a great deal about construction. A sense of adventure helps, too. You might find yourself at the top of a skyscraper or at the bottom of an underground parking lot.

This job is about making sure that buildings are safe. You might be asked to inspect the progress on a new one as it goes up. You will need to determine whether the work is going as it should and whether all the safety measures are being taken.

What parts of a building need to be inspected? All of them! The walls, windows, and roof get looked over, as do the furnace, air conditioner, pipes, and wires. In homes, an inspection includes things like the connections for the washing machine, dryer, and stove, too.

Most people can see obvious problems, such as the absence of a floor tile or chipped paint. But it is harder to tell whether something is wrong with wires inside a wall. That is why this is not a job for anyone who is scornful of hard, dirty work on your hands and knees. You might have to crawl into a tight space to look at wood beams that hold up a floor or pipes that run under it.

If you find permanent damage, you can help the owners. They will be glad to have your sensible suggestions. You can tell them reasonable ways to replace the parts of a building that cannot be fixed.

For this career, it would also be a good idea to know about geography. Climate can have a big effect on a building; so can location. For example, there are special rules about building materials that can be used in areas where there are lots of earthquakes or high winds.

So think about it. Are you interested in what buildings are made from and how they fit together? Do you like helping people live and work in safe places? If the answer is yes, then this might be just the job for you

1. Underline the words in a nearby sentence that have a similar meaning to inspector. Then, write a sentence using the word *inspector.*

2. Underline the words that have a similar meaning to progress. Then, write a sentence using the word *progress.*

3. Circle the words that tell what isn't always obvious. Then, tell what *obvious* means.

4. According to this article, most people might notice the absence of what? Write the answer, and then write a word that means the opposite of *absence.*

5. Underline the words that refer to the part of the job that some people might be scornful of. Then, write a sentence using the word *scornful.*

6. Underline the words that explain what permanent means. Then, write a sentence using the word *permanent.*

7. Circle the word in a nearby sentence that has a similar meaning to sensible. Then, write a sentence using the word *sensible.*

8. Underline the words that explain why it would be good to know geography. Then, write a sentence using the word *geography.*

"**The Fun They Had**" by Issac Asimov
"**Feathered Friend**" by Arthur C. Clarke

Reading Warm-up B

Read the following passage. Pay special attention to the underlined words. Then, read it again, and complete the activities. Use a separate sheet of paper for your written answers.

Liz had been born in the colony and had lived there for her entire life. She had never visited Earth or even dreamed about going there. It had never occurred to her to leave Mars. One day, however, workers were shocked to <u>detect</u> a problem with the power plant. They were even more alarmed to discover it was failing extremely fast.

Expert engineers had built the plant using the most modern <u>mechanical</u> equipment available: magnetic pumps, solar-powered engines, and fuel rods containing energy-producing chemicals. To avoid a crisis, workers tried to <u>insert</u> new wires into the chambers containing the fuel rods. Unfortunately, these efforts failed. Every-one would have to leave the colony, the only one on Mars.

At a meeting in the central dome, the experts informed the residents. Most people already knew the bad news; <u>concealing</u> it had been impossible. Word of the situation had spread from person to person in just hours.

Only two ships were available to transport the resi-dents to other planets. Where should they go? Some wanted to travel to Earth; others believed Venus or Jupiter were better choices. Each proposed destination was con-sidered carefully, for it was the biggest decision the col-ony's residents had ever had to make. People discussed the reasons for their preferences calmly without arguing or trying to <u>dispute</u> each other's ideas. They agreed that all of the choices were <u>satisfactory</u>.

In the end, a decision was made that half the resi-dents would travel to Venus, while the <u>remainder</u> would voyage to Earth. People could then transfer to other colo-nies if they chose to do so.

Liz and her family decided to journey on the ship that was destined for Earth. Liz's parents wanted her to see it even if they decided not to stay there. Just two days later, the ships departed from the colony.

Liz stared out the window at the <u>vacant</u> settlement as the rocket sped away. She was sad about leaving her home but excited about the opportunity to see Earth.

1. Underline the nearby word with a similar meaning to <u>detect</u>. Then, use the word *detect* in a sentence.

2. Circle the words that describe <u>mechanical</u> parts of the power plant. Then, tell what *mechanical* means.

3. Circle the words that tell what the workers were trying to <u>insert</u> and where they were trying to do it. Then, use the word *insert* in a sentence.

4. Circle the words that explain why <u>concealing</u> the news was impossible. Then, use the word *concealing* in a sentence.

5. Underline a word that has a similar meaning to <u>dispute</u>. Give an antonym for *dispute*.

6. In this passage, which choices were <u>satisfactory</u>? Use the word *satisfactory* in a sentence.

7. Circle the words that tell what would happen to the <u>remainder</u>. Then, use the word *remainder* in a sentence.

8. Circle the word that tells what is <u>vacant</u>. Then, explain why it is *vacant*.

"**The Fun They Had**" by Isaac Asimov
"**Feathered Friend**" by Arthur C. Clarke

Writing About the Big Question

Is conflict always bad?

Big Question Vocabulary

argue	battle	challenge	compete	conclude
convince	defend	game	issue	lose
negotiate	oppose	resolve	survival	win

A. *Use one or more words from the list above to complete each sentence.*

1. Bullying is an important _____ in many schools.

2. Students facing bullies alone are often unable to _____ themselves.

3. Sometimes students can work together to _____ a bully.

4. A strong group can _____ a bully to back down.

B. *Respond to each item with a complete sentence.*

1. Describe an incident you have seen or heard about in which someone was bullied.

_____

_____

2. What are some ways to stop bullying? Use at least two Big Question vocabulary words in your answer.

_____

_____

C. *Complete this sentence. Then, write a brief paragraph in which you connect this idea to the Big Question.*

When humans rely on animals or computers to do their work, _____

_____

_____

_____

_____

_____

_____

Name _____ Date _____

"The Fun They Had" by Isaac Asimov
"Feathered Friend" by Arthur C. Clarke
Literary Analysis: Comparing Setting and Theme

Setting is the time and place of a story's action. In most stories, the setting serves as a background for the plot and creates a feeling or atmosphere. Setting can be real or make-believe. Details of setting can include the year, the time of day, or even the weather. The time may be a historical era, the present, or the future. The place may be a specific home, neighborhood, or state, or even outer space.

The **theme**, or central idea, of a story is the thought, message, or lesson about life that the story conveys. A theme can be expressed in a sentence, such as "Hard work leads to success" or "Every member of a team counts." Sometimes the theme is directly stated, and sometimes it is not. To determine the theme, consider the events; the characters' thoughts, words, actions, and feelings; and the title.

A. DIRECTIONS: *Read the following passage from "The Fun They Had" by Isaac Asimov. Write the details of the setting.*

> Margie went into the schoolroom. It was right next to her bedroom, and the mechanical teacher was on and waiting for her. It was always on at the same time every day except Saturday and Sunday, because her mother said little girls learned better if they learned at regular hours.

> The screen was lit up, and it said: "Today's arithmetic lesson is on the addition of proper fractions. Please insert yesterday's homework in the proper slot."

Past, Present, or Future? _____

Place: _____

Time of Day and Week: _____

B. DIRECTIONS: *Read the following passage from "Feathered Friend" by Arthur C. Clarke. Then, list three events or details that suggest the story's theme. On the last line, write a sentence stating the theme.*

> For the last few minutes, something had been tugging at my memory. My mind seemed to be very sluggish that morning, as if I was still unable to cast off the burden of sleep. I felt that I could do with some of that oxygen—but before I could reach the mask, understanding exploded in my brain. I whirled on the duty engineer and said urgently:

> "Jim! There's something wrong with the air! That's why Claribel's passed out. I've just remembered that miners used to carry canaries down to warn them of gas."

Detail: _____

Detail: _____

Detail: _____

Theme: _____

"The Fun They Had" by Isaac Asimov
"Feathered Friend" by Arthur C. Clarke
Vocabulary Builder

Word List

    calculated   ceased   fusing   loftily   nonchalantly   regulation

DIRECTIONS: *Use a thesaurus to find a* **synonym,** *a word with nearly the same meaning, for each word in the Word List. Use each synonym in a sentence that makes the meaning of the word clear. The first one is done for you as an example.*

1. regulation

    Synonym: <u>rule</u>

    Sentence: <u>The new rule stated that no dogs were allowed in the park.</u>

2. calculated

    Synonym: _____

    Sentence: _____

3. loftily

    Synonym: _____

    Sentence: _____

4. nonchalantly

    Synonym: _____

    Sentence: _____

5. regulation

    Synonym: _____

    Sentence: _____

6. fusing

    Synonym: _____

    Sentence: _____

7. ceased

    Synonym: _____

    Sentence: _____

Name _____ Date _____

"The Fun They Had" by Isaac Asimov
"Feathered Friend" by Arthur C. Clarke
Integrated Language Skills: Support for Writing an Essay

Before you draft your essay comparing the themes, complete this graphic organizer. In the first row, write the nonhuman helper in each story. In the second row, describe the helper's usefulness. In the third row, describe any problems the helper causes. Finally, write a possible theme about the usefulness of animals and computers.

	"The Fun They Had"	"Feathered Friend"
Nonhuman helper		
Usefulness		
Problems		
Theme		

Now, use your notes to write an essay comparing the theme each story presents about the usefulness of animals and computers.

Name _____ Date _____

Open-Book Test

Short Answer *Write your responses to the questions in this section on the lines provided.*

1. Tommy explains the concept of a traditional school to Margie in "The Fun They Had." As he does, he speaks loftily. Describe Tommy's attitude toward Margie. Base your response on the definition of *loftily*.

   _____

   _____

   _____

2. In "The Fun They Had," how does Tommy feel about the book he found and the school it describes? Cite two details from the story to support you answer.

   _____

   _____

   _____

   _____

   _____

3. In "The Fun They Had," what does Margie seem to dislike about her form of education? Cite two details from the story to support your answer.

   _____

   _____

   _____

4. In "Feathered Friend," Sven waits for several days before confessing to being the owner of Claribel, the canary. Explain why the delay turns out to have been a good plan.

   _____

   _____

   _____

5. In "Feathered Friend," the air filter has ceased working. Explain what the word *ceased* tells you about the air filter. Base your response on the definition of *ceased*.

   _____

   _____

   _____

6. Think about the crew's feelings for Claribel in "Feathered Friend." Next, complete this chart. Then, on the lines below, state the larger point about pets that Arthur C. Clarke may have been making.

How Does Claribel Help the Crew?	How Does the Narrator View Claribel at the End?

_____

_____

7. Think about the setting of "The Fun They Had" and "Feathered Friend." In particular, consider when the stories take place. Explain how the setting of the two stories is alike.

_____

_____

8. Both "The Fun They Had" and "Feathered Friend" say something about human dependence on technology. Cite one detail of setting in each story that supports this theme. Explain how the detail relates to the theme.

_____

_____

_____

_____

9. Both "The Fun They Had" and "Feathered Friend" contain comparisons with the past. Why are those comparisons important to the stories? Cite one detail from each story in your answer.

_____

_____

_____

_____

10. "The Fun They Had" and "Feathered Friend" share a theme, a central thought or message about life. What is that theme? Cite one detail from each story to support your answer.

_____

_____

_____

_____

_____

Essay

Write an extended response to the question of your choice or to the question or questions your teacher assigns you.

11. The title of a story often gives clues about the story's central message. Think about the central message of both "The Fun They Had" and "Feathered Friend." In an essay, discuss what each title reveals about each story's central message.

12. The writers of both "The Fun They Had" and "Feathered Friend" use details of setting to bring their stories to life. In an essay, explain how these details help the reader relate to the stories. Support your points with at least two details from each story.

13. Both "The Fun They Had" and "Feathered Friend" are science-fiction stories. In an essay, state which story seems more believable. Focus on the characters and situations. How convincing are they? Cite two details from each story to support your argument.

14. **Thinking About the Big Question: Is conflict always bad?** Both Margie in "The Fun They Had" and the narrator in "Feathered Friend" face conflict. In an essay, discuss whether these characters would likely agree that conflict is always bad. Cite at least one detail from each story to support your ideas.

Oral Response

15. Go back to question 1, 4, 7, or 8 or to the question your teacher assigns you. Take a few minutes to expand your answer and prepare an oral response. Find additional details in "The Fun They Had" and "Feathered Friend" that support your points. If necessary, make notes to guide your oral response.

"The Fun They Had" by Isaac Asimov
"Feathered Friend" by Arthur C. Clarke
Selection Test A

Critical Reading *Identify the letter of the choice that best answers the question.*

____ 1. In "The Fun They Had," what does Tommy find?
A. a robot
B. a teacher
C. a book
D. a computer

____ 2. In "The Fun They Had," how do Margie's feelings about the old school change by the end of the story?
A. She decides it must have been nice to go to school.
B. She decides old schools must have been boring.
C. She decides old schools must have been scary.
D. She decides old schools were much harder than her school.

____ 3. When does "The Fun They Had" take place?
A. long ago
B. far in the future
C. in the present
D. fifty years ago

____ 4. Why does Margie's mother send for the inspector?
A. Margie has gotten into trouble.
B. Margie needs to take a test.
C. Margie won't stop talking about school.
D. Margie's mechanical teacher isn't working right.

____ 5. In "Feathered Friend," why does the crew adopt Claribel as a pet?
A. They appreciate having a bird on board.
B. Sven refuses to send her back to Earth.
C. She nearly died.
D. They do not want to hurt Sven's feelings.

____ 6. What has the canary become at the end of "Feathered Friend"?
A. an annoyance
B. an important crew member
C. a source of disagreement
D. the narrator's own pet

____ 7. In "Feathered Friend," which of the following is a challenge to the crew members?
   A. bad food
   B. limited room
   C. unfair rules
   D. loud noise

____ 8. Which sentence from the story *best* states the main message of "Feathered Friend"?
   A. Don't ask me why Sven wanted a pet, or why he chose the one he did.
   B. Certainly when I woke that "morning" it felt like 6:00 A.M. on Earth.
   C. Without Claribel, we should soon have been slightly dead.
   D. To our delighted surprise, she revived at once.

____ 9. How are the settings of "The Fun They Had" and "Feathered Friend" alike?
   A. They take place in the present.
   B. They are set in space.
   C. They take place in winter.
   D. They happen in the future.

____ 10. What do the titles "The Fun They Had" and "Feathered Friend" tell you about the stories' characters?
   A. that they think about friendship
   B. that they are fearful
   C. that they behave in silly ways
   D. that they work harder than others

____ 11. Which is true of a story's theme?
   A. A story's theme is always stated by a main character.
   B. A story can have more than one theme.
   C. A story's theme is never directly stated.
   D. The author usually disagrees with the theme of the story.

____ 12. Which sentence *best* states a theme of both "The Fun They Had" and "Feathered Friend"?
   A. Animals are better friends than people.
   B. Hard work is your only friend.
   C. Sometimes living things are best for the job.
   D. True friendship lasts forever.

Vocabulary

____ 13. If you boast loftily, how are you speaking?
   A. coldly
   B. shyly
   C. angrily
   D. proudly

____ 14. Which of the following is a regulation?
   A. If at first you do not succeed, try again.
   B. Please call for an appointment.
   C. No running in the hallways.
   D. Stop right where you are!

____ 15. If the rain has ceased and the sun is coming out from behind the clouds, what has happened?
   A. The rain has stopped.
   B. The rain has become heavier.
   C. The rain has become lighter.
   D. It has begun to rain.

Essay

16. The title of a story often gives clues about the story's theme, or main message. In an essay, state what you think is the theme of "The Fun They Had" and the theme of "Feathered Friend." Then, explain how each story's title does or does not express that idea.

17. Some stories tell about group efforts, and others tell about an individual's efforts. Which kind of effort does "The Fun They Had" describe? Which kind does "Feathered Friend" describe? What lesson can be learned from each story?

18. **Thinking About the Big Question: Is conflict always bad?** In "Feathered Friend," the narrator lives and works as part of a group. In "The Fun They Had," Margie imagines life in a group at a school. Both characters know that in groups, conflicts happen. In an essay, discuss whether each character would agree that conflict is always bad. Cite at least one detail from each story to support your ideas.

Name _____ Date _____

"**The Fun They Had**" by Isaac Asimov
"**Feathered Friend**" by Arthur C. Clarke
Selection Test B

Critical Reading *Identify the letter of the choice that best completes the statement or answers the question.*

____ 1. What can you tell about the future in "The Fun They Had"?
   A. There are no computers.
   B. There are no books.
   C. There are few humans left.
   D. There are no cars.

____ 2. In "The Fun They Had," why couldn't Margie do well in geography?
   A. She doesn't understand the subject.
   B. There are no more countries.
   C. Her mechanical teacher is not working right.
   D. She is not smart enough.

____ 3. In "The Fun They Had," why does Margie hate the teacher?
   A. It does not interact with Margie in a human way.
   B. It is always wrong.
   C. It doesn't listen when she speaks to it.
   D. It says unkind things to her.

____ 4. Why does Tommy laugh at Margie?
   A. She doesn't do well on her geography.
   B. She doesn't know how to read.
   C. She has never seen a book before.
   D. She doesn't know anything about old schools.

____ 5. Why does Margie change her mind about old schools?
   A. She likes the idea of being with other kids.
   B. She thinks she could do better on geography in those schools.
   C. She decides humans are smarter than computers.
   D. She thinks old schools were easier.

____ 6. In "Feathered Friend," the crew adopts Claribel as a pet because
   A. she nearly died.
   B. they like Sven and do not want to hurt his feelings.
   C. they have no way of sending the bird back to Earth.
   D. they appreciate having the bird on board.

____ 7. Short, wiry people like Sven are preferred to taller people for space station work because
   A. they fit into spacesuits more easily and are quicker on their feet.
   B. they take up less room.
   C. they are smarter and have more endurance than bigger workers.
   D. they are easier to train.

____ 8. By the end of "Feathered Friend," the canary has proved to be
   A. an obstacle to the crew's work.
   B. an important member of the crew.
   C. nothing more than a lovable pet.
   D. a source of disagreement among the crew.

____ 9. Once you know the ending of "Feathered Friend," which story event first suggests that something is wrong with the space station's air supply?
   A. The narrator wakes up with a headache.
   B. The narrator bumps his head on a beam.
   C. The canary is found unconscious.
   D. The canary revives after getting oxygen.

____ 10. Which sentence from "Feathered Friend" states a main message of the story?
   A. So now, if you visit any space station, don't be surprised if you hear an inexplicable snatch of birdsong.
   B. Don't ask me why Sven wanted a pet, or why he chose the one he did.
   C. Without Claribel, we should soon have been slightly dead.
   D. To the best of my knowledge, there's never been a regulation that forbids one to keep pets in a space station.

____ 11. Both Margie in "The Fun They Had" and Claribel in "Feathered Friend"
   A. are overwhelmed by the challenges they face.
   B. pester the people closest to them.
   C. are unafraid to take risks.
   D. are helped by nonhumans.

____ 12. Which sentence best expresses a theme that both stories share?
   A. Children and animals make better friends than grown-ups.
   B. Living things can be better than technology.
   C. True friendship lasts forever.
   D. In challenging times, hard work is your only friend.

____ 13. How are the narrators of "The Fun They Had" and "Feathered Friend" alike?
   A. They appreciate something from an earlier time.
   B. They work as a team toward a goal.
   C. They help a character break a rule.
   D. They grow to greatly dislike someone.

____ 14. Which is *not* true of a story's theme?

A. There is always only one theme per story.

B. A theme can be directly stated.

C. Sometimes a theme is not directly stated.

D. A theme is a message that the author wants to convey.

____ 15. Based on the titles "The Fun They Had" and "Feathered Friend," you can tell that both authors

A. think poorly of the title characters.

B. are writing an amusing story.

C. are writing about living creatures.

D. feel sorry for the title characters.

Vocabulary

____ 16. Which word is most alike in meaning to the word *ceased* as used in this sentence?

When the stars had ceased to explode before my eyes, I had my first view of Claribel.

A. begun

B. burst

C. happened

D. stopped

____ 17. If a job is done *nonchalantly*, how is it done?

A. easily

B. sloppily

C. carefully

D. perfectly

____ 18. If there had been a *regulation* against pets in "Feathered Friend," what might have happened?

A. Claribel might have died.

B. Everyone on the space station might have died.

C. The narrator would have quit his job.

D. The narrator would have been very lonely.

Essay

19. The title of a story often expresses the story's theme. In an essay, evaluate the titles of "The Fun They Had" and "Feathered Friend." State what you think is each story's theme. Then, go on to show how the story's title does or does not express that idea.

20. Some stories tell about team efforts, and others tell about individual efforts. In an essay, discuss the types of effort in "The Fun They Had" and "Feathered Friend." Use examples from the stories to support your ideas.

21. The central characters in "The Fun They Had" and "Feathered Friend" face challenges. In an essay, discuss Margie's challenge and the challenge faced by the space station's crew. Then, give your opinion as to which character or characters face the greater challenge. Support your ideas and opinions with examples from the stories.

22. **Thinking About the Big Question: Is conflict always bad?** Both Margie in "The Fun They Had" and the narrator in "Feathered Friend" face conflict. In an essay, discuss whether these characters would likely agree that conflict is always bad. Cite at least one detail from each story to support your ideas.

Name _____ Date _____

Writing Workshop—Unit 2, Part 2
Narration: Short Story

Prewriting: Narrowing Your Topic

Answer the questions in the following chart to help identify the conflict of your story.

What does my main character want?	
Who or what is getting in the way?	
What will the character do to overcome the person or thing that is getting in the way?	

Drafting: Developing a Plot

Use the following graphic organizer to organize the plot, or sequence of events, in your short story.

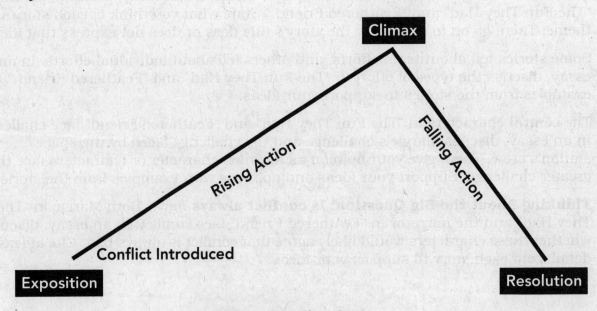

Writing Workshop—Unit 2, Part 2
Short Story: Integrating Grammar Skills

Revising to Maintain Verb Tense

A verb tense shows the time—past, present, or future—of an action or a state of being that is expressed by a verb.

Verb Tense and What It Shows	Example
Present Tense indicates an action in the present, or one that occurs regularly.	Ian is helping build a backyard deck. Carla teaches swimming every summer.
Past Tense shows an action in the past.	Mark traveled to Turkey last March.
Future Tense shows an action in the future.	I will clean my room this weekend.

Using different verb tenses in a story, if you are not careful, can lead to errors.

Incorrect use of verb tenses: As Carlos *waited* outside the gym he sees his friend Raul.

Correction: As Carlos *waited* outside the gym, he *saw* his friend Raul.

Tenses to show sequence of events: Since Amy *studied* hard, she *will go* to the movies.

Identifying Verb Tenses

A. DIRECTIONS: *On the line, identify the tense of the verb in italics.*

_____ 1. Luz *is memorizing* her lines for the play.

_____ 2. She *was chosen* for the part last week.

_____ 3. The dress rehearsal *will be held* Thursday night.

_____ 4. Her mother *worked* on the costume all last weekend.

Fixing Verb-Tense Errors

B. DIRECTIONS: *Rewrite each sentence to correct errors in verb tenses.*

1. While Luz practices her lines, she learned the cue words.

_____

2. All of the actors are nervous because they wanted to do well.

_____

3. The performance will take place on Saturday if all went as planned.

_____

4. Everyone expects a large audience, but we never knew for sure.

_____

Unit 2 Vocabulary Workshop—1
Word Origins

Many of the words we use every day are based on the names of people we may never have heard of.

DIRECTIONS: *Each of the following words is based on a personal name. Use the definitions to help you match the names of the people to their descriptions.*

___ 1. **Braille:** a system of printing and writing for the blind; named for Louis Braille (1809-52)

___ 2. **dunce:** a dull, ignorant person; named for John Duns Scotus (1265–1308)

___ 3. **guillotine:** a machine for beheading; named for Joseph Ignace Guillotin (1738–1814)

___ 4. **leotard:** a tight-fitting, one-piece garment worn by dancers and acrobats; named for Júles Léotard (1839–70)

___ 5. **pasteurization:** a process of destroying harmful bacteria in milk and other beverages; named for Louis Pasteur (1822–95)

___ 6. **sandwich:** two or more slices of bread with a filling between them; named for John Montagu, 4th Earl of Sandwich (1718–92)

___ 7. **silhouette:** a portrait that is the outline of a figure; named for Etienne de Silhouette (1709–67)

    A. government official who was known for making amateur portraits

    B. public figure who liked to eat a specific type of meal at the gaming table

    C. aerial performer

    D. chemist and bacteriologist

    E. teacher of blind students and an inventor

    F. scholar of theology and philosophy whose writings were considered ignorant

    G. doctor who suggested a certain method of killing prisoners during the French Revolution

Unit 2 Vocabulary Workshop—2
Word Origins

Learning word origins and their meanings can often help you understand unfamiliar words.

DIRECTIONS: *Use the word origins given to match each word to its synonym.*

1. **incredible:** Latin *incredibilis* *in-* not *credibilis* believable _____
   A. blame

2. **increment:** Latin *incrementum* to increase _____
   B. raise

3. **incriminate:** Latin *incriminare* to accuse _____
   C. hatch

4. **incubate:** Latin *incubatus* to lie in _____
   D. deadly

5. **incurable:** Latin *incurabilis* *in* -not *curabilis* – curable _____
   E. absurd

DIRECTIONS: *Fill in the blanks with the words above.*

"I have an _____ story," said Don. "Our pet hen kept losing feathers and we did not know what was wrong. Finally, we called the vet, who told us that Henny had an _____ disease. Now, I don't mean to _____ anyone, but Henny caught the disease from one of the people living in our home! Anyway, the vet told us that there was only one hope for Henny. If we could increase her food in tiny _____ (s) every day, she might recover. We are taking his advice. If all goes well, perhaps Henny will be back to herself soon, _____ (ing) her eggs as usual.

Name _____   Date _____

Evaluating a Persuasive Message

After choosing a television advertisement, fill out the following chart to evaluate what you see.

Topic of television advertisement: _____

What is the purpose of the advertisement?
Who is delivering the information?
What is the advertisement's message? Is this message fact or opinion? Explain.
What persuasive techniques are used in place of factual information?
What mood is created by the words, sounds, and pictures?
Are you presuaded? Why or why not?

Unit 2: Short Stories
Benchmark Test 4

MULTIPLE CHOICE

Reading Skill: Drawing Conclusions

1. What are the two main things to consider when you draw conclusions as you read a literary work?
   A. the time and place of the setting
   B. the author's background and other works
   C. the plot and the title of the work
   D. your prior knowledge and the story details

2. Why is it important to ask questions when you need to draw conclusions?
   A. to gather people's opinions
   B. to identify relevant details
   C. to check facts for accuracy
   D. to understand background information

Read the selection. Then, answer the questions that follow.

The day was sunny but cool. Ernie kicked the leaves on the sidewalk as he walked home from the gym. Frowning, he kept replaying the game in his mind. For just a couple of seconds he had let his guard slip, and McGirk had taken advantage of the lapse to toss a long one right through the hoop. Ernie's team had fallen further and further behind after that. Not that Ernie was playing by then. After his terrible lapse, Coach had benched him. Ernie sighed. He resolved to practice doubly hard all week.

3. From the details in the selection and your own prior knowledge, what conclusion do you draw about when the events in the selection occur?
   A. a spring morning
   B. a summer evening
   C. an autumn afternoon
   D. a winter night

4. Which detail most clearly helps you conclude that Ernie was playing basketball?
   A. Ernie keeps replaying the game in his mind.
   B. During the game, Ernie let his guard slip.
   C. McGirk tossed a long one through the hoop.
   D. Coach benched Ernie for the rest of the game.

5. Why do you think the author included the detail about Ernie's team falling behind?
   A. to show that the team lost by several points
   B. to show that the game was close
   C. to show that Ernie is the best player on the team
   D. to show that the team is terrible

6. From the selection, what can you conclude is Ernie's attitude toward the game?
   A. He regrets his performance and will try to do better in the future.
   B. He resents being removed from the game and is very angry with Coach.
   C. He regrets his lapse but is otherwise happy about the outcome of the game.
   D. He is not worried about his performance because his teammates also performed poorly.

Reading: Comparison-and-Contrast Organization

Read this brief comparison-and-contrast article. Then, answer the questions that follow.

(1) Vermont and New Hampshire are often confused by people unfamiliar with New England. (2) Located right next to each other, both New England states are long and narrow, stretching from Massachusetts north to the Canadian border. (3) New Hampshire has a bit of coast on the Atlantic Ocean. (4) Vermont, on the other hand, is an inland state, although Lake Champlain, a large lake on the border with New York State, does provide a small shipping industry. (5) Both Vermont and New Hampshire have large forested areas and mountains popular with skiers. (6) In fact, New Hampshire's White Mountains include Mount Washington, the tallest mountain in the Northeast.

7. What sort of organization does this comparison-and-contrast article use?
   A. block organization
   B. point-by-point organization
   C. chain reaction
   D. chronological order

8. Which of these sentence pairs contrasts the same categories of information?
   A. sentences 1 and 2
   B. sentences 3 and 4
   C. sentences 4 and 5
   D. sentences 3 and 6

9. What comparison does the writer support with the details in sentence 6?
   A. the comparison of the two states' mountainous areas
   B. the comparison of the two states' forested areas
   C. the comparison of the two states' long and narrow shape
   D. the comparison of the two states' waterfront resorts

10. Which of these changes would most improve the comparison-and-contrast article?
    A. Drop the detail about Lake Champlain in sentence 4.
    B. Add a detail mentioning the nearby New England state of Maine right after sentence 4.
    C. Add a detail identifying Vermont's Green Mountains right after sentence 6.
    D. Drop the detail about New Hampshire's White Mountains in sentence 6.

Literary Analysis: Theme

11. Which statement about the theme of a work is true?
    A. The theme of a work is usually directly stated at the end.
    B. The theme of a work is never directly stated in the work.
    C. Characters' thoughts and feelings often point to the theme.
    D. The title of a work rarely has anything to do with its theme.

Read the selection. Then, answer the questions that follow.

A Curious Incident

Every Friday, Mia worked as a babysitter for the Homers. The couple had only one child, but he was very noisy. If he woke up, he would cry and cry. Mia would rock him and walk with him and sing to him until he would finally quiet down.

This Friday, all was quiet as usual when Mia arrived. "I sure hope he won't wake up," she whispered to Mrs. Homer. Just then she noticed a large, oddly shaped box on the living room coffee table. "What's that?" she asked.

"Oh, it's nothing," Mrs. Homer answered. "Just don't touch it."

Sitting in the living room trying to read, Mia kept glancing at the box. What on earth can it be? she wondered. Finally, she decided to peek inside. But as she lifted the lid, the whole thing fell off the coffee table with a loud crash . . . which, of course, woke Baby up.

Mia was still trying to calm the screaming baby when the Homers came home. "I see Baby is awake," Mrs. Homer commented. "And I also see you touched the box."

"I admit I was going to take a look inside," Mia confessed. "But I accidentally knocked it off the table, and that woke Baby up, so I never did see what was inside."

"I guess you learned your lesson," Mrs. Homer commented. "Nothing good comes of being too curious."

12. What is the stated theme of this story?
    A. If he woke up, he would cry and cry.
    B. What on earth can it be?
    C. I guess you learned your lesson.
    D. Nothing good comes of being too curious.

13. Which of these events from the story most clearly points to the stated theme?
    A. The Homer baby always cries a lot if he wakes up.
    B. Mia arrives for her babysitting job.
    C. Mrs. Homer tells Mia not to look in the box.
    D. Mia tries to read.

14. Which of these additional themes does the story also convey?
    A. Only a person who is not curious can be a good babysitter.
    B. Babies are adorable even when they are hard to manage.
    C. Never interrupt one thing to do another.
    D. When things are going well, try not to do anything to disturb them.

Literary Analysis: Setting

15. Which of these is the best definition of the setting of a literary work?
  A. The setting is the time and place of the action.
  B. The setting is the historical era in which a work takes place.
  C. The setting is the central idea of a work.
  D. The setting is the season of the year in which a work takes place.

Read the selection. Then, answer the questions that follow.

On a cold December evening in 1773, a group of about fifty American colonists gathered in Boston Harbor. They called themselves the Sons of Liberty, but they were disguised as Mohawk Indians so that they would not be recognized. Crossing Griffin's Wharf to the inky harbor waters, they boarded three British ships: the *Eleanor,* the *Beaver,* and the *Dartmouth.* The ships contained tea owned by the British East India Company that the dockworkers had refused to unload and the colonists had refused to buy because of the high tax the British government had placed on the tea. When the British governor of Massachusetts tried to make the dockworkers unload the tea, the colonists felt further protest was called for. After boarding the three boats, they split open 342 chests of tea and proceeded to dump forty-five tons into Boston Harbor as cheering crowds looked on from the wharf. The famous protest became known as the Boston Tea Party.

16. In what historical period do the events of the selection take place?
  A. ancient times
  B. the American Revolution
  C. the American Civil War
  D. World War II

17. Which aspect of the setting does the selection give the most detailed information about?
  A. the time of day
  B. the time of year
  C. the historical period
  D. the city

Vocabulary: Prefixes and Roots

18. In what language does the word *migratory* have its origin?
  A. German   **C.** Greek
  B. Italian   **D.** Latin

19. Based on your understanding of the root *-clin-*, which of these is an *incline*?
  A. the end of a road
  B. the side of a hill
  C. the shape of the moon
  D. the top of a table

20. From your knowledge of the prefix *com-*, what do people who *commune* do?
  A. take frequent trips
  C. know each other well
  B. travel regularly to work
  D. talk together intimately

21. How does the meaning of the word *contemporary* reflect the meaning of the root *-tempor-*?
  A. Something contemporary is always in style.
  B. Something contemporary is of use to everyone.
  C. Something contemporary is of the present time.
  D. Something contemporary is usually popular.

22. How does the word *recline* reflect the meaning of the root *-clin-*?
  A. When you recline, you lean back.
  B. When you recline, you relax.
  C. When you recline, you are tired.
  D. When you recline, you are on a couch.

23. Based on your understanding of the root *-migra-*, what do *migrant* workers do?
  A. stay in one place for a long period of time
  B. work both day and night
  C. work for more than one person at a time
  D. move from place to place

Grammar: Verbs

24. How do you form the simple past tense of regular verbs?
  A. Add *-ed* or *-d*.
  B. Add *-ed* or *-en*.
  C. Add *-s* or *-es*.
  D. Use the helping verb *have*.

25. Which sentence uses a verb in the simple future tense?
  A. Paula usually eats in the school cafeteria.
  B. Paula will probably eat in the school cafeteria today.
  C. Since September, Angela has eaten every day in the school cafeteria.
  D. Angela had eaten in the school cafeteria until she went on a diet.

26. What is the tense of the verb in this sentence?
  Marta has composed a song.
  A. present
  B. past
  C. present perfect
  D. past perfect

27. How do you form perfect tenses of verbs?
  A. Use the helping verb *will* and the base form of the verb.
  B. Use a form of the helping verb *be* and the past participle of the verb.
  C. Use a form of the helping verb *have* and the present participle of the verb.
  D. Use a form of the helping verb *have* and the past participle of the verb.

28. Which sentence uses verbs correctly?
    A. As Marylou walked down the street, she is excited to see the first robin of the year.
    B. Since the robin has arrived, maybe spring will begin.
    C. Nowadays there are lots of mockingbirds but in the past we see more robins.
    D. The robin gets caught in the rain and looked all wet.

Spelling

29. Which word is spelled correctly?
    A. responsably
    B. admirible
    C. canceling
    D. typicly

30. In which sentence is the italic word spelled correctly?
    A. That would be a *nottable* achievement.
    B. I need a *workible* solution.
    C. That idea is very *appealling*.
    D. Please speak a bit more *quietly*.

31. To spell words correctly, when should you change *y* to *i* before adding a suffix?
    A. when the original word ends in a consonant and *y*
    B. when the original word ends in a vowel and *y*
    C. whenever the original word ends in *y*
    D. only when the original word ends in a double consonant and *y*

ESSAY

Writing

32. Think of a person whom you find interesting. It might be someone you know or someone you encountered in movies or on TV. Then, on your paper or a separate sheet, write a brief description of this person as if he or she were a story character. Begin your description with one or two words that capture the character's personality.

33. Recall a time in your life when you experienced something new and interesting. It might be a trip you took or a new outdoor activity you tried to learn. On your paper or a separate sheet, recount your experience in a brief personal narrative.

34. Think of an incident in your own life that you might turn into a short story. It could be a challenge you faced or an unusual experience you had. On your paper or a separate sheet, create an outline of the story you will write. Your outline should provide details about the characters, the setting or settings, and the different elements of the plot.

Vocabulary in Context

Identify the answer choice that best completes the statement.

1. At their Thanksgiving feast, many families have pumpkin pie for_____ .
   A. turkey
   B. dessert
   C. vegetables
   D. popular

2. Our baseball team is part of our town's_____ .
   A. sport
   B. government
   C. league
   D. record

3. Our armed forces are trained to protect us from any_____ .
   A. enemy
   B. citizen
   C. council
   D. dangerous

4. Slow down, because there is a sharp_____ in the road ahead.
   A. mound
   B. curve
   C. accident
   D. pause

5. To knit the scarf, I used different-colored_____ .
   A. embroider
   B. equipment
   C. velvet
   D. yarns

6. The butterfly broke out of its_____ and flew away.
   A. swarm
   B. mass
   C. roost
   D. cocoon

7. Grandma rarely forgets people's names because she has a good_____ .
   A. detail
   B. concentration
   C. memory
   D. conscious

8. Downtown shoppers now have many more choices because of the _____ opened stores.
   A. newly
   B. generally
   C. naturally
   D. properly

9. The car seat protected the baby because he was _____ in tightly.
   A. defended
   B. strapped
   C. battered
   D. formed

10. The walls of the cave were covered with beautiful drawings and _____ .
    A. interesting
    B. symbol
    C. entertainment
    D. carvings

11. When you borrowed your library books, did you write down when they were _____ ?
    A. due
    B. scheduled
    C. connected
    D. chapters

12. I woke up when a nice dream suddenly turned into a _____ .
    A. rhyme
    B. nightmare
    C. diary
    D. punishment

13. The naughty little child took a crayon and _____ on the wall.
    A. sprinkled
    B. incident
    C. appreciated
    D. scribbled

14. If you do not know the meaning of a word, look at the _____ around it.
    A. published
    B. context
    C. guidelines
    D. documents

15. The soldiers live in the _____ .
 A. household
 B. terrace
 C. barracks
 D. association

16. The wedding cake was decorated in an interesting, _____ way.
 A. romance
 B. composed
 C. elaborate
 D. specialize

17. After she brought it home, Savah wasn't sure she liked the pink _____ sweater.
 A. fuzzy
 B. obvious
 C. equal
 D. genuine

18. Although it was his first year playing major league baseball, the _____ played very well.
 A. cadet
 B. predator
 C. introduction
 D. rookie

19. Many people believe that to stay healthy, they must take _____ .
 A. formula
 B. vitamins
 C. aged
 D. applications

20. Perhaps because I like to laugh, I prefer movies that are _____ .
 A. dramas
 B. comedies
 C. traditional
 D. tragic

Diagnostic Tests and Vocabulary in Context
Use and Interpretation

The Diagnostic Tests and Vocabulary in Context were developed to assist teachers in making the most appropriate assignment of *Prentice Hall Literature* program selections to students. The purpose of these assessments is to indicate the degree of difficulty that students are likely to have in reading/comprehending the selections presented in the *following* unit of instruction. Tests are provided at six separate times in each grade level—a *Diagnostic Test* (to be used prior to beginning the year's instruction) and a *Vocabulary in Context,* the final segment of the Benchmark Test appearing at the end of each of the first five units of instruction. Note that the tests are intended for use not as summative assessments for the prior unit, but as guidance for assigning literature selections in the upcoming unit of instruction.

The structure of all Diagnostic Tests and Vocabulary in Context in this series is the same. All test items are four-option, multiple-choice items. The format is established to assess a student's ability to construct sufficient meaning from the context sentence to choose the only provided word that fits both the semantics (meaning) and syntax (structure) of the context sentence. All words in the context sentences are chosen to be "below-level" words that students reading at this grade level should know. All answer choices fit *either* the meaning or structure of the context sentence, but only the correct choice fits *both* semantics and syntax. All answer choices—both correct answers and incorrect options—are key words chosen from specifically taught words that will occur in the subsequent unit of program instruction. This careful restriction of the assessed words permits a sound diagnosis of students' current reading achievement and prediction of the most appropriate level of readings to assign in the upcoming unit of instruction.

The assessment of vocabulary in context skill has consistently been shown in reading research studies to correlate very highly with "reading comprehension." This is not surprising as the format essentially assesses comprehension, albeit in sentence-length "chunks." Decades of research demonstrate that vocabulary assessment provides a strong, reliable prediction of comprehension achievement— the purpose of these tests. Further, because this format demands very little testing time, these diagnoses can be made efficiently, permitting teachers to move forward with critical instructional tasks rather than devoting excessive time to assessment.

It is important to stress that while the Diagnostic Tests and Vocabulary in Context were carefully developed and will yield sound assignment decisions, they were designed to *reinforce,* not supplant, teacher judgment as to the most appropriate instructional placement for individual students. Teacher judgment should always prevail in making placement—or indeed other important instructional—decisions concerning students.

Diagnostic Tests and Vocabulary in Context Branching Suggestions

These tests are designed to provide maximum flexibility for teachers. Your *Unit Resources* books contain the 40-question **Diagnostic Test** and 20-question **Vocabulary in Context** tests. At *PHLitOnline*, you can access the Diagnostic Test and complete 40-question Vocabulary in Context tests. Procedures for administering the tests are described below. Choose the procedure based on the time you wish to devote to the activity and your comfort with the assignment decisions relative to the individual students. Remember that your judgment of a student's reading level should always take precedence over the results of a single written test.

Feel free to use different procedures at different times of the year. For example, for early units, you may wish to be more confident in the assignments you make—thus, using the "two-stage" process below. Later, you may choose the quicker diagnosis, confirming the results with your observations of the students' performance built up throughout the year.

The **Diagnostic Test** is composed of a single 40-item assessment. Based on the results of this assessment, make the following assignment of students to the reading selections in Unit 1:

Diagnostic Test Score	Selection to Use
If the student's score is 0–25	more accessible
If the student's score is 26–40	more challenging

Outlined below are the three basic options for administering **Vocabulary in Context** and basing selection assignments on the results of these assessments.

1. For a one-stage, quicker diagnosis using the *20-item* test in the *Unit Resources:*

Vocabulary in Context Test Score	Selection to Use
If the student's score is 0–13	more accessible
If the student's score is 14–20	more challenging

2. If you wish to confirm your assignment decisions with a *two-stage* diagnosis:

Stage 1: Administer the 20-item test in the *Unit Resources*	
Vocabulary in Context Test Score	Selection to Use
If the student's score is 0–9	more accessible
If the student's score is 10–15	(Go to Stage 2.)
If the student's score is 16–20	more challenging

Stage 2: Administer items 21–40 from *PHLitOnline*	
Vocabulary in Context Test Score	Selection to Use
If the student's score is 0–12	more accessible
If the student's score is 13–20	more challenging

3. If you base your assignment decisions on the full 40-item **Vocabulary in Context** from *PHLitOnline:*

Vocabulary in Context Test Score	Selection to Use
If the student's score is 0–25	more accessible
If the student's score is 26–40	more challenging

Name _____ Date _____

Grade 6—Benchmark Test 3
Interpretation Guide

For remediation of specific skills, you may assign students the relevant Reading Kit Practice and Assess pages indicated in the far-right column of this chart. You will find rubrics for evaluating writing samples in the last section of your Professional Development Guidebook.

Skill Objective	Test Items	Number Correct	Reading Kit
Reading Skill			
Make Inferences	1, 2, 3, 4, 5		pp. 52, 53
Use text aids and text features	6, 7, 8		pp. 54, 55
Literary Analysis			
Characterization (indirect and direct)	9, 10, 13, 14		pp. 56, 57
Conflict (internal/external)	11, 12, 15		pp. 58, 59
Character's Motives	16, 17,18		pp. 60, 61
Vocabulary			
Prefixes *re-, dis-, ex-, in-*	19, 20, 21, 22, 23, 24		pp. 62, 63
Grammar			
Action and Linking Verbs	25, 26, 27		pp. 64, 65
Principle Parts of Verbs	28, 29, 30		pp. 66, 67
Irregular and Troublesome Verbs	31, 32		pp. 68, 69
Writing			
Help-Wanted Ad	33	Use rubric	pp. 70, 71
Persuasive Speech	34	Use rubric	pp. 72, 73
Review	35	Use rubric	pp. 74, 75

Grade 6—Benchmark Test 4
Interpretation Guide

For remediation of specific skills, you may assign students the relevant Reading Kit Practice and Assess pages indicated in the far-right column of this chart. You will find rubrics for evaluating writing samples in the last section of your Professional Development Guidebook.

Skill Objective	Test Items	Number Correct	Reading Kit
Reading Skill			
Draw Conclusions	1, 2, 3, 4, 5, 6		pp. 76, 77
Compare-and-Contrast Organization	7, 8, 9, 10		pp. 78, 79
Literary Analysis			
Theme	11, 12, 13, 14		pp. 80, 81, 84, 85
Setting	15, 16, 17		pp. 82, 83
Vocabulary			
Roots -*migra*-, -*com*-, -*clin*-, -*tempor*-	18, 19, 20, 21, 22, 23		pp. 86, 87
Grammar			
Simple Verb Tenses	24, 25		pp. 88, 89
Perfect Tenses	26, 27		pp. 90, 91
Revise to Maintain Verb Tense	28		pp. 92, 93
Spelling			
Adding Suffixes	29, 30, 31		pp. 94, 95
Writing			
Description	32	Use rubric	pp. 96, 97
Personal Narrative	33	Use rubric	pp. 98, 99
Short Story	34	Use rubric	pp. 100, 101

ANSWERS

Big Question Vocabulary—1, p. 1

Sample Answers

1. My friend Katie and I *argued* over who would keep the invention that we made together. The *issue* was that she was leaving for the summer, and I did not want her to take it with her. We had both worked so hard on it.

2. I worked hard to *convince* Katie that she should leave our invention safely at home with me. It was too big to take on an airplane anyway.

3. We *concluded* the issue in two days. We *resolved* that Katie would leave the invention with me for the summer and then, in the fall, she would keep it at her house.

Big Question Vocabulary—2, p. 2

Sample Answers

1. I love to play the *game* of Scrabble. It is a *challenge* to think of long words and spell them correctly with the random letters you pick.

2. I *compete* with my friend Esther every Saturday morning.

3. Most of the time, Esther *wins* and I *lose*, but I have won twice and I am going to keep trying.

Big Question Vocabulary—3, p. 3

Sample Answers

1. The settlers could have chosen to *negotiate* with the Native Americans to find a good solution sharing the land. OR The settlers could have chosen to *battle* with the Native Americans over the land.

2. The end result of negotiation would have been that they work out their differences and there is *survival* for everyone. OR The end result of a battle would have been that the Native Americans would *defend* their land and there would have been death and destruction.

"The Wounded Wolf"
by Jean Craighead George

Vocabulary Warm-up Exercises, p. 8

A.
1. presence
2. clan
3. lunges
4. gulps
5. flesh
6. whimpers
7. squints
8. blinding

B. Sample Answers

1. This lamp <u>shatters</u> easily, so I'm very careful moving it.
2. The mountain is <u>massive</u>; it will take hours or days to climb it.
3. The wind is <u>frigid</u>; I'll wear a down coat and a hat when I go outside.
4. Terrence can't get along with anyone, so we're not surprised that he has <u>foes</u>.
5. The fish <u>flits</u> through the water so quickly that it's hard to catch.
6. J.J. walked by the pit bull so <u>boldly</u> that I never would have guessed that he was afraid of dogs.
7. This desert is a <u>barren</u> place, without a single tree, plant, or animal.

Reading Warm-up A, p. 9

Sample Answers

1. <u>its eyes</u>: Looking directly at bright sunlight makes me *squint*.
2. (light); Something that is *blinding* makes it hard to see.
3. (making small soft sounds); A human baby *whimpers*.
4. <u>a brother or sister pup</u>; The *presence* of my dog on the bed made it uncomfortable to sleep.
5. The pup's *clan* includes its mother and its brother and sister pups.
6. <u>its mother's milk</u>; *Gulps* means "to eat or drink in a greedy way."
7. (its prey); *Lunges* means "to move forward very quickly."
8. (deer, elk, and caribou); *Flesh* means "the meat of an animal."

Reading Warm-up B, p. 10

Sample Answers

1. <u>some of the coldest days and nights on the planet</u>; Winter is the season most likely to have *frigid* weather.
2. (as tall as apartment buildings); *Massive* means "really, really big."
3. (a small chicken-like bird); *Flits* means "moves around quickly."
4. When an iceberg *shatters*, it cracks and breaks into smaller pieces.
5. (full of life); *Barren* means "without a lot of life."
6. <u>smaller birds</u>; *Foe* means "enemy."
7. <u>those that can't find food</u>; *Starvation* is "the suffering or dying from lack of food."
8. If a seal goes about too *boldly*, without fear or caution, it will end up as food for a polar bear.

Jean Craighead George

Listening and Viewing, p. 11

Sample answers and guidelines for evaluation:

Segment 1: Jean Craighead George became a nature writer because she was exposed to nature at a young age and learned to love it. Her experience of living so closely with nature in the woods in Michigan helped her decide to write about nature.

Segment 2: She uses the short-story form when a story dictates it. The anecdote she learns from Dr. Haber provided her with a beginning, a dramatic interior, and an ending that she can use as the basis of her story.

Segment 3: Jean Craighead George spends up to a year researching for a single book. It is important that her writing be scientifically accurate so she can portray animal species and their behaviors and environments factually.

Segment 4: George is rewarded if she can inspire her audience to view the world differently and to get them to act independently. Her audience learns to be more independent and learns more about the world.

Unit 2: Learning About Short Stories, p. 12

1. external conflict
2. stated theme
3. character trait
4. theme
5. plot

"The Wounded Wolf" by Jean Craighead George

Model Selection: Short Story, p. 13

Sample Answers

A. 1. He is brave and determined to defend himself.
   2. He must fight off the scavenging animals in order to survive.
   3. He faces an external conflict. He is wounded, he is cold, he must find a safe place for shelter, and he must defend himself against animals who want to eat him.
   4. The setting is an icy, high ridge above an Arctic valley.
   5. The cold increases his need for shelter. Lack of food makes him a target.

B. 1. It has a suggested theme, because the message is not directly stated.
   2. Sample response: The theme of the story is that personal courage and the help of friends lead to survival. Roko had to be brave and strong to withstand the attacks of the scavenging animals. The help of Kiglo and the other wolves made his survival possible.

Open-Book Test, p. 14

Short Answer

1. As the problem in a short story gets worse, the plot builds to the point of greatest tension. This is the climax.
   Difficulty: *Easy* **Objective:** *Literary Analysis*

2. An internal conflict takes place in the mind of a character, while an external conflict is one in which a character struggles with an outside force.
   Difficulty: *Easy* **Objective:** *Literary Analysis*

3. The sentence describes the theme because it is a message about or insight into life.
   Difficulty: *Average* **Objective:** *Literary Analysis*

4. The sentence describes one of the characters, people or animals who take part in the action.
   Difficulty: *Average* **Objective:** *Literary Analysis*

5. Sample answers for web: massive spine of rock and ice, blinding whiteness, barren ground. The story's action is based partly on the frozen setting.
   Difficulty: *Average* **Objective:** *Literary Analysis*

6. The herd of musk-ox circle to protect themselves from an enemy. The word *fort* suggests that the solid line of heads and horns and fur will offer this protection.
   Difficulty: *Challenging* **Objective:** *Interpretation*

7. Roko's position gives him protection on three sides so he can be in a better situation to face his foes.
   Difficulty: *Easy* **Objective:** *Interpretation*

8. The wolves each howl in turn, as if they are calling roll. Kiglo, the leader, finds Rocko and brings him meat to build up his strength.
   Difficulty: *Challenging* **Objective:** *Interpretation*

9. Since *gnashes* means "bites with grinding teeth," the wolf is eating vigorously and hungrily.
   Difficulty: *Average* **Objective:** *Vocabulary*

10. The wolves are pleased that Roko has regained his strength. This conclusion is supported by the fact that the sounds begin right after Roko strongly barks out his name during roll call.
    Difficulty: *Average* **Objective:** *Interpretation*

Essay

11. Student essays should indicate that Roko feels greatly relieved and grateful. After seeing his foes on deathwatch attack, Roko knew it would be only a matter of time until he would not be able to fight them off. The appearance of Kiglo means that the pack knows where he is and will now help and protect him. The food Kiglo brings means that he will have the nourishment to be able to recover.
    Difficulty: *Easy* **Objective:** *Essay*

12. Student essays should note that Roko is brave, determined, and clever. He bravely fights off his enemies, and his determination does not let him give up even when the odds are against him. He is clever in how he positions himself for the best protection. All these qualities allow him to survive even though he is weak from hunger, his wounds, and the cold. His motives include a will to survive and a desire to defend himself.

Difficulty: *Average* **Objective:** *Essay*

13. Student essays should note that the setting of the frozen Artic plays a large role in the events of the story. In this harsh locale, food is scarce and survival always in question. Animals must fight one another to survive. They do this by hunting each other or preying on the weak and the wounded. When Roko is wounded, his foes come in for the kill. The setting drives the action of the story. Without the bad weather and threatening animals, the story has no conflict.

Difficulty: *Challenging* **Objective:** *Essay*

14. Students should make some of these observations: Roko's struggle is certainly a hard one. Nature and his enemies have no sympathy for the fact that he is injured. He comes very close to dying. On the other hand, the conflict does have positive aspects. The wolf's determination and courage are put to the test and pass. Another positive aspect is the loyalty and caring of the pack. They do not desert him and actually save his life.

Difficulty: *Average* **Objective:** *Essay*

Oral Response

15. Oral responses should be clear, well organized, and well supported by appropriate examples from the selection.

Difficulty: *Average* **Objective:** *Oral Interpretation*

Selection Test A, p. 17

Learning About Short Stories

1. ANS: C	DIF: Easy	OBJ: Literary Analysis
2. ANS: C	DIF: Easy	OBJ: Literary Analysis
3. ANS: A	DIF: Easy	OBJ: Literary Analysis
4. ANS: A	DIF: Easy	OBJ: Literary Analysis
5. ANS: C	DIF: Easy	OBJ: Literary Analysis

Critical Reading

6. ANS: B	DIF: Easy	OBJ: Literary Analysis
7. ANS: D	DIF: Easy	OBJ: Comprehension
8. ANS: A	DIF: Easy	OBJ: Comprehension
9. ANS: C	DIF: Easy	OBJ: Interpretation
10. ANS: B	DIF: Easy	OBJ: Comprehension
11. ANS: D	DIF: Easy	OBJ: Interpretation
12. ANS: C	DIF: Easy	OBJ: Interpretation
13. ANS: A	DIF: Easy	OBJ: Interpretation
14. ANS: C	DIF: Easy	OBJ: Literary Analysis
15. ANS: B	DIF: Easy	OBJ: Literary Analysis

Essay

16. Students can support the statement with specific details involving the ravens, the herd of musk-ox, and the pack of wolves.

Difficulty: *Easy*

Objective: *Essay*

17. Students will probably say that he is greatly relieved to see both his leader and the food that his leader brings. He has help and protection at last.

Difficulty: *Easy*

Objective: *Essay*

18. Students will probably say the conflict is not totally bad but certainly hard. Roko comes very close to dying. The other animals want a meal. The wind is brutal. On the other hand, good things do come of the conflict. The wolf proves he is strong and brave. The pack shows their loyalty. They do not desert him and actually save his life.

Difficulty: *Easy*

Objective: *Essay*

Selection Test B, p. 20

Learning About Short Stories

1. ANS: B	DIF: Average	OBJ: Literary Analysis
2. ANS: C	DIF: Average	OBJ: Literary Analysis
3. ANS: A	DIF: Challenging	OBJ: Literary Analysis
4. ANS: C	DIF: Challenging	OBJ: Literary Analysis
5. ANS: C	DIF: Challenging	OBJ: Literary Analysis
6. ANS: D	DIF: Average	OBJ: Literary Analysis

Critical Reading

7. ANS: B	DIF: Average	OBJ: Literary Analysis
8. ANS: B	DIF: Average	OBJ: Literary Analysis
9. ANS: C	DIF: Challenging	OBJ: Comprehension
10. ANS: A	DIF: Challenging	OBJ: Comprehension
11. ANS: C	DIF: Average	OBJ: Comprehension
12. ANS: B	DIF: Challenging	OBJ: Interpretation
13. ANS: B	DIF: Challenging	OBJ: Interpretation
14. ANS: D	DIF: Challenging	OBJ: Interpretation
15. ANS: C	DIF: Challenging	OBJ: Interpretation
16. ANS: B	DIF: Average	OBJ: Comprehension
17. ANS: D	DIF: Average	OBJ: Interpretation
18. ANS: D	DIF: Average	OBJ: Comprehension
19. ANS: D	DIF: Challenging	OBJ: Interpretation
20. ANS: D	DIF: Average	OBJ: Literary Analysis

Essay

21. Students should note that Roko acts bravely and shows determination, even when he is weak from hunger, his wounds, and the cold, and even though he faces many

enemies. His motives include a will to survive and a desire to defend himself.

Difficulty: *Average*

Objective: *Essay*

22. Students may say that Roko learns to watch the older wolves when hunting so that he might avoid getting injured again. Additionally, he may have learned how to defend himself against enemies. Finally, he probably gains a greater appreciation for the other wolves and an understanding of the importance of teamwork.

Difficulty: *Challenging*

Objective: *Essay*

23. Students should make some of these observations: Roko's struggle is certainly a hard one. Nature and his enemies have no sympathy for the fact that he is injured. He comes very close to dying. On the other hand, the conflict does have positive aspects. The wolf's determination and courage are put to the test and pass. Another positive aspect is the loyalty and caring of the pack. They do not desert him and actually save his life.

Difficulty: *Average*

Objective: *Essay*

"The Tail" by Joyce Hansen

Vocabulary Warm-up Exercises, p. 24

A. 1. hiking
2. stoop
3. entrance
4. overlooking
5. filthy
6. ridiculous
7. elderly
8. centuries

B. Sample Answers

1. F; *To blackmail* means "to threaten," an action that is normally not considered friendly.
2. F; On the contrary, it's an example of disobedience.
3. F; Most kittens are cute, not scary looking.
4. T; Those are two jobs that a fireman has to perform.
5. F; On the contrary, you are helping end suffering, not causing it.
6. T; If the joke is funny enough, it could produce a sudden burst of laughter.
7. T; The face is where dimples are found, usually on the cheeks or on the chin.
8. F; An annual event happens once a year.

Reading Warm-up A, p. 25

Sample Answers

1. just a few hundred years; I was not alive *centuries* ago.

2. (through the woods); *Hiking* means "walking in the country."
3. (paying about $25 in goods); The payment of $25 is an unbelievably low price for all of Manhattan.
4. of a building; A *stoop* is "a set of steps in front of a building."
5. (the highway); My classroom window is *overlooking* the playground.
6. playgrounds, benches; An *entrance* is the place where people enter, or walk into, a place.
7. (relax and enjoy good weather); *Elderly* means "old."
8. clean, garbage-free; *Filthy* means "very dirty."

Reading Warm-up B, p. 26

Sample Answers

1. First, the two of you must clean all your old stuff out of the attic. Then, you will help me and your father in the basement. Finally, the two of you will bring all the stuff over to the thrift shop; One of my *responsibilities* is folding the laundry.
2. (spring-cleaning Sunday); This family does this event once every year.
3. (a week without dessert, or worse, permanent grounding); *Obedience* means "doing what you are told to do."
4. Cleaning would *torment* Rebecca since she hates to get dirty.
5. (in their face); *Dimples* are little hollows some people have in their cheeks.
6. of fear; *Spasm* means "a burst of emotion."
7. shadows creepy, dark corners; Halloween masks and movie monsters might appear *monstrous*.
8. She would threaten to lock me in there if I didn't obey her commands. *Blackmail* means "to threaten a person to make them do what you want."

Writing About the Big Question, p. 27

A. 1. game
2. argue
3. win
4. negotiate

B. Sample Answers

1. I argued with my big brother over who got to visit my grandmother this summer. I also argued with my mother about whether I could go to my friend's birthday party.
2. I **negotiated** with my mother by promising to finish all my homework before the party, so we were both able to **win** the argument.

C. Sample Answer

Conflicts between kids and their parents can have positive outcomes when both sides listen carefully to each other and try to understand each other's viewpoints. Therefore, conflict can sometimes bring people together.

"The Tail" by Joyce Hansen

Reading: Use Details to Make Inferences, p. 28
Sample Answers

A. *Detail:* It began as the worst summer of my life.

Detail: My heart came to a sudden stop.

Inference: Tasha does not want summer responsibilities.

B. *Detail:* We were so good that some of the boys in the stickball game watched us.

Detail: We had an audience, so I really showed off. . . .

Inference: Tasha likes attention.

C. *Detail:* A part of me was gone and I had to find it.

Detail: "Dear God," I said out loud, "please let me find him."

Inference: Tasha loves her brother.

Literary Analysis: Characterization, p. 29
Sample Answers

Character's Words, Thoughts, and Actions: I'd rather be in school than minding Junior all day; I was too embarrassed; A part of me was gone and I had to find it; I couldn't believe how brave I was.

Others' Words, Thoughts, and Actions: Your father and I decided that you're old enough now to take on certain responsibilities; Tasha, I'm depending on you; Tasha, you're not going in there, are you?

Direct Statements: I couldn't believe how brave I was.

Vocabulary Builder, p. 30
Sample Answers

A. 2. attacked

The cat attacked and shredded the side of the sofa.

3. promise

My friend and I made a promise to talk to each other every day.

4. burst

I felt a burst of fear when the floorboards creaked.

5. worried

I felt *worried* about the play tryouts.

6. habit

Josie had the same *habit* every time she cleaned her room.

B. 1. T; *Discomfort* is the opposite of comfort. A person in discomfort would feel sick or hurt.

2. F; To *disappear* is to go away. You want a lost item to show up.

3. F; You connect something by plugging it in. To *disconnect* it, you would unplug it.

Enrichment: The Cloisters, p. 31
Sample Answers

The Cloisters

1. The Cloisters includes parts of five medieval French monasteries.

2. Some of the gardens include plants found in medieval writings.

3. There are about 5,000 works of art in the Cloisters.

The Unicorn Tapestries

1. Tapestries were woven in wool and silk.

2. Fabric includes silver and gold threads.

3. Tapestries show the unicorn coming to a young woman and later being hunted by a group of hunters on horseback with dogs.

Students' paragraphs should include factual information as well as speculation on what Tasha and Junior might find interesting in the museum.

Open-Book Test, p. 32
Short Answer

1. The narrator says that there are no kids Junior's age on the block, suggesting that he has nobody to play with living nearby.

   Difficulty: *Average* **Objective:** *Reading*

2. The passage tells that Junior always bothers his sister when their parents are not around.

   Difficulty: *Average* **Objective:** *Literary Analysis*

3. Ma is very strict and expects her children to do what she says without arguing. She tells Tasha "Life ain't always fair," when Tasha argues about babysitting. She gives Tasha a long list of rules and chores for the day and expects them to be carried out.

   Difficulty: *Challenging* **Objective:** *Literary Analysis*

4. Because Tasha misses him so much, the reader can infer that she loves her brother.

   Difficulty: *Easy* **Objective:** *Reading*

5. The word *mauled* means "badly injured by being attacked." A toy mouse that was mauled by a cat would be torn and falling apart.

   Difficulty: *Average* **Objective:** *Vocabulary*

6. Tasha is afraid that Junior is lost and might get hurt. Concern for her brother gives her courage to climb the steps to find him.

   Difficulty: *Average* **Objective:** *Interpretation*

7. Junior is mischievous. He runs away and hides from his sister while she is desperately looking for him.

   Difficulty: *Easy* **Objective:** *Literary Analysis*

8. Tasha and Junior fight and tease each other, but they are very close. When she thinks Junior is lost, Tasha is very upset and just wants her brother back. Junior also loves his sister as evidenced by the fact that he always hangs around her.

   Difficulty: *Challenging* **Objective:** *Interpretation*

9. First example: indirect; Junior knows how to bug his sister.

   Second example: direct; Junior is less of a bother than he was

   Difficulty: *Average* **Objective:** *Literary Analysis*

10. Tasha learns that she didn't realize how she felt about her brother until he was missing.

Difficulty: *Easy* **Objective:** *Interpretation*

Essay

11. Students' essays should note that at the beginning of the story, Tasha does not want the responsibility of taking care of her brother. She also thinks he is a pest. However, the near-loss of her brother causes her to realize that he is important to her. By the end of the story, she accepts the responsibility of looking after him. She takes good care of him and is happy to do so. Students might say that Tasha learns to appreciate her brother and her responsibility.

Difficulty: *Easy* **Objective:** *Essay*

12. Student essays should indicate that Tasha is a stubborn, spirited, loving person. She is shown to be stubborn by her initial refusal to baby-sit for Junior and her bossy treatment of him. Her behavior after he is lost shows her spirited nature and her loving side. Tasha is willing to risk personal harm to find him. Her prayer for Junior's safety and her statement that "a part of me was gone" also show her love for him.

Difficulty: *Average* **Objective:** *Essay*

13. Student essays should note that the reader would know Junior's thoughts and feelings but not Tasha's. As a result, Junior would become the main character and his conflict the basis of the plot. There would be no suspense about Junior's safety since the reader would be with him. Most students would find this takes away from the story. Some might like the idea of watching Tasha searching for her brother knowing he is safe.

Difficulty: *Challenging* **Objective:** *Essay*

14. Student essays should make some of the following observations: Tasha feels burdened by having to take care of Junior, who follows her like "a tail." Because of Junior, she cannot leave the block and freely play with her friends. She breaks her mother's rules by going to play in the park and telling Junior to get lost. After he does just that, Tasha realizes how much he means to her. By the end of the story, she has learned the importance of living up to her responsibilities. Therefore, the conflict has helped her learn some important lessons.

Difficulty: *Average* **Objective:** *Essay*

Oral Response

15. Oral responses should be clear, well organized, and well supported by appropriate examples from the literary work.

Difficulty: *Average* **Objective:** *Oral Interpretation*

Selection Test A, p. 35

Critical Reading

1. ANS: D   DIF: Easy   OBJ: Comprehension
2. ANS: B   DIF: Easy   OBJ: Literary Analysis
3. ANS: B   DIF: Easy   OBJ: Reading

4. ANS: A   DIF: Easy   OBJ: Comprehension
5. ANS: B   DIF: Easy   OBJ: Comprehension
6. ANS: A   DIF: Easy   OBJ: Comprehension
7. ANS: C   DIF: Easy   OBJ: Interpretation
8. ANS: A   DIF: Easy   OBJ: Literary Analysis
9. ANS: C   DIF: Easy   OBJ: Reading
10. ANS: D   DIF: Easy   OBJ: Interpretation
11. ANS: B   DIF: Easy   OBJ: Interpretation

Vocabulary and Grammar

12. ANS: D   DIF: Easy   OBJ: Vocabulary
13. ANS: A   DIF: Easy   OBJ: Vocabulary
14. ANS: C   DIF: Easy   OBJ: Grammar
15. ANS: A   DIF: Easy   OBJ: Grammar

Essay

16. Student essays might mention that Tasha is spirited and stubborn, as shown by her initial refusal to watch her brother and her bossy way with him. Her behavior after he is lost reveals her spirited nature and her loving side. Essays might note that Tasha is willing to risk personal harm to find Junior and bring him home safely. Her prayer for her brother's safety and her statement that "a part of me was gone" also show her love for him.

Difficulty: *Easy*

Objective: *Essay*

17. Student essays should note that at the beginning of the story, Tasha does not want the responsibility of her brother's care and thinks he is a pest. However, the near-loss of her brother leads her to realize that he is important to her and that he is her responsibility. By the end of the story, Tasha takes good care of her brother and is glad to do it. Essays might say that Tasha learned to enjoy her brother and her responsibility.

Difficulty: *Easy*

Objective: *Essay*

18. Student essays should make some of the following observations: Tasha is unhappy about having to take care of Junior, who follows her like "a tail." Because of Junior, she cannot leave the block to play with her friends. She breaks her mother's rules by going to play in the park and telling Junior to get lost. After he does just that, Tasha realizes how much he means to her. By the end of the story, she has learned how to make things work for everybody. Therefore, the conflict turns out to be good for her.

Difficulty: *Easy*

Objective: *Essay*

Selection Test B, p. 38

Critical Reading

1. ANS: B   DIF: Challenging   OBJ: Reading
2. ANS: B   DIF: Average   OBJ: Literary Analysis
3. ANS: D   DIF: Challenging   OBJ: Reading

4. ANS: C	DIF: Challenging	OBJ: Literary Analysis
5. ANS: A	DIF: Challenging	OBJ: Reading
6. ANS: B	DIF: Average	OBJ: Comprehension
7. ANS: A	DIF: Average	OBJ: Comprehension
8. ANS: C	DIF: Average	OBJ: Reading
9. ANS: A	DIF: Challenging	OBJ: Reading
10. ANS: B	DIF: Average	OBJ: Comprehension
11. ANS: D	DIF: Challenging	OBJ: Interpretation
12. ANS: B	DIF: Average	OBJ: Literary Analysis
13. ANS: C	DIF: Challenging	OBJ: Interpretation

Vocabulary and Grammar

14. ANS: B	DIF: Average	OBJ: Vocabulary
15. ANS: C	DIF: Average	OBJ: Vocabulary
16. ANS: D	DIF: Average	OBJ: Grammar
17. ANS: A	DIF: Average	OBJ: Grammar

Essay

18. Student essays should note that Tasha is a spirited, stubborn, loving person. She is shown to be stubborn by her initial refusal to watch her brother and her bossy treatment of him. Her behavior after he is lost reveals her spirited nature and her loving side. Tasha is willing to risk personal harm to find him and bring him home safely. Her prayer for her brother's safety and her statement that "a part of me was gone" also show her love for him.

    Difficulty: *Average*

    Objective: *Essay*

19. Student essays should note that at the beginning, Tasha does not want the responsibility of her brother's care. However, the near-loss of her brother leads her to realize that he is important to her and that he is indeed her responsibility. Essays should note that by the end of the story, Tasha is obeying her mother's commands and taking good care of her brother. Tasha has learned to be responsible and to enjoy her responsibility.

    Difficulty: *Average*

    Objective: *Essay*

20. Student essays should make some of the following observations: Tasha feels burdened by having to take care of Junior, who follows her like "a tail." Because of Junior, she cannot leave the block and freely play with her friends. She breaks her mother's rules by going to play in the park and telling Junior to get lost. After he does just that, Tasha realizes how much he means to her. By the end of the story, she has learned the importance of living up to her responsibilities. Therefore, the conflict has helped her learn some important lessons.

    Difficulty: *Average*

    Objective: *Essay*

"Dragon, Dragon" by John Gardner

Vocabulary Warm-up Exercises, p. 42

A. 1. novels
2. poems
3. lair
4. labored
5. maidens
6. slicing
7. strolled
8. merely

B. Sample Answers
1. The eldest person in my house is my grandfather.
2. In *The Hobbit*, Bilbo has to slay Smaug, the dragon.
3. I had to show patience while waiting for my appointment in the dentist's office.
4. *Finding Nemo* made a big impression on me.
5. I was annoyed when it started to rain yesterday since I had no umbrella.
6. If you don't act in a decent way, people will not like you.
7. I prefer pizza to chicken.
8. The mouse was tempted by the cheese to walk into the mousetrap.

Reading Warm-up A, p. 43

Sample Answers
1. stories; *Novels* are books that tell long, made-up stories.
2. a dragon's home
3. (dragons' heads); *Slicing* means "cutting."
4. They are *only* make-believe.
5. mermaids; *Maidens* are young women.
6. (to find a real mermaid); I have *labored* to improve my grades.
7. it always has a single long horn sticking out of its forehead; I like the rhythm and rhyme of *poems*.
8. (no unicorn); *Strolled* means "walked in a slow and relaxed way."

Reading Warm-up B, p. 44

Sample Answers
1. send his knights to slay it; I was *tempted* to eat all the ice cream, but I decided not to do it.
2. The knights would *slay* the dragon.
3. No; *eldest* means "oldest," so there are no children older than the *eldest* son.
4. (terrible); My report card made a big impression on me; it was the first time I had ever gotten straight A's.
5. Attila would *prefer* not to kill the dragon.
6. It seems to me that dragons are probably good and honest creatures all in all.

7. his younger brother didn't agree with his suggestion; *Annoyed* means "feeling bothered or disturbed."

8. (with this dragon); *Patience* is "the ability to wait without getting upset."

Writing About the Big Question, p. 45

A. 1. defend
   2. challenge
   3. battle; win
   4. lose

B. Sample Answers

   1. I defended my friend when a group of kids were teasing and frightening her.
   2. When I **challenged** the kids, I learned that I was braver than I thought, and that I could **oppose** others when I needed to.

C. Sample Answer

   If there was someone terrorizing my neighborhood, I would get the neighbors together to try to stop the menace. This conflict would not be bad because we would stop the person.

"Dragon, Dragon" by John Gardner

Reading: Use Details to Make Inferences, p. 46

Sample Answers

A. *Detail:* The dragon stops up chimneys.
   Detail: The dragon sets clocks back.
   Inference: The dragon is more annoying than dangerous.

B. *Detail:* The cobbler wonders if marrying the princess is a good deal.
   Detail: The cobbler feels the kingdom is too much responsibility.
   Inference: The cobbler is a sensible man.

C. *Detail:* The youngest son trembles before the dragon.
   Detail: The youngest son keeps on with his mission.
   Inference: The youngest son, while afraid, is very brave.

Literary Analysis: Characterization, p. 47

Sample Answers

Character's Words, Thoughts, and Actions: He was perfectly sure he could slay the dragon; The old man is not as wise as I thought; If I say something like that to the dragon, he will eat me up in an instant; The way to kill a dragon is to outfox him.

Others' Words, Thoughts, and Actions: The second eldest son looked at him enviously; The dragon lunged and swallowed him in a single gulp.

Direct Statements: Now the cobbler's eldest son was very clever; he didn't feel he needed his wise old father's advice.

Vocabulary Builder, p. 48

Sample Answers

A. 2. thinking
   I spent hours thinking about my poor performance in the piano recital.
   3. ruined
   The storm ruined the campground, downing trees and flooding campsites.
   4. stretched
   I stretched my neck so I could see the stage.
   5. bad ruler
   The *tyrant* put people in jail for no reason.
   6. jealously
   Tomas stared *enviously* at Paul's new soccer ball.

B. 1. F; A *refund* is money you get back, so you would receive extra money.
   2. T; A cool swim can make you feel less hot.
   3. T; People like to play the songs they enjoy over and over again.

Enrichment: Fairy Tales, p. 49

A. 1. a dragon
   2. the princess's hand in marriage and half the kingdom
   3. the cobbler's two older sons
   4. the cobbler's youngest son
   5. the poem the cobbler gives his sons
   6. The hero kills the dragon, marries the princess, and wins half the kingdom.

B. Students' original tales should include a monster, a reward offered by a king or queen, one or more unsuccessful heroes, a successful hero, a magic charm or object, and a happy ending.

"The Tail" by Joyce Hansen
"Dragon, Dragon" by John Gardner

Integrated Language Skills: Grammar, p. 50

A. Answers

       L
   1. It <u>was</u> that time of year again.
                   A   A
   2. When I <u>opened</u> the front door to the shack, I <u>stopped</u>.
                  A   L
   3. No sooner had he <u>said</u> that than I <u>felt</u> sick to my stomach.
       A   L
   4. I <u>knew</u> he <u>was</u> sad.
            L   A   A
   5. I still <u>felt</u> a little dizzy when we <u>took</u> a break to <u>eat</u> lunch.

B. Sample Answers

1. Roberto feels sad when his brother does not go to school.
2. The fruit pickers struggle to make enough money for their families.
3. Panchito reads poorly at first, but he works hard and gets better at it.
4. The heat seems like a heavy blanket laid over the workers.
5. Panchito's family moves often, going where work can be found.

Open-Book Test, p. 53

Short Answer

1. The Dragon is really more bothersome than dangerous. The "ravaging" is a series of tricks he plays to annoy people.
   Difficulty: *Average*   **Objective:** *Reading*
2. The wizard is not very good at his job and seems a bit of a fool.
   Difficulty: *Easy*   **Objective:** *Literary Analysis*
3. It tells you he is clever and thinks things through.
   Difficulty: *Average*   **Objective:** *Interpretation*
4. The oldest son tries to trick the dragon. The middle son tries to use sheer strength on the dragon. They both get eaten, so being tricky or strong will not work.
   Difficulty: *Easy*   **Objective:** *Reading*
5. The older brothers learn to always take their father's advice.
   Difficulty: *Easy*   **Objective:** *Interpretation*
6. Sample answers: obedient, responsible. These traits agree with the narrator's description: "a decent, honest boy who always minded his elders."
   Difficulty: *Average*   **Objective:** *Literary Analysis*
7. He may be reflecting, or thinking seriously, that he has made a huge mistake and should have stayed at home.
   Difficulty: *Challenging*   **Objective:** *Vocabulary*
8. The word *craned* means "stretched out for a better look." The man stretched his neck to see the parade.
   Difficulty: *Average*   **Objective:** *Vocabulary*
9. The youngest son becomes angry because the dragon is insulting the boy's father and the boy. He doesn't like to be laughed at, and he doesn't want his father to be laughed at.
   Difficulty: *Challenging*   **Objective:** *Interpretation*
10. The Dragon's belief that he cannot be defeated leads to his defeat. Because he can't stop laughing at "the poor dear boy" and his "ridiculous" poem, the boy is able to chop his head off.
    Difficulty: *Challenging*   **Objective:** *Literary Analysis*

Essay

11. Student essays may make some of these observations: The dragon ravages the countryside in silly ways that are not dangerous as in traditional fairy tales. Such details as the mention of spark plugs and cars are out of place and therefore humorous. The incompetent wizard is silly and unlike the powerful wizards in traditional tales. The eldest brother pretends to sell brushes, which is a contemporary detail. The dragon gets killed because he laughs too much.
    Difficulty: *Easy*   **Objective:** *Essay*
12. Student essays should include an appropriate moral, such as "Never disregard the advice of your elders." This moral is appropriate because ignoring their father is what made the two eldest sons fail. Essays might also refer to the king and the wizard, who learn that the wise cobbler is able to get rid of the dragon where they have failed.
    Difficulty: *Average*   **Objective:** *Essay*
13. Student essays should note an example both of direct and indirect characterization. For example, the following passage is direct characterization: "Now the cobbler's eldest son was very clever and was known far and wide for how quickly he could multiply fractions in his head." Gardner probably chose direct characterization here because it would have taken too much time to have the cobbler's eldest son actually multiply fractions in the story. The following passage is an example of indirect characterization: ". . . the king smiled, pleased with the impression he had made." Gardner probably chose indirect characterization because the actions of the self-satisfied king add humor to the story.
    Difficulty: *Challenging*   **Objective:** *Essay*
14. Student essays should make some of the following observations. The conflict is bad because of the confusion and inconvenience the dragon causes by doing such things as frightening maidens, changing house numbers, and changing around roads. The solution is a good thing because it brings to light the wisdom of the cobbler and the good qualities of his youngest son. By listening to his father's advice, the young man slays the dragon and claims the princess and half the kingdom. This is a very happy ending for all (except the dragon).
    Difficulty: *Average*   **Objective:** *Essay*

Oral Response

15. Oral responses should be clear, well organized, and well supported by appropriate examples from the literary work.
    Difficulty: *Average*   **Objective:** *Oral Interpretation*

Selection Test A, p. 56

Critical Reading

1. ANS: B   DIF: Easy   OBJ: Literary Analysis
2. ANS: C   DIF: Easy   OBJ: Literary Analysis
3. ANS: B   DIF: Easy   OBJ: Interpretation
4. ANS: C   DIF: Easy   OBJ: Comprehension
5. ANS: B   DIF: Easy   OBJ: Reading
6. ANS: A   DIF: Easy   OBJ: Literary Analysis
7. ANS: C   DIF: Easy   OBJ: Comprehension
8. ANS: B   DIF: Easy   OBJ: Comprehension
9. ANS: C   DIF: Easy   OBJ: Comprehension
10. ANS: A   DIF: Easy   OBJ: Comprehension
11. ANS: A   DIF: Easy   OBJ: Interpretation

Vocabulary and Grammar

12. ANS: C   DIF: Easy   OBJ: Vocabulary
13. ANS: A   DIF: Easy   OBJ: Vocabulary
14. ANS: C   DIF: Easy   OBJ: Grammar
15. ANS: A   DIF: Easy   OBJ: Grammar

Essay

16. Student essays should include at least three character traits from the character they choose. For example, they may characterize the king as vain, silly, and not very smart; the cobbler, as humble, wise, and patient. Students should illustrate their description with story details.

    Difficulty: *Easy*

    Objective: *Essay*

17. Student essays might include the following: The things the dragon does to ravage the countryside are funny because they are silly and are not violent or dangerous as in traditional fairy tales. The incompetent wizard is in contrast to powerful wizards in traditional tales. The eldest brother pretends to sell brushes, which is a contemporary, not a traditional, detail. The dragon is slain with laughter, not with force as in traditional tales.

    Difficulty: *Easy*

    Objective: *Essay*

18. Student essays should make some of the following observations. The conflict is bad because the dragon does things such as frightening maidens, changing house numbers, and changing around roads. The solution is good because it gets rid of the dragon, shows the wisdom of the cobbler, and shows the good qualities of his youngest son. It is a very happy ending for all (except the dragon).

    Difficulty: *Easy*

    Objective: *Essay*

Selection Test B, p. 59

Critical Reading

1. ANS: B   DIF: Challenging   OBJ: Reading
2. ANS: B   DIF: Average   OBJ: Comprehension
3. ANS: D   DIF: Average   OBJ: Literary Analysis
4. ANS: B   DIF: Challenging   OBJ: Literary Analysis
5. ANS: A   DIF: Challenging   OBJ: Reading
6. ANS: B   DIF: Average   OBJ: Literary Analysis
7. ANS: B   DIF: Average   OBJ: Interpretation
8. ANS: B   DIF: Average   OBJ: Literary Analysis
9. ANS: B   DIF: Challenging   OBJ: Reading
10. ANS: D   DIF: Challenging   OBJ: Reading
11. ANS: C   DIF: Average   OBJ: Comprehension
12. ANS: D   DIF: Challenging   OBJ: Literary Analysis
13. ANS: A   DIF: Average   OBJ: Interpretation
14. ANS: A   DIF: Average   OBJ: Comprehension

Vocabulary and Grammar

15. ANS: A   DIF: Average   OBJ: Vocabulary
16. ANS: A   DIF: Average   OBJ: Vocabulary
17. ANS: A   DIF: Average   OBJ: Grammar

Essay

18. Student essays should include a moral, such as "Never disregard the advice of those who are older and wiser." Support for the moral should cite the failure of the two sons to complete the task because they did not take their father's advice. Essays might also refer to the king and the wizard, who learn that the wise cobbler is able to get rid of the dragon.

    Difficulty: *Average*

    Objective: *Essay*

19. Student essays should compare and contrast heroes, antagonists, obstacles, and rewards. Essays should note that comical and modern touches, such as the detail that the dragon "stole spark plugs out of people's cars," make "Dragon, Dragon" different from traditional tales.

    Difficulty: *Average*

    Objective: *Essay*

20. Student essays should make some of the following observations. The conflict is bad because of the confusion and inconvenience the dragon causes by doing such things as frightening maidens, changing house numbers, and changing around roads. The solution is a good thing because it brings to light the wisdom of the cobbler and the good qualities of his youngest son. By listening to his father's advice, the young man slays the dragon and claims the princess and half the kingdom. This is a very happy ending for all (except the dragon).

    Difficulty: *Average*

    Objective: *Essay*

"Zlateh the Goat" by Isaac Bashevis Singer

Vocabulary Warm-up Exercises, p. 63

A. 1. blanketed
2. mild
3. flakes
4. blizzard
5. experienced
6. dense
7. mighty
8. cuddled

B. Sample Answers

1. F; If you <u>resist</u> doing something, you don't want to do it.
2. F; A sense of <u>satisfaction</u> comes after a job well done.
3. T; Goats make <u>bleating</u> noises.
4. F; A <u>hesitation</u> is a pause before acting.
5. F; A person who has <u>regained</u> his or her health feels well.
6. T; "Almost every day" is often, or <u>frequently</u>.
7. T; Lettuce and tomatoes are common salad ingredients.
8. F; When you are <u>accustomed</u> to doing something, you do it often.

Reading Warm-up A, p. 64

Sample Answers

1. (this heavy snowstorm); A *blizzard* is a scary type of snowstorm.
2. <u>Temperatures were between 40 and 50 degrees</u>; *Mild* weather is neither very hot nor very cold.
3. <u>individual, snow</u>; Both snow and breakfast cereal come in *flakes*.
4. <u>people could barely see through it</u>; The fog was very *dense*.
5. (strong), (force); I think that airplanes travel at *mighty* speeds.
6. <u>pressing their bodies up against each other to stay warm</u>; It feels good to be *cuddled*.
7. <u>in a thick covering of snow</u>; The floor of my room was *blanketed* with laundry.
8. People suffered and many died; I have *experienced* traveling to another country and that was enjoyable.

Reading Warm-up B, p. 65

Sample Answers

1. <u>he was used to seeing</u>; I am *accustomed* to going to school every day.
2. A *bleating* goat sounds like a baby crying.
3. Victor was trying to <u>resist</u> watching the goats. He thought it was too scary a job.
4. <u>was also made up of</u>; The herd of goats *consisted* of a ram, three nannies, and two kids.

5. Lechuga <u>frequently</u> quarreled with the other goats and ran away; I *frequently* go hiking on the weekends.
6. Victor *regained* his feet after falling down. *Regained* means "got back."
7. (Victor stopped to think); I have moments of *hesitation* very often.
8. Victor wasn't afraid of the goats anymore; After I finish a big project, I always feel a sense of *satisfaction*.

Writing About the Big Question, p. 66

A. 1. lose
2. survival
3. challenge
4. battle

B. Sample Answers

1. My hometown was hit by a terrible hurricane two summers ago. The high winds and heavy rains flooded nearly the whole town and caused a lot of damage.
2. The hurricane **challenged** me to stay calm even though the winds were terrifying. I played a **game** with my little brothers for hours and hours to keep them from being scared.

C. Sample Answer

One positive outcome of hardship or conflict can be finding inner strength to face difficulties and becoming a stronger and better person because of them.

"Zlateh the Goat" by Isaac Bashevis Singer

Reading: Use Prior Knowledge to Make Inferences, p. 67

Sample Answers

1. Aaron and Zlateh will be caught in a dangerous snowstorm.
2. Zlateh is right that it is too dangerous to go farther.
3. Aaron will value Zlateh more than ever.

Literary Analysis: Conflict and Resolution, p. 68

A. 1. External. The opposing forces are the peasant farmers who need to grow grain and the dry weather.
2. Internal. The opposing forces are Aaron's fondness for the goat and his obedience toward his father.

B. 1. The conflict is resolved after the storm, because it brings the needed moisture to grow grain.
2. The conflict is resolved when Zlateh helps save Aaron's life and is no longer in danger of being sold.

Vocabulary Builder, p. 69

Sample Answers

A. 2. F; Someone who *exuded* despair would feel great unhappiness.

3. F; *Astray* means "lost." A sheep that has gone *astray* is probably far from the other sheep.

4. T; A *trace* is a small hint, and civilizations leave evidence of themselves even when they perish.

5. T; People in families are tied together by affection and shared values.

6. T; A breeze would make a candle flame waver, or *flicker*.

7. T; A huge palace would be rich and beautiful to see.

B. Sample answers

1. You would *explain* an idea when it was complicated and you were trying to go beyond a simple definition.

2. A clam has a shell on the outside.

3. *Extreme* sports are sports that go beyond the usual rules of safety.

Enrichment: A Map of Poland, p. 70

1. Warsaw
2. about 80 miles
3. about 40 miles
4. the Baltic Sea
5. Germany, the Czech Republic, Slovakia, Ukraine, Belarus, Lithuania, and Russia (any three)

Open-Book Test, p. 71

Short Answer

1. Aaron understands that the butcher will slaughter the goat for meat to sell to his customers.
Difficulty: *Easy*   **Objective:** *Reading*

2. Aaron is twelve and old enough to understand what hard times mean for his family. He is respectful of his father's leadership and able to set aside his own feelings to do what has to be done.
Difficulty: *Average*   **Objective:** *Interpretation*

3. The word *bound* means "tied." The two are tied together, or made closer, by their ordeal.
Difficulty: *Challenging*   **Objective:** *Vocabulary*

4. The story states, "In his twelve years Aaron had seen all kinds of weather, but he had never experienced a snow like this one."
Difficulty: *Average*   **Objective:** *Reading*

5. Inside the haystack, Aaron finds shelter, warmth, and food for Zlateh.
Difficulty: *Easy*   **Objective:** *Literary Analysis*

6. Conflict: The snow piles high, making it difficult to get enough air. Solution: Aaron bores a window through the hay and keeps the passage clear.
It is an external conflict. Aaron is struggling against nature.
Difficulty: *Average*   **Objective:** *Literary Analysis*

7. Aaron and Zlateh are very fond of each other and grow closer with their time in the haystack. Being Aaron's only companion, Zlateh becomes more like a family member than a pet. In turn, the goat totally trusts and relies on Aaron.
Difficulty: *Easy*   **Objective:** *Interpretation*

8. Aaron feels like the world of sun and family is a dream, and life in the cold, quiet, dark haystack is his "real" life.
Difficulty: *Challenging*   **Objective:** *Interpretation*

9. The word *trace* means "mark left behind by something." A person might leave footprints in the snow.
Difficulty: *Average*   **Objective:** *Vocabulary*

10. Since Zlateh helps save Aaron's life, selling her is no longer an option. Also, the snowstorm brings the cold weather, allowing Reuven to sell his furs and make the money he needs without selling the goat.
Difficulty: *Challenging*   **Objective:** *Literary Analysis*

Essay

11. Student essays will probably focus on Aaron as having the more difficult time. His only food is goat milk, and he has no one to talk to and nothing to do. He longs for companionship and thinks of the goat as family, talking to her. Meanwhile, Zlateh has plenty of patience and food (hay). She has a human on whom she depends and no complex thoughts to disturb her. So, she has little difficulty.
Difficulty: *Easy*   **Objective:** *Essay*

12. Student essays should indicate that Aaron changes his mind because his relationship with the goat changes during the storm. Aaron and Zlateh not only save each other's life but become close friends. Students should cite examples of how they take care of each other: Aaron provides shelter for Zlateh; Zlateh gives Aaron milk; they comfort each other with companionship. Aaron's internal conflict is between his obedience to his father and his loyalty to Zlateh. After what happens in the haystack, the boy sides with Zlateh.
Difficulty: *Average*   **Objective:** *Essay*

13. Student essays should indicate that Aaron both accepts and does not accept what he is given in life. He is accepting of his father's decision when he sets off to deliver the beloved goat to the butcher. Some students may indicate that he does not seem accepting of the storm since he fights for survival. Other may say that accepting his situation allows him to remain calm during the storm and thus make good decisions. During the storm, he accepts the warmth and food Zlateh has to offer and does not struggle against the darkness and silence. He waits out the storm. At the end of the story, he does not accept his father's decision that Zlateh should go to the butcher and he brings her home.
Difficulty: *Challenging*   **Objective:** *Essay*

14. Student essays should make a case and support it with some of the following observations: The storm is bad for the characters in that it threatens their lives. Aaron realizes that if he does not find shelter, they will

freeze to death. Ironically, it is nature that provides shelter in the form of the haystack. There, the boy and goat are warm, and the hay serves as food for Zlateh. The storm also solves another conflict. The cold weather accompanying the storm brings the need for the furrier's services, and Reuven no longer needs the money he was to make by selling Zlateh to the butcher.

Difficulty: *Average*   **Objective:** *Essay*

Oral Response

15. Oral responses should be clear, well organized, and well supported by appropriate examples from the selection.

Difficulty: *Average*   **Objective:** *Oral Interpretation*

Selection Test A, p. 74

Critical Reading

1. ANS: B	DIF: Easy	OBJ: Comprehension
2. ANS: A	DIF: Easy	OBJ: Reading
3. ANS: C	DIF: Easy	OBJ: Reading
4. ANS: C	DIF: Easy	OBJ: Literary Analysis
5. ANS: D	DIF: Easy	OBJ: Literary Analysis
6. ANS: A	DIF: Easy	OBJ: Interpretation
7. ANS: A	DIF: Easy	OBJ: Comprehension
8. ANS: C	DIF: Easy	OBJ: Interpretation
9. ANS: B	DIF: Easy	OBJ: Interpretation
10. ANS: D	DIF: Easy	OBJ: Comprehension
11. ANS: D	DIF: Easy	OBJ: Comprehension

Vocabulary and Grammar

12. ANS: B	DIF: Easy	OBJ: Vocabulary
13. ANS: C	DIF: Easy	OBJ: Vocabulary
14. ANS: A	DIF: Easy	OBJ: Grammar

Essay

15. Student essays should note that nature provides Aaron and Zlateh with shelter and food during the storm. The haystack is made up of dried hay, grass, and field flowers. It keeps them warm and becomes food for Zlateh.

Difficulty: *Easy*

Objective: *Essay*

16. Student essays will most likely focus on Aaron. He faced a more difficult ordeal because he ran out of food and began to have waking dreams because of the tedium. Meanwhile, Zlateh, with plenty of patience and food, had little difficulty.

Difficulty: *Easy*

Objective: *Essay*

17. Most students will make the case that on the whole the conflict is good. The storm itself is dangerous, but Aaron finds shelter for them in the haystack. There, the boy and goat are warm, and the hay serves as food for

Zlateh, who in turn provides milk for Aaron, In the end, the storm solves another conflict: The family cannot imagine selling Zlateh, and with the cold weather the furrier's services are needed. The family has enough money without selling Zlateh.

Difficulty: *Easy*

Objective: *Essay*

Selection Test B, p. 77

Critical Reading

1. ANS: A	DIF: Average	OBJ: Comprehension
2. ANS: B	DIF: Challenging	OBJ: Reading
3. ANS: A	DIF: Average	OBJ: Comprehension
4. ANS: C	DIF: Average	OBJ: Comprehension
5. ANS: D	DIF: Challenging	OBJ: Reading
6. ANS: B	DIF: Average	OBJ: Literary Analysis
7. ANS: C	DIF: Average	OBJ: Literary Analysis
8. ANS: B	DIF: Challenging	OBJ: Reading
9. ANS: C	DIF: Average	OBJ: Comprehension
10. ANS: C	DIF: Average	OBJ: Interpretation
11. ANS: A	DIF: Average	OBJ: Literary Analysis
12. ANS: B	DIF: Average	OBJ: Interpretation
13. ANS: D	DIF: Challenging	OBJ: Literary Analysis

Vocabulary and Grammar

14. ANS: A	DIF: Average	OBJ: Vocabulary
15. ANS: D	DIF: Average	OBJ: Vocabulary
16. ANS: C	DIF: Average	OBJ: Grammar
17. ANS: A	DIF: Average	OBJ: Grammar

Essay

18. Student essays should note that Aaron's difficulties include the cold, a lack of air, minimal food, and a dreamlike state brought on by the tedium. Zlateh provides warmth and food. Aaron pokes holes in the hay and snow to bring in air, and he talks to Zlateh like a sister, for company.

Difficulty: *Average*

Objective: *Essay*

19. Student essays should explain that Aaron and Zlateh not only save each other's life but become close friends during the snowstorm. Students should cite examples of how Aaron and Zlateh take care of each other: Aaron provides a shelter for Zlateh; Zlateh gives Aaron milk to drink; Aaron comforts Zlateh by talking to her; Zlateh comforts Aaron by keeping him company. Students should note that in Aaron's conflict between his obedience to his father and his loyalty and gratefulness to Zlateh, Zlateh won out.

Difficulty: *Average*

Objective: *Essay*

20. Student essays should make a case and support it with some of the following observations: The storm is bad for the characters in that it threatens their lives. Aaron realizes that if he does not find shelter, they will freeze to death. Ironically, it is nature that provides shelter in the form of the haystack. There, the boy and goat are warm, and the hay serves as food for Zlateh. The storm also solves another conflict. The cold weather accompanying the storm brings the need for the furrier's services, and Reuven no longer needs the money he was to make by selling Zlateh to the butcher.

Difficulty: *Average*
Objective: *Essay*

"The Old Woman Who Lived With the Wolves"
by Chief Luther Standing Bear

Vocabulary Warm-up Exercises, p. 81

A. 1. wherever
2. considered
3. seek
4. borders
5. territory
6. odor
7. shaggy
8. pure

B. Sample Answers

1. I would be angry to see someone on my property where they don't belong.
2. I would be sad to no longer be able to see my favorite animal.
3. A <u>foothill</u> is easier to climb because it is smaller than a mountain.
4. I would open a window to help get rid of the smell all through the house. Then I would look to see where it came from.
5. I find lying <u>offensive</u> because I don't like it when people are dishonest.
6. Yes, a <u>determined</u> person wants to achieve what he or she set out to do.
7. Yes, I would go find <u>another</u> <u>place</u> to play.

Reading Warm-up A, p. 82

Sample Answers

1. <u>thick, fur</u>; My little brother's hair is *shaggy*.
2. (the land in which the pack lives and hunts); My bedroom at home is my *territory*.
3. <u>the edges of this area of land</u>; *Borders* are the boundaries around a specific area.

4. (scent, smell); I don't like the *odor* of garbage.
5. <u>two wolves, a male and a female</u>; I *considered* my old teacher to be very important.
6. Wolves *seek* places to hunt and sleep.
7. (in the open) I like to eat lunch *wherever* I can find the best food.
8. <u>unspoiled, wilderness</u>; *Pure* means "whole and genuine."

Reading Warm-up B, p. 83

Sample Answers

1. (traveling to different locations); I once *journeyed* to Philadelphia on a bus.
2. <u>If food supplies were running low or if the weather became too harsh</u>; When I am bored in class, I often wish I were *elsewhere*.
3. (low, hilly land); The *foothills* of the Appalachian Mountains are near the town where I live.
4. The Sioux thought it was *offensive* to have other tribes on their land. To be *offensive* is "to be unpleasant and irritating."
5. <u>came onto their land</u>; I think it is wrong to *trespass* on other people's land; to trespass means you are there without permission.
6. The Sioux were *determined* to protect their land because it was under attack from foreigners.
7. Sioux warriors *perished* in the attack.
8. All sorts of fruits and vegetables grow *all through* the state of California, including strawberries, grapes, and lettuce.

Writing About the Big Question, p. 84

A. 1. convince
2. survival
3. resolve

B. Sample Answers

1. I was lost once on a hiking trip with my family. I was looking at a weird mushroom and didn't notice everyone had gone ahead of me. I stayed where I was until they found me.
2. I would **convince** a friend who is lost to stay in one place or find a place nearby that is protected. My own experience helped me **conclude** that staying put is the safest way to get found.

C. Sample Answer

Sometimes when we choose to trust instead of fear something, we learn that the thing we feared isn't nearly as scary as we had thought it was. Trusting someone, for example, can be the start of overcoming a conflict.

"The Old Woman Who Lived With the Wolves"
by Chief Luther Standing Bear

Reading: Use Prior Knowledge to Make Inferences, p. 85

Sample Answers

1. Marpiyawin loves her dog enough to face danger for him.
2. Marpiyawin believes that the wolves are friendly.
3. Marpiyawin has become part of the wolf group.

Literary Analysis: Conflict and Resolution, p. 86

A. 1. External. The opposing forces are the dog's disappearance and Marpiyawin's wanting him to be near her.

2. External. The opposing forces are the snowfall and Marpiyawin's desire to be warm and comfortable.

3. Internal. The opposing forces are Marpiyawin's desire to rejoin her people and her desire to stay with the wolves.

B. 1. The conflict is never fully resolved, as Marpiyawin does not find the dog.

2. The conflict is resolved when Marpiyawin finds shelter in the cave and is taken care of by the wolves.

3. The conflict is resolved when Marpiyawin rejoins her people but retains contact with the wolves.

Vocabulary Builder, p. 87

Sample Answers

A. 2. F; Someone who *traversed* a frozen pond would have walked across the surface.

3. T; *Coaxed* means "gently urged," and a frightened child should be gently urged.

4. F; An *offensive* smell is a bad smell, and people most likely would not buy an offensive-smelling pizza.

5. F; Marpiyawin was cared for by the wolves and did not die.

6. T; Someone who *trespasses* is going where they aren't supposed to go.

7. F; *Scarce* means "rare," and there are a lot of people in cities.

8. T; It would be strange and unexplainable to see someone disappear, so it would *mystify* you.

B. **Sample Answers**

1. An *indecisive* person would have trouble making up his or her mind about which ice cream flavor to choose.

2. You might not be able to describe a view that is really beautiful or dramatic.

3. You should dress in casual clothes for an *informal* party.

Enrichment: Reintroducing Wolves, p. 88

Students should choose one position, pro or con, and support their position with points from the chart and facts from their own research.

"The Old Woman Who Lived With the Wolves"
by Chief Luther Standing Bear
"Zlateh the Goat" by Isaac Bashevis Singer

Integrated Language Skills: Grammar, p. 89

A. Answers

2. present participle
3. present
4. past participle
5. past participle
6. present participle
7. past

B. Sample Answers

1. Mary and Pam decide to take the bus instead of walking home.
2. Kevin became my best friend this fall.

Open-Book Test, p. 92

Short Answer

1. Since they move with their tipis and their families, the Sioux always feel at home.
   Difficulty: *Easy*   **Objective:** *Interpretation*

2. During the move, Marpiyawin loses her dog.
   Difficulty: *Average*   **Objective:** *Literary Analysis*

3. What I Know: a person like that is sure of herself.
   Inference: Marpiyawin is very independent and confident.
   Difficulty: *Average*   **Objective:** *Reading*

4. Marpiyawin is trapped in a blizzard.
   Difficulty: *Easy*   **Objective:** *Literary Analysis*

5. She shows no fear of the wolves when she wakes up, because in her dream the wolves told her they would help her. Showing no fear is a clue that she believes in her dreams.
   Difficulty: *Easy*   **Objective:** *Reading*

6. The word *traversed* means "went across." To go across a river, the tribe might have used boats.
   Difficulty: *Challenging*   **Objective:** *Vocabulary*

7. The word *offensive* means "unpleasant." Students may choose any unpleasant odor, such as that of rotten eggs or a skunk.
   Difficulty: *Average*   **Objective:** *Vocabulary*

8. Marpiyawin is sad to say good-bye to the wolves, but she wants to rejoin her people.
   Difficulty: *Challenging*   **Objective:** *Literary Analysis*

9. The wolves helped Marpiyawin stay alive during the storm and ask her for this favor in return. She is very grateful to them for their kindness and wants to repay them by providing the meat.
   Difficulty: *Average*   **Objective:** *Interpretation*

10. The relationship is one of fondness and mutual respect. Marpiyawin continues to feed the wolves when food is

scarce. They, in turn, give her warnings about blizzards and enemies.

Difficulty: *Challenging* **Objective:** *Interpretation*

Essay

11. Student essays should note that Marpiyawin's action of taking off by herself with no fear of getting lost shows that she is independent and confident. When she shows no fear of the wolves, she reveals that she is courageous and trusting. Later, when she continues to feed the wolves, she shows that she is loyal and true to her word.
    Difficulty: *Easy* **Objective:** *Essay*

12. Student essays should indicate that the Sioux are wary and distrustful of wolves at the beginning of the story. Marpiyawin feels the same way until she has her dream, which tells her to trust the wolves. Students should note that the wolves' kindness toward her reinforces the trust in them that she gained through her vision. Her people change their attitude when they realize that the wolves saved Marpiyawin. They then gain an attitude of respect toward the wolves, anxious to hear what the animals tell Marpiyawin.
    Difficulty: *Average* **Objective:** *Essay*

13. Student essays should note that the quotation illustrates the lesson that humans and animals have similar opinions of each other. For example, the humans in the story are uneasy about the wolves, and the wolves are not used to being with humans. Students might note that if both humans and animals realize that they view each other in a similar way, they might gain a new respect for each other and be better able to coexist.
    Difficulty: *Challenging* **Objective:** *Essay*

14. Student essays will probably indicate that Marpiyawin would not think that conflict is always bad. She starts out to find a lost dog and is caught in a bad storm. Because she seeks shelter from the storm, she finds the wolves. Her experience with the wolves is very positive and changes her attitude toward them. When she finally rejoins her people, her story causes the Sioux to have a new respect and fondness for the wolves. Marpiyawin's new identity becomes "The Old Woman Who Lived with the Wolves." All of these positive results came from her original conflict.
    Difficulty: *Average* **Objective:** *Essay*

Oral Response

15. Oral responses should be clear, well organized, and well supported by appropriate examples from the selection.
    Difficulty: *Average* **Objective:** *Oral Response*

Selection Test A, p. 95

Critical Reading

1. ANS: C	DIF: Easy	OBJ: Comprehension
2. ANS: D	DIF: Easy	OBJ: Interpretation
3. ANS: B	DIF: Easy	OBJ: Literary Analysis
4. ANS: B	DIF: Easy	OBJ: Reading
5. ANS: A	DIF: Easy	OBJ: Literary Analysis
6. ANS: A	DIF: Easy	OBJ: Reading
7. ANS: D	DIF: Easy	OBJ: Comprehension
8. ANS: D	DIF: Easy	OBJ: Comprehension
9. ANS: B	DIF: Easy	OBJ: Interpretation
10. ANS: B	DIF: Easy	OBJ: Interpretation

Vocabulary and Grammar

11. ANS: A	DIF: Easy	OBJ: Vocabulary
12. ANS: B	DIF: Easy	OBJ: Vocabulary
13. ANS: C	DIF: Easy	OBJ: Grammar
14. ANS: B	DIF: Easy	OBJ: Grammar

Essay

15. Student essays should note that Marpiyawin's action of taking off by herself to find her dog shows that she is brave, independent, and thinks for herself. For example, she is not afraid of the wolves and she shows no fear during the blizzard.
    Difficulty: *Easy*
    Objective: *Essay*

16. Student essays should note that as a member of the wolf pack, Marpiyawin's life would have remained the same because she would have been part of a close-knit group and she would have traveled looking for food and water. Her life would have been different because she would not have lived in a tipi and she would not be engaged in Native American customs and traditions with her people.
    Difficulty: *Easy*
    Objective: *Essay*

17. Student essays will probably indicate that Marpiyawin would not think that conflict is always bad. When she seeks shelter from the storm, she finds the wolves. Her experience with the wolves is very positive and changes her attitude toward them. When she finally rejoins her people, the Sioux and the wolves begin a friendship that is good for all of them.
    Difficulty: *Easy*
    Objective: *Essay*

Selection Test B, p. 98

Critical Reading

1. ANS: D	DIF: Average	OBJ: Interpretation
2. ANS: C	DIF: Average	OBJ: Comprehension
3. ANS: B	DIF: Average	OBJ: Reading
4. ANS: B	DIF: Average	OBJ: Literary Analysis
5. ANS: A	DIF: Challenging	OBJ: Reading
6. ANS: C	DIF: Average	OBJ: Interpretation
7. ANS: A	DIF: Average	OBJ: Literary Analysis

8. ANS: B	DIF: Average	OBJ: Interpretation	
9. ANS: C	DIF: Challenging	OBJ: Interpretation	
10. ANS: A	DIF: Average	OBJ: Reading	
11. ANS: B	DIF: Average	OBJ: Reading	
12. ANS: D	DIF: Average	OBJ: Comprehension	
13. ANS: B	DIF: Challenging	OBJ: Interpretation	

Vocabulary and Grammar

14. ANS: C	DIF: Average	OBJ: Vocabulary	
15. ANS: A	DIF: Average	OBJ: Vocabulary	
16. ANS: A	DIF: Average	OBJ: Grammar	
17. ANS: C	DIF: Average	OBJ: Grammar	

Essay

18. Student essays should point out that the quotation illustrates the lesson that humans and animals have similar opinions of each other. For example, the humans in the story are uneasy about the wolves, and the wolves are not used to being with humans. Students might note that if both humans and animals realize that they view each other in a similar way, they might be better able to coexist.

    Difficulty: Average

    Objective: Essay

19. Student essays should point out that at the beginning of the story, the Sioux are wary and distrustful of wolves. Marpiyawin feels the same way until she has her dream. The dream tells her to trust the wolves. Students should note that the wolves' kindness toward Marpiyawin reinforces the trust in them that she gained through her vision. Her people change their attitude when they realize that the wolves saved Marpiyawin.

    Difficulty: Average

    Objective: Essay

20. Student essays will probably indicate that Marpiyawin would not think that conflict is always bad. She starts out to find a lost dog and is caught in a bad storm. Because she seeks shelter from the storm, she finds the wolves. Her experience with the wolves is very positive and changes her attitude toward them. When she finally rejoins her people, her story causes the Sioux to have a new respect and fondness for the wolves. Marpiyawin's new identity becomes "The Old Woman Who Lived With the Wolves." All of these positive results came from her original conflict.

    Difficulty: Average

    Objective: Essay

"Becky and the Wheels-and-Brake Boys"
by James Berry
"The Southpaw" by Judith Viorst

Vocabulary Warm-up Exercises, p. 102

A. 1. quarrel
2. broad
3. interfere
4. terrific
5. average
6. crushed
7. envy
8. sympathy

B. Sample Answers

1. I would notice if someone barged into the room because he or she would be loud and rude.
2. Yes, a trophy is an award for having played well, so my friend should be congratulated.
3. I am uncertain about my plans for the future; I don't know just what I want to do.
4. A permanent change would last forever—that is what the word means.
5. Since baseball is a team sport, it doesn't necessarily prove that one ballplayer is good. Usually, however, most players on a winning team are good.
6. That would be unreasonable, because six hours is too long to practice something every day.
7. A person who plays in the outfield can't cover home plate because he or she is too far away.

Reading Warm-up A, p. 103

Sample Answers

1. She was jealous; I feel *envy* toward people who get A's without studying.
2. (get involved with); I don't like to *interfere* in other people's business.
3. when we argue; The last *quarrel* I had was with my brother this morning over who would take out the dog.
4. Mom; I don't have *sympathy* for people who are selfish.
5. (hopes); *Crushed* means "squashed or destroyed."
6. She scores a lot of goals and is a really good soccer player; I am *terrific* at making chocolate chip cookies.
7. (two goals a game); My *average* in baseball is .231.
8. (filled her whole face); The word *broad* means "full or wide."

Reading Warm-up B, p. 104

Sample Answers

1. (stadiums); A *ballplayer* is an athlete who plays some sort of ballgame.
2. They thought the rules of the game made it too hard for women to play well; I think it's *unreasonable* for my parents to think I can always do just what they ask.
3. Women's teams *abruptly came* onto the baseball scene in 1942; To have *barged* means to have "entered loudly or suddenly."
4. It would feel great to win the *trophy* for my league, because it means you are the best.
5. The *outfield* is the part of the baseball field that is far outside the baseball diamond.

6. She became a *menace* by being a great pitcher; Having great skills would make an opposing player a *menace*.

7. It means that the AAGBL did not last; I hope that women have a *permanent* position in professional base-ball soon.

8. The league owners were *uncertain* that women should play professional sports along with men. I am *uncertain* about my own ability to play baseball.

Writing About the Big Question, p. 105

A. 1. game
2. oppose
3. win; lose
4. resolve

B. Sample Answers

1. My volleyball team played against a team whose players were much taller and tougher than we were.

2. We were able to **win** the game because we wore the **opposing** team down. We kept returning their shots until they were exhausted!

C. Sample Answer

When a person uses force in a conflict to get what he or she wants, he or she might find that winning that way is not as satisfying as if he or she had won by doing something clever or brave.

Literary Analysis: Comparing Characters' Traits and Motives, p. 106

Sample Answers

A. 1. She is thoughtful and a little vain.
2. The external factor is that the boys will see her when she goes out.
3. Becky's internal motivation is her desire to look nice.

B. 1. pride, a sense of humor
2. friendliness, practicality
3. Dear Richard,

   I have to have my tonsils taken out tomorrow. I know that my throat will be too sore for me to catch at next week's game. Maybe Janet could take my place.
   Alfie

Vocabulary Builder, p. 107

A. Sample Answers

2. Eating junk food is a <u>menace</u> to your health.
3. I would find an eight o'clock curfew <u>unreasonable</u>.
4. A <u>reckless</u> driver might run a red light.
5. My <u>envy</u> shows when my friend wears her new tennis shoes.

B. Sample Answers

1. I might find it *enviable* if someone had a horse.
2. I saw someone jump *recklessly* into a river.

3. I have always found singing *enviable*.
4. I think people are sometimes *reckless* because they don't think before they act.

Open-Book Test, p. 109

Short Answer

1. Granny-Liz means that some things are just for boys, and girls should not try to do them.
   Difficulty: *Challenging*   **Objective:** *Interpretation*

2. Becky and her mother love each other, but they do not always agree. Becky's mother does not see why her daughter needs a bike, but she does want the girl to be happy. Because she loves her daughter, she does allow Becky to have a bike at the end of the story.
   Difficulty: *Average*   **Objective:** *Interpretation*

3. The word *envy* means "unhappy feeling of wanting what someone else has." Becky feels envy as she watches the Wheels-and-Brake Boys ride their bikes at the beginning of the story.
   Difficulty: *Average*   **Objective:** *Vocabulary*

4. The word *former* means "past." In the past, Becky made her centipede crawl up Shirnette's back. As payback, Shirnette lets a cockroach fly into Becky's blouse.
   Difficulty: *Challenging*   **Objective:** *Vocabulary*

5. Since Richard wants Janet to once more name her gold-fish after him, the two seem to be friends again.
   Difficulty: *Easy*   **Objective:** *Interpretation*

6. Becky's reason for fighting is that Shirnette lets a cock-roach fly into her blouse. Even though this is payback for one of Becky's pranks, she picks a fight with her friend. Janet's reason for fighting is that Richard will not allow her on his team because she is a girl.
   Difficulty: *Easy*   **Objective:** *Literary Analysis*

7. The main idea shared by both stories is that it pays to continue to work toward a goal. Becky never gives up asking for a bike. Janet does not give up trying to per-suade Richard to let her pitch on his baseball team.
   Difficulty: *Challenging*   **Objective:** *Interpretation*

8. Becky and Janet are both very determined to get what they want. Becky does not give up her hopes of getting a bike. Janet does not give up until she convinces Richard to let her pitch on his team.
   Difficulty: *Average*   **Objective:** *Literary Analysis*

9. Becky's mom: fireman Mr. Dean, buys a bike; Richard: big losing streak, asks Janet to play The external factors play a big part in each main character's success.
   Difficulty: *Average*   **Objective:** *Literary Analysis*

10. Students who say external should cite examples, such as the influence of the losing streak and the fireman on the outcome. Students who say internal should cite Becky's desire to have a bike and Janet's desire to be on the team.
    Difficulty: *Challenging*   **Objective:** *Literary Analysis*

Essay

11. Student essays should note that both Becky and Janet feel that girls can and should partake in activities that boys do. Becky believes she should be able to ride a bike with boys, and Janet believes she should be able to play baseball with boys. Some students may say that the girls' ideas create problems and conflicts with family and friends. Others may note that the girls' strong beliefs help them to succeed in changing people's minds.

   Difficulty: *Easy*   **Objective:** *Essay*

12. Student essays might note that because the focus of the stories as written is that girls can do anything boys can do, the stories would be radically different. They might point out that the conflict in "Becky. . ." would not exist, because neither the mother nor the grandmother would object to a boy having a bike or not helping at home. In "The Southpaw," the conflict would also disappear because the issue of a girl being on a boys' team would be gone.

   Difficulty: *Average*   **Objective:** *Essay*

13. Student essays might focus on Becky's attempt to sell her father's helmet to the fireman. The external factor is that her mother does not have enough money to buy Becky a bike. The internal factors are the sadness she feels for her mother and her desire for the bike. Students might point out that Janet writes to Richard in "The Southpaw." The external factor is that Richard will not let her play on his baseball team. The internal factors are anger at Richard for his ideas about girls and her pride in her own abilities.

   Difficulty: *Challenging*   **Objective:** *Essay*

14. Student essays will probably say that the conflicts are good for the girls since they serve to make the characters stronger. Becky's conflict involves her trying to get a bike even though her mother cannot afford to buy it, and others' beliefs that bike riding is not a proper activity for a girl. As a result of the conflict, she learns the importance of perseverance and gains a new insight into her mother's financial limitations. Janet's conflict is with her friend Richard, who refuses to allow a girl on his baseball team. By not giving in and presenting her abilities in a positive light, she gets Richard to change his mind.

   Difficulty: *Average*   **Objective:** *Essay*

Oral Response

15. Oral responses should be clear, well organized, and well supported by appropriate examples from the selections.

   Difficulty: *Average*   **Objective:** *Oral Interpretation*

Selection Test A, p. 112

Critical Reading

1. ANS: D   DIF: Easy   OBJ: Comprehension
2. ANS: A   DIF: Easy   OBJ: Interpretation
3. ANS: C   DIF: Easy   OBJ: Comprehension
4. ANS: C   DIF: Easy   OBJ: Literary Analysis
5. ANS: B   DIF: Easy   OBJ: Literary Analysis
6. ANS: D   DIF: Easy   OBJ: Comprehension
7. ANS: D   DIF: Easy   OBJ: Literary Analysis
8. ANS: A   DIF: Easy   OBJ: Interpretation
9. ANS: A   DIF: Easy   OBJ: Literary Analysis
10. ANS: B   DIF: Easy   OBJ: Comprehension
11. ANS: C   DIF: Easy   OBJ: Interpretation
12. ANS: B   DIF: Easy   OBJ: Interpretation

Vocabulary

13. ANS: D   DIF: Easy   OBJ: Vocabulary
14. ANS: A   DIF: Easy   OBJ: Vocabulary

Essay

15. Student essays should point out that both Becky and Janet believe that girls can and should share activities that boys do. Essays should include that Becky believes she should be able to ride bikes with boys and Janet believes she should be able to play baseball with boys. Some students may say that the girls' ideas create problems and conflicts within their family and/or friendships. Others may say that the girls' strong beliefs help them to be the first to challenge stereotypes and obstacles.

   Difficulty: *Easy*

   Objective: *Essay*

16. Student essays should note that in "Becky and the Wheels-and-Brake Boys," Becky tries to sell her father's helmet because her mother does not have enough money to buy Becky a bike. She feels sorry for her mother, and she wants the bike. In "The Southpaw," Janet writes to Richard because Richard will not let her play on his baseball team. She is angry with him because of his ideas about girls, and she has pride in her own abilities. The characters both want to prove to others that girls can be successful in activities usually designated for boys.

   Difficulty: *Easy*

   Objective: *Essay*

17. Student essays will probably indicate that Becky and Janet would not think that these conflicts were bad for them. Instead, by asserting themselves with determination and facing conflict with confidence, they were able to succeed.

   Difficulty: *Easy*

   Objective: *Essay*

Selection Test B, p. 115

Critical Reading

1. ANS: B	DIF: Average	OBJ: Comprehension
2. ANS: B	DIF: Challenging	OBJ: Literary Analysis
3. ANS: D	DIF: Challenging	OBJ: Comprehension
4. ANS: C	DIF: Average	OBJ: Interpretation
5. ANS: A	DIF: Average	OBJ: Literary Analysis
6. ANS: A	DIF: Average	OBJ: Interpretation
7. ANS: C	DIF: Average	OBJ: Literary Analysis
8. ANS: C	DIF: Average	OBJ: Comprehension
9. ANS: C	DIF: Challenging	OBJ: Literary Analysis
10. ANS: D	DIF: Average	OBJ: Literary Analysis
11. ANS: D	DIF: Average	OBJ: Interpretation
12. ANS: B	DIF: Challenging	OBJ: Comprehension
13. ANS: C	DIF: Average	OBJ: Interpretation
14. ANS: A	DIF: Challenging	OBJ: Literary Analysis
15. ANS: C	DIF: Average	OBJ: Comprehension

Vocabulary

16. ANS: C	DIF: Average	OBJ: Vocabulary
17. ANS: B	DIF: Average	OBJ: Vocabulary
18. ANS: D	DIF: Average	OBJ: Vocabulary

Essay

19. Student essays should point out that both Becky and Janet believe that girls can and should do activities that may be regarded as proper only for boys. Essays should include the following: Becky believes that she should be able to ride bikes with the boys, while Becky's mother and grandmother believe that riding a bike is improper for a girl. Janet believes that she should be able to play on a baseball team with boys, while Richard believes that girls aren't good ballplayers. Essays might include that the girls' attitudes create problems and conflicts in their relationships or that the girls' attitudes help them overcome the problems that others create.

    Difficulty: *Average*

    Objective: *Essay*

20. Student essays might say that in "Becky and the Wheels-and-Brake Boys," Becky experiences a change in the way she sees her mother's financial situation. This allows her to take action to earn money for a bicycle. As a result, she acquires the bike she wants. In "The Southpaw," Richard experiences a change in the way he sees girls. Once he realizes how talented Janet is, he also has to view other girls as potentially good athletes. This change in perspective leads to a renewed friendship with Janet.

    Difficulty: *Average*

    Objective: *Essay*

21. Student essays might discuss that in "Becky and the Wheels-and-Brake Boys," Becky tries to sell her father's helmet to the fireman. The external factor is that her mother doesn't have enough money to buy Becky a bike. The internal factors are the sadness she feels for her mother and her desire for the bike. Her actions reflect her determination and caring. In "The Southpaw," Janet writes to Richard. The external factor is that Richard will not let her play on his baseball team. The internal factors are anger at Richard for his ideas about girls and her pride in her own abilities. Her actions reflect her stubbornness and pride.

    Difficulty: *Challenging*

    Objective: *Essay*

22. Student essays will probably say that the conflicts are good for the girls since they serve to make the characters stronger. Becky's conflict involves her trying to get a bike even though her mother cannot afford to buy it and others' beliefs that bike riding is not a proper activity for a girl. As a result of the conflict, she learns the importance of perseverance and gains a new insight into her mother's financial limitations. Janet's conflict is with her friend Richard, who refuses to allow a girl on his baseball team. By not giving in and presenting her abilities in a positive light, she gets Richard to change his mind.

    Difficulty: *Average*

    Objective: *Essay*

Writing Workshop

Review: Integrating Grammar Skills, p. 119

A. 1. B; 2. C; 3. A; 4. B

B. 1. rang; 2. striving; 3. lying; 4. driven

Benchmark Test 3, p. 120

MULTIPLE CHOICE

1. ANS: A
2. ANS: B
3. ANS: C
4. ANS: D
5. ANS: A
6. ANS: C
7. ANS: C
8. ANS: C
9. ANS: A
10. ANS: B
11. ANS: D
12. ANS: B

13. ANS: A
14. ANS: B
15. ANS: C
16. ANS: C
17. ANS: C
18. ANS: B
19. ANS: C
20. ANS: B
21. ANS: C
22. ANS: B
23. ANS: A
24. ANS: D

ESSAY

25. Students' ads should make clear the task or job that needs to be done, the hours and days, the pay, and the qualifications of those who should apply. Ads should be short and might use abbreviations.

26. Students should clearly state a general point of view and then list reasons and examples to support that view.

27. Reviews should include a summary of important features of the work, the writer's feelings about the work, a clear organization, and details that support each main idea.

"The Circuit" by Francisco Jiménez

Vocabulary Warm-up Exercises, p. 128

A.
1. signaling
2. hesitantly
3. accompanied
4. original
5. dizzy
6. sunset
7. peak
8. stained

B. Sample Answers
1. A *husky* man might help carry a heavy suitcase.
2. You could not type with your hands *clasped* because you need your hands apart, not held together, for typing.
3. He would have less space because he received the comics and would need a place to put them.
4. Reading is not something that comes naturally but is something we think about. It is not an *instinct*.
5. Yes, I would check carefully and completely to make sure that nothing was burning if I noticed a strange smell.
6. No, he would be supervising, not doing the work.

Reading Warm-up A, p. 129

Sample Answers

1. world stops spinning; I might get *dizzy* after riding on a Ferris wheel.
2. (perfect ripeness); I like to eat tomatoes at their *peak* when they are juicy.
3. the arrival of spring; *Signaling* means "calling attention to."
4. Peaches are stained; *Stained* means "colored or marked."
5. (yellow and red); I love watching the *sunset* down by the river.
6. (better farming methods); A cookie might be *accompanied* by a glass of milk.
7. New farming methods produced hardier plants than the *original* methods.
8. fruit and vegetables becoming available all year; I might make new friends *hesitantly*.

Reading Warm-up B, p. 130

Sample Answers

1. (weak); A *husky* person is large and powerful.
2. tightly together; I *clasped* my hands together the first time I heard my favorite band.
3. She felt she needed to try everything; It's important to do a job carefully and completely because otherwise things can go wrong.
4. The *foreman* works at the mill and hires workers.
5. Dawn could *sense* the frustration in her father's voice when he said the mill wasn't hiring. To *detect* means to "sense or pick up on something."
6. The *drone* of machinery is a constant humming sound that is probably very annoying.
7. No, she just did it without thinking. *Instinct* means you don't think about it.
8. He *acquired* a car. I just *acquired* a new sound wave radio.

Writing About the Big Question, p. 131

A.
1. challenge
2. resolve
3. convince
4. conclude

B. Sample Answers
1. I moved to Portland two years ago and was the new kid. The first day of school was really scary because the school was so big, and I felt shy and afraid.
2. I forced myself to smile at one girl, and she smiled back. She was friendly, and I guess she **concluded** that I was, too. She **convinced** me to join a club she was in, and we're still friends.

C. Sample Answer

When I talk through conflicts with my family, I learn to defend my position on issues, and we often negotiate a solution that pleases everyone. Conflicts can give me the opportunity to express my opinions.

"The Circuit" by Francisco Jiménez

Reading: Draw Conclusions, p. 132

Sample Answers

A. 1. No, Papa does not want the boys to go to school. He warns them about the approach of the bus so they can hide.

2. Panchito is nervous and afraid he cannot read well enough.

3. Panchito feels comfortable and willingly asks for help.

B. I thought they were happy to see me, but when I opened the door to our shack, I saw that everything we owned was neatly packed in cardboard boxes.

Conclusion: When a family's belongings are packed in boxes, it usually means they are moving.

Literary Analysis: Theme, p. 133

Sample Answers

A. Theme: Without education, the family must continually work, move, and struggle to survive.

B. 1. The family is ready to move again. Panchito, the narrator, feels the weight of the work he has done and the work he knows he will have to continue doing.

2. Panchito's brother cannot go to school because he must work.

3. Panchito's family is moving again, interrupting his short time at school.

Vocabulary Builder, p. 134

A. Sample Answers

1. *Surplus* means "extra," so if there were extra food, people would not have been hungry.

2. *Drone* is a low-pitched hum, so it would make concentration hard.

3. When you *enroll*, you join. Megan would not have gone home to join a school club.

4. *Instinctively* means "automatically," which is how you would move if something were coming toward your face.

5. *Savoring* is tasting slowly, so you couldn't do it if you ate so fast you almost choked.

6. *Accompanied* means "went with," so it makes sense that they went with each other to the fair.

B. Sample Answers

1. Yes, you could put together peanut butter and jelly in a sandwich.

2. Yes, a *companion* is someone who keeps you company, which a pet can do.

3. No, it would be easier to close a suitcase if the items were pressed together.

Enrichment: César Chávez and Migrant Workers, p. 135

Answers

A. March 31, 1927: César Chávez is born

September 30, 1962: first convention of Chávez's National Farm Workers Association

March–April 1966: Chávez and other strikers walk 340 miles to draw attention to the suffering of farm workers

December, 1970: Chávez goes to jail for refusing to stop a lettuce boycott

April 23, 1993: Chávez dies

August 8, 1994: Chávez is awarded the Medal of Freedom

B. Student paragraphs should note that with better wages and other benefits, Panchito and his brother would probably have gone to school, had better housing and more personal possessions, and may have moved less frequently.

Open-Book Test, p. 136

Short Answer

1. Panchito does not like the thought of leaving familiar people and surroundings. He knows that he has months of very hard work ahead of him.

   Difficulty: *Challenging*   **Objective:** *Interpretation*

2. Since Papá examines the car so thoroughly, the logical conclusion is that he is a very careful man. He does not have money to waste, so he must be very careful with his purchase.

   Difficulty: *Average*   **Objective:** *Reading*

3. Sample answers: buzzing insects; wet sweat; hot dry dust. The field work is boring, difficult, and exhausting.

   Difficulty: *Average*   **Objective:** *Interpretation*

4. Panchito feels guilty that he is going to school while Roberto cannot.

   Difficulty: *Easy*   **Objective:** *Reading*

5. Panchito dislikes constantly moving from place to place because it keeps him from going to school for any length of time. He is always the new kid in school and never has time to learn or take part in new activities.

   Difficulty: *Easy*   **Objective:** *Literary Analysis*

6. Panchito looks forward to going to school and learning. He asks for help because he wants to do his best in school and learn as much as he can.

   Difficulty: *Easy*   **Objective:** *Interpretation*

7. This event highlights the theme, the pain of Panchito's constant moving, by providing a contrast. Playing the trumpet represents excitement and possibility. This is a clear contrast to the letdown Panchito feels when he comes home to find the boxes packed once again.

Difficulty: *Challenging*   Objective: *Literary Analysis*

8. The boxes represent the constant moving that Panchito's family does, the cause of his unhappiness.

Difficulty: *Average*   Objective: *Literary Analysis*

Essay

9. Student essays should suggest that Panchito's attitude is that he appreciates education and does not take it for granted. He has never settled in one place, gone to the same school for very long, or made lasting friendships. His education is frequently interrupted and is difficult to obtain, making him appreciate it all the more. Panchito's desire for extra help with English and his joy of learning music support this idea.

Difficulty: *Easy*   Objective: *Essay*

10. Student essays should note sensory images, such as the heat in the field, Panchito's thirst and getting sick to his stomach after drinking water, and his dizziness. Essays should also point out Panchito's sadness at the prospect of moving and the contrast of his joy in school with the hopelessness of his everyday life.

Difficulty: *Average*   Objective: *Essay*

11. Student essays should note that the story begins with the family moving and ends with them preparing to move again. Students should explain that Panchito's life is a circuit in which he can never get enough education to take another path in life. Essays should also note that the idea of a circuit supports the theme of growing up without education, constantly moving but never getting anywhere.

Difficulty: *Challenging*   Objective: *Essay*

12. Some students might see Panchito's conflict as bad. He has a very harsh childhood, always moving from place to place. These moves make gaining an education very difficult. These students will see Panchito's life as unfair with few redeeming qualities. Other students might not find Panchito's conflict all bad. His way of life has given him a desire and respect for education. Because Francisco Jiménez gained this respect, he was able to study and lead a successful life. Panchito can do the same thing, and perhaps even be a better person for it.

Difficulty: *Average*   Objective: *Essay*

Oral Response

13. Oral responses should be clear, well organized, and well supported by appropriate examples from the selection.

Difficulty: *Average*   Objective: *Oral Interpretation*

Selection Test A, p. 139

Critical Reading

1. ANS: A	DIF: Easy	OBJ: Literary Analysis
2. ANS: C	DIF: Easy	OBJ: Interpretation
3. ANS: D	DIF: Easy	OBJ: Interpretation
4. ANS: B	DIF: Easy	OBJ: Comprehension
5. ANS: B	DIF: Easy	OBJ: Reading
6. ANS: D	DIF: Easy	OBJ: Comprehension
7. ANS: B	DIF: Easy	OBJ: Interpretation
8. ANS: C	DIF: Easy	OBJ:Reading
9. ANS: A	DIF: Easy	OBJ: Literary Analysis
10. ANS: B	DIF: Easy	OBJ: Comprehension
11. ANS: A	DIF: Easy	OBJ: Literary Analysis

Vocabulary and Grammar

12. ANS: C	DIF: Easy	OBJ: Vocabulary
13. ANS: C	DIF: Easy	OBJ: Vocabulary
14. ANS: A	DIF: Easy	OBJ: Grammar
15. ANS: D	DIF: Easy	OBJ: Grammar

Essay

16. Student essays should note sensory images, such as the heat in the field, Panchito's thirst and getting sick to his stomach after drinking water, and his dizziness. Essays should point out Panchito's sadness at the prospect of moving and how relieved he is to go to school rather than going to work.

Difficulty: *Easy*

Objective: *Essay*

17. Student essays should note that Panchito's attitude is that he appreciates education and does not take education for granted. He has never settled in one place, gone to the same school for very long, or made lasting friendships. His education is frequently interrupted and is difficult to obtain, making him appreciate it all the more. Panchito's desire for extra help with English and his joy of learning music support this conclusion.

Difficulty: *Easy*

Objective: *Essay*

18. Some students might see Panchito's conflict as bad. He moves from place to place and has to work very hard. He is not able to go to school for long periods of time. These students will see Panchito's life as unfair and generally negative. Other students might not find Panchito's conflict all bad. His life leads him to want and respect education, just like Francisco Jiménez. Jiménez was able to study and lead a successful life. Perhaps Panchito can do the same thing.

Difficulty: *Easy*

Objective: *Essay*

Selection Test B, p. 142

Critical Reading

1. ANS: C	DIF: Challenging	OBJ: Interpretation
2. ANS: C	DIF: Challenging	OBJ: Reading
3. ANS: D	DIF: Average	OBJ: Interpretation
4. ANS: B	DIF: Average	OBJ: Comprehension
5. ANS: C	DIF: Challenging	OBJ: Interpretation
6. ANS: B	DIF: Average	OBJ: Interpretation
7. ANS: B	DIF: Average	OBJ: Reading
8. ANS: A	DIF: Average	OBJ: Comprehension
9. ANS: B	DIF: Average	OBJ: Comprehension
10. ANS: D	DIF: Challenging	OBJ: Literary Analysis
11. ANS: A	DIF: Challenging	OBJ: Literary Analysis
12. ANS: C	DIF: Challenging	OBJ: Literary Analysis
13. ANS: A	DIF: Average	OBJ: Literary Analysis

Vocabulary and Grammar

14. ANS: D	DIF: Average	OBJ: Vocabulary
15. ANS: D	DIF: Average	OBJ: Vocabulary
16. ANS: D	DIF: Average	OBJ: Grammer
17. ANS: A	DIF: Average	OBJ: Grammer

Essay

18. Student essays should note that the cycles include poverty, in which the pay for work keeps the family in poverty. Moving to find work keeps the family from having a home and acquiring an education for the children, which would help them break out of poverty.

    Difficulty: *Average*

    Objective: *Essay*

19. Student essays might use words such as *serious, solemn, despairing,* or *pessimistic* to describe "The Circuit." They should support their choice of word with examples, such as descriptions of the family's preparations for moving, the living conditions in Mr. Sanchez's garage, and Panchito's disappointing discovery that the family is moving again.

    Difficulty: *Average*

    Objective: *Essay*

20. Student essays should note that the story begins with the family moving and ends with their preparing to move again. Essays should explain that Panchito's life is a circuit in which he can never get enough education to move beyond the confines of the circular trap. Essays should also note that the idea of a circuit supports the theme of growing up without education, constantly moving but never getting anywhere.

    Difficulty: *Challenging*

    Objective: *Essay*

21. Some students might see Panchito's conflict as bad. He has a very harsh childhood, always moving from place to place. These moves make gaining an education very difficult. These students will see Panchito's life as unfair with few redeeming qualities. Other students might not find Panchito's conflict all bad. His way of life has given him a desire and respect for education. Because Francisco Jiménez gained this respect, he was able to study and lead a successful life. Panchito can do the same thing, and perhaps even be a better person for it.

    Difficulty: *Average*

    Objective: *Essay*

"The All-American Slurp" by Lensey Namioka

Vocabulary Warm-up Exercises, p. 146

A. 1. constantly
2. western
3. local
4. dictionary
5. peculiar
6. shreds
7. raw
8. dumping

B. Sample Answers

1. Diane resolved to eat more healthfully, so she stopped eating candy and drinking soda.
2. Don't draw on your face with this marker; it uses permanent ink.
3. I want a promotion; I need a better job.
4. There is a lot of food to carry, so we may need to use the platters.
5. Since Barry is the waiter, his job is to deliver the food to the table.
6. Turn on the lights! It's too murky in here.
7. I guess you must think about Jack a lot because that's the third reference you've made to him.

Reading Warm-up A, p. 147

Sample Answers

1. Soups that are made from ingredients gathered nearby; *Local* means "from the area near where you live."
2. (for lunch or dinner); Eggs, cereal, and toast are common breakfast foods in this *western* country.
3. (strange); I think it would be *peculiar* to take a bath in soup.
4. herbs and vegetables; *Raw* means "uncooked."
5. of pork or other meats; *Shreds* means "long, thin strips or pieces."
6. A *dictionary* is used to look up the meaning of words.

7. (letting the whole thing simmer); *Dumping* means "tossing or throwing something."

8. (food that offers this combination/nutritious *and* great tasting); *Constantly* means "always."

Reading Warm-up B, p. 148

Sample Answers

1. when school started again he would have to leave; *Permanent* means "long-lasting."

2. (a shortage of employees); A *reference* is a mention of something.

3. browsing through the food choices; A *menu* is a list of foods you can choose to order at a restaurant.

4. ". . . I'm very hardworking," Richard nearly shouted; I *resolved* to study hard and bring up my grades in science.

5. (a position with more responsibility); A *promotion* is a move to a better job with greater responsibilities.

6. take orders from the customers, deliver food, and figure out the checks; A *waiter* delivers food to the table in a restaurant.

7. plates of food; *Platters* are large trays used to serve or carry food.

8. (There weren't many lights); *Murky* means "hard to see in or through."

Writing About the Big Question, p. 149

A. 1. battle
2. issue
3. convince
4. negotiate

B. Sample Answers

1. My friend Mona's parents refused to let her eat any sweets at all. It was terrible to go there for dinner!

2. Mona **negotiated** with her parents and **convinced** them that when other people come to dinner, they can have a nice dessert. Now I eat there all the time!

C. Sample Answer

Getting used to differences in a new country can be a huge challenge for anyone, even for people who try to fit in. The differences can lead to conflicts that need to be resolved.

"The All-American Slurp" by Lensey Namioka

Reading: Draw Conclusions, p. 150

Sample Answers

A. 1. The attention of the party guests has turned toward the actions of the Chinese guests.

2. She realizes that the two cultures are similar in some ways.

3. She is feeling embarrassed and out-of-place.

B. Next day we took the bus downtown and she bought me a pair of jeans. In the same week, my brother made the baseball team of his junior high school. Father started taking driving lessons, and Mother discovered rummage sales.

Conclusion: Buying jeans to wear, playing baseball, driving a car, and shopping at rummage sales are American culture activities that are different from Chinese life.

Literary Analysis: Theme, p. 151

Sample Answers

A. **Theme:** Though cultures have many differences, people are alike in many ways.

B. 1. The narrator worries that she won't look like American girls, thinking her differences will set her apart.

2. Though the narrator's parents react to the teacher as Chinese, their pride in their daughter is the same as that of American parents.

3. The narrator realizes that Americans and Chinese are similar in the way they eat.

Vocabulary Builder, p. 152

A. Sample Answers

1. *Etiquette* is accepted social manners, and it is good manners to thank a host.

2. *Consumption* means "eating or drinking," so consumption is something Charley would do, not something he had.

3. *Systematic* means "orderly," so it is more likely that Luis's systematic method of studying would result in success, not failure, on the test.

4. *Smugly* means "in a self-satisfied way" and not kindly, so when the girls smiled smugly, Rachel would have felt embarrassed and left out.

5. *Emigrated* means "left one country to go to another," such as to go from Chile to America.

6. *Acquainted* means "got to know each other," so it makes sense that they got acquainted on the first day of school.

B. Sample Answers

1. Yes, an *emigrant* moves from his or her home country to a new place.

2. No, *migration* is the movement of animals from one place to another.

3. Yes, *immigrants* moved to North America from many places in the 1600s and 1700s.

Enrichment: Community Diversity, p. 153

Answers

A. Students' charts should be filled out like the example. Charts should include at least two businesses, each representing a different country or culture.

B. Student paragraphs should include at least two ways in which diversity enriches a community. Students might choose from the ways suggested: arts, crafts, music, language, literature, food, fashions, and traditions.

"The All-American Slurp" by Lensey Namioka
"The Circuit" by Francisco Jiménez

Integrated Language Skills: Grammar, p. 154

A. 1. grow, present; 2. will pick, future; 3. display, present; 4. sell, present; 5. will grow, future; 6. planted, past; 7. was, past; ate, past
B. Guidelines for evaluation: Students should write a sensible sentence with verbs in the past tense. They should then rewrite the sentence using the same verbs in the present tense. They should then rewrite the sentences using the same verbs in the future tense.

Open-Book Test, p. 157

Short Answer

1. Details: stiffly in a row, children glancing at their parents for a clue on what to do next. Conclusion: The Lins are anxious and unsure.
   Difficulty: *Average* **Objective:** *Reading*
2. The narrator is embarrassed the first time her family eats raw celery. She sees everyone staring at her family as they pull the strings out of the stalks.
   Difficulty: *Easy* **Objective:** *Interpretation*
3. The statement points out how the two families are alike. It helps the narrator realize that Americans and Chinese are not so different.
   Difficulty: *Easy* **Objective:** *Literary Analysis*
4. The narrator's father learns English in a scientific, methodical manner, suggesting he is organized and precise.
   Difficulty: *Challenging* **Objective:** *Interpretation*
5. The word *smugly* means "in a way that shows satisfaction with oneself." The father is very proud about his accomplishment.
   Difficulty: *Average* **Objective:** *Vocabulary*
6. The word *etiquette* means "acceptable social manners." At the dinner party, the narrator gets up to see if her guests need more food. When she goes with Meg for a milkshake, she insists on paying because she is the hostess.
   Difficulty: *Challenging* **Objective:** *Vocabulary*
7. Since the Lins are so startled when different foods are mixed together, they must usually eat one type of food at a time.
   Difficulty: *Average* **Objective:** *Interpretation*
8. Both families show they are unfamiliar with the other's culture. Neither family judges the other for their

behavior. This highlights the theme because it shows that people are basically the same everywhere.
   Difficulty: *Challenging* **Objective:** *Literary Analysis*
9. Sample answers: The family tries to learn English; the mother buys blue jeans for the narrator; the family celebrates the father's promotion at a fancy French restaurant recommended by his coworkers.
   Difficulty: *Easy* **Objective:** *Reading*
10. The narrator was embarrassed when her family slurped their soup in the French restaurant. Now she finds that Americans slurp too. Meg's statement illustrates the theme: cultures may be different, but people are not so different.
    Difficulty: *Average* **Objective:** *Literary Analysis*

Essay

11. Student essays will probably suggest that the title "The All-American Slurp" is a good one because it successfully reflects the theme. In the story, the narrator is embarrassed when her family slurps soup inappropriately at a restaurant. But at the end, she sees that her friend slurps her milkshake. So the slurp stands for more than a slurp. It represents how people with different customs are more alike than they think, which is the theme of the story.
    Difficulty: *Easy* **Objective:** *Essay*
12. Student essays should mention that the narrator has to deal with an unfamiliar language, learn social customs, and dress as Americans do. Problem solving includes adjusting her perspective, sharing her customs with a friend, cleverly convincing her mother of the necessity of a pair of jeans, and being a good observer of the culture around her.
    Difficulty: *Average* **Objective:** *Essay*
13. Student essays may focus on the narrator and her father. The narrator is a bit shy and easily embarrassed, as evidenced by her behavior at the French restaurant. She proceeds cautiously, speaking English slowly so as not to make mistakes. Desperately feeling the need to fit in at school, she tricks her mother into buying her a pair of jeans. The father is not at all shy and tackles challenges head on. He takes a scientific approach to learning English and confidently exhibits his mastery of difficult verb tenses. He is unafraid to try a French restaurant, even though the family members are out of their element.
    Difficulty: *Challenging* **Objective:** *Essay*
14. Student essays will probably indicate that the conflict is not a bad thing. The narrator does suffer embarrassment as she and her family try new things. She is mortified when they become the object of stares at the dinner party and when they slurp their soup at the French restaurant. However, the narrator slowly does manage to adapt. And she learns an important lesson in the process: Although customs are different, people are basically the same.
    Difficulty: *Average* **Objective:** *Essay*

Oral Response

15. Oral responses should be clear, well organized, and well supported by appropriate examples from the selection.

    Difficulty: *Average* **Objective:** *Oral Interpretation*

Selection Test A, p. 160

Critical Reading

1. ANS: B	DIF: Easy	OBJ: Interpretation
2. ANS: C	DIF: Easy	OBJ: Reading
3. ANS: B	DIF: Easy	OBJ: Comprehension
4. ANS: A	DIF: Easy	OBJ: Comprehension
5. ANS: C	DIF: Easy	OBJ: Interpretation
6. ANS: D	DIF: Easy	OBJ: Literary Analysis
7. ANS: D	DIF: Easy	OBJ: Comprehension
8. ANS: B	DIF: Easy	OBJ: Reading
9. ANS: A	DIF: Easy	OBJ: Literary Analysis
10. ANS: B	DIF: Easy	OBJ: Interpretation
11. ANS: C	DIF: Easy	OBJ: Comprehension
12. ANS: C	DIF: Easy	OBJ: Comprehension

Vocabulary and Grammar

13. ANS: A	DIF: Easy	OBJ: Vocabulary
14. ANS: C	DIF: Easy	OBJ: Grammar
15. ANS: D	DIF: Easy	OBJ: Grammar

Essay

16. Student essays should conclude that the narrator learns how to adapt or fit in to new surroundings, or that she learns that Americans and Chinese are not as different as she first thought. Ideas can be supported with details about how the narrator learns to eat, dress, and socialize.

    Difficulty: *Easy*

    Objective: *Essay*

17. Student essays might take the position that the title, "The All-American Slurp," reflects the themes of fitting in and similarities of cultures. Essays should point out that *slurp* in the title symbolizes how people with different customs are more alike than they think.

    Difficulty: *Easy*

    Objective: *Essay*

18. Student essays will probably indicate that the conflict is not a bad thing. The narrator is certainly embarrassed as she and her family try new things. She is horrified when others stare at them at the dinner party and when her family slurps their soup at the French restaurant. However, the narrator learns to adjust to her new life and that people are all basically the same.

    Difficulty: *Easy*

    Objective: *Essay*

Selection Test B, p. 163

Critical Reading

1. ANS: B	DIF: Challenging	OBJ: Reading
2. ANS: A	DIF: Average	OBJ: Literary Analysis
3. ANS: D	DIF: Challenging	OBJ: Interpretation
4. ANS: B	DIF: Average	OBJ: Interpretation
5. ANS: C	DIF: Average	OBJ: Interpretation
6. ANS: A	DIF: Average	OBJ: Comprehension
7. ANS: D	DIF: Challenging	OBJ: Reading
8. ANS: C	DIF: Average	OBJ: Comprehension
9. ANS: B	DIF: Average	OBJ: Literary Analysis
10. ANS: C	DIF: Average	OBJ: Comprehension
11. ANS: D	DIF: Average	OBJ: Literary Analysis
12. ANS: B	DIF: Challenging	OBJ: Literary Analysis

Vocabulary and Grammar

13. ANS: B	DIF: Average	OBJ: Vocabulary
14. ANS: B	DIF: Average	OBJ: Vocabulary
15. ANS: C	DIF: Average	OBJ: Grammar
16. ANS: B	DIF: Average	OBJ: Grammar
17. ANS: A	DIF: Challenging	OBJ: Grammar

Essay

18. Student essays should note that the narrator has to deal with an unfamiliar language, learning social customs, and dressing as other Americans do. Problem solving involves adjustment, sharing her own customs with a friend, convincing her parents that she needs to change, and being a good observer of the culture around her.

    Difficulty: *Average*

    Objective: *Essay*

19. Student essays should note that similarities between the Lins' dinner party and the Gleasons' dinner party are that the guests at each party made etiquette mistakes. The Gleasons do everything "wrong," according to Chinese custom, just as the Lins thought they did everything "wrong" at the Gleasons'. This supports the theme that people of any culture, who are in new situations, may make mistakes.

    Difficulty: *Average*

    Objective: *Essay*

20. Student essays will probably indicate that the conflict is not a bad thing. The narrator does suffer embarrassment as she and her family try new things. She is mortified when they become the object of stares at the dinner party and when they slurp their soup at the French restaurant. However, the narrator slowly does manage to adapt. And she learns an important lesson in the process: Although customs are different, people are basically the same.

    Difficulty: *Average*

    Objective: *Essay*

"The King of Mazy May" by Jack London

Vocabulary Warm-up Exercises, p. 167

A.
1. labor
2. delayed
3. glimpses
4. streak
5. increase
6. proceeded
7. objected
8. slackened

B. Sample Answers
1. Some people associate courage with <u>manliness</u>.
2. People on a plane would be scared if it flew <u>perilously</u> close to a mountain.
3. Too much <u>haste</u> can be dangerous when driving.
4. I read about <u>prospectors</u> when my class studied the Gold Rush.
5. It usually takes <u>newcomers</u> a while to do something well.
6. Scary movies often give me a feeling of <u>suspense</u>.
7. You are not leading in a race if people <u>overtake</u> you.
8. A <u>thermometer</u> can let you know what kind of clothes you need to wear.

Reading Warm-up A, p. 168

Sample Answers
1. <u>middle of his black beard</u>; A *streak* is a thin strip.
2. <u>disagree with</u>; I *objected* when my mother took away my allowance.
3. (write down a list of items); *Proceeded* means "went ahead and did something."
4. <u>a black-bearded man</u>; Through the window, I caught *glimpses* of cars pulling into our driveway.
5. (work); I put in some hard *labor* when we shoveled our walkway after a blizzard.
6. (the size of your muscles; the size of your wallet); *Increase* means "make larger."
7. <u>The last discoveries of gold in this area were made about two hundred years ago</u>; *Delayed* means "waited."
8. (desire to look for gold); *Slackened* means "weakened or died down."

Reading Warm-up B, p. 169

Sample Answers
1. <u>were looking for gold</u>; *Prospectors* are people who make a living by looking for gold.
2. The numbers on the *thermometer* are scary because they show that it's likely well below freezing.
3. (first-time); *Newcomers* are people who haven't done something before.

4. <u>watching to see who will win</u>; I felt <u>suspense</u> while watching the last game of the World Series.
5. (Iditarod); Butcher showed that you didn't have to be a man to win the race.
6. Racers need speed, but they also need to be careful.
7. <u>The leading team</u>; *Overtake* means "catch up to and pass."
8. (to get lost in the fierce snowstorms); *Perilously* means "dangerously."

Writing About the Big Question, p. 170

A.
1. challenge
2. defend
3. oppose
4. compete

B. Sample Answers
1. I was very small when my big brother tried to take my stuffed dinosaur away from me.
2. I **won** the battle because I screamed and cried and told our mother, and she **defended** me and got my toy back.

C. Sample Answer

If someone tried to steal my friend's property, I would defend my friend and do my best to win the item back. It would mean confronting someone, but my friendships are important to me. This conflict would not be so bad because I would be doing the right thing.

"The King of Mazy May" by Jack London

Reading: Use Prior Knowledge to Draw Conclusions, p. 171

Sample Answers

A. 2. *Prior knowledge:* A young person who can do these things is very independent.
   Conclusion: Walt is very independent.
3. *Prior knowledge:* In the Far North, winter has very short days and long nights.
   Conclusion: The story takes place in winter.
4. *Prior knowledge:* Desperate people might try to commit murder.
   Conclusion: The stampeders are desperate to stake their claim.

B. Walt is deserving of his title "King of Mazy May." Walt's actions to save Loren's claim were brave and heroic. The title of king is bestowed on a worthy leader.

Literary Analysis: Setting, p. 172

A. 1. The Klondike, at the Mazy May camp; the author states this outright
2. winter of a time in the past, during the gold rush in the Klondike; details state that the prospectors are looking for gold; the author states that the days are short and nights long

3. from Mazy May Creek to the town of Dawson; the author describes the route
4. during a day and night; details tell about the cold and the dark

B. Sample Answer

The setting is important to the story because it is necessary that it take place during the historical period of the gold rush in the Far North Klondike region, sometime after 1896.

Vocabulary Builder, p. 173

Answers

A. Sample Answers

1. No, when you *endure* something, you suffer through it.
2. No, when you *decline*, you say no.
3. Yes, he or she is likely to spring a quiz.
4. He or she is already at the top when at the *summit*.
5. Yes, you would be moving quickly.
6. Yes, *pursuing* means "chasing."

B. Sample Answers

1. You might be climbing a hill or mountain.
2. You might already be full.
3. You might be relaxing and watching television.

Enrichment: The Iditarod, p. 174

A. 1. Today's Iditarod race is about 1,150 miles long.
2. The race goes from Anchorage to Nome, Alaska.
3. A team is limited to 16 dogs. Dogs can be of any kind but are usually called "huskies." They might be Malamutes or Siberians.

B. Sample Answer

A musher must have determination and courage to complete the long, dangerous race; often they face wolves, bears, or angry moose. He or she must be able to endure cold and other uncomfortable and life-threatening weather conditions. He or she should have a rapport with dogs, which would make leading the sled dogs easier. He or she must have the physical strength to do the work and endure the hardships that occur on the trail.

Open-Book Test, p. 175

Short Answer

1. The word *manliness* suggests that Walt is on his way to being a strong adult.
   Difficulty: *Challenging*   **Objective:** *Interpretation*
2. Since life in the Yukon is primitive and rough, Walt has grown up to be tough—"talking big" with men, trading on his own, shooting moose, and driving wild wolf dogs.
   Difficulty: *Easy*   **Objective:** *Literary Analysis*

3. The word *endured* means "suffered through." Loren Hall endured breaking through the ice on Rosebud Creek and badly freezing his feet.
   Difficulty: *Average*   **Objective:** *Vocabulary*
4. Walt dislikes the claim jumpers because they steal what others have worked hard to get.
   Difficulty: *Easy*   **Objective:** *Interpretation*
5. The fact that Mr. Masters leaves Walt alone and allows him to be responsible for Loren Hall's claim means that he has confidence in Walt.
   Difficulty: *Average*   **Objective:** *Interpretation*
6. Sample answers: Gold is found in the creek; Walt follows the creek on his journey; curves along the creek make it easy for the men to catch up.
   Difficulty: *Average*   **Objective:** *Literary Analysis*
7. Walt has to run beside the sled to keep from freezing to death.
   Difficulty: *Easy*   **Objective:** *Reading*
8. The word *summit* means "highest point." If the sled is at the highest point on the ice jam, it would be most visible to the claim jumpers.
   Difficulty: *Challenging*   **Objective:** *Vocabulary*
9. The route is winding, uneven, and slippery. The dangerously low temperatures force Walt to get out of the sled and run for part of the trip.
   Difficulty: *Challenging*   **Objective:** *Literary Analysis*
10. **Sample answers: Details**: bitter cold air, men shooting at him; **Prior Knowledge**: people who are determined don't let anything stop them; **Conclusion**: Walt is brave and determined.
    Difficulty: *Average*   **Objective:** *Reading*

Essay

11. Student essays should include Walt's good qualities—his "good heart," the strength he inherited from his father, his refusal to tolerate injustice, as well as several examples of his courage. Essays should include the bad qualities of the claim jumpers' determination to steal what others have worked so hard to earn and their willingness to shoot Walt to keep him from ruining their plans.
    Difficulty: *Easy*   **Objective:** *Essay*
12. Student essays should note the extreme nature of the Klondike climate: the bitter cold and constant presence of snow and ice. Essays should also mention that there are few people, no law enforcement, and no modern communication. Prospectors have to travel to Dawson to register a claim. The cold, ice, and rugged terrain make the claim jumpers' pursuit of Walt especially exciting, and the lack of a surrounding community makes the threat posed by the claim jumpers much more menacing.
    Difficulty: *Average*   **Objective:** *Essay*

13. Student essays may note that Walt was born with a sense of justice and bravery; that his ability to react quickly in a crisis and to keep functioning through hardship are qualities that may be inborn but are also brought out in the harsh and demanding environment. Essays may indicate that Walt developed qualities of independence and self-confidence because of the demands of his environment.

    Difficulty: *Challenging*   **Objective:** *Essay*

14. Student essays should mention that Walt was in mortal danger while being pursued by the claim jumpers. Things could have turned out very badly for Walt. However, the new respect he gains from his actions is a very positive outcome, as is the fact that he saves Loren Hall's claim. Some students might mention that Walt gains more confidence from the experience. Most students should say that Walt would undertake such a conflict again since he hates injustice and has the self-confidence that he can succeed.

    Difficulty: *Average*   **Objective:** *Essay*

Oral Response

15. Oral responses should be clear, well organized, and well supported by appropriate examples from the literary work.

    Difficulty: *Average*   **Objective:** *Oral Interpretation*

Selection Test A, p. 178

Critical Reading

1. ANS: D	DIF: Easy	OBJ: Comprehension
2. ANS: A	DIF: Easy	OBJ: Literary Analysis
3. ANS: B	DIF: Easy	OBJ: Literary Analysis
4. ANS: B	DIF: Easy	OBJ: Interpretation
5. ANS: C	DIF: Easy	OBJ: Comprehension
6. ANS: B	DIF: Easy	OBJ: Reading
7. ANS: A	DIF: Easy	OBJ: Comprehension
8. ANS: C	DIF: Easy	OBJ: Reading
9. ANS: D	DIF: Easy	OBJ: Interpretation
10. ANS: C	DIF: Easy	OBJ: Interpretation
11. ANS: A	DIF: Easy	OBJ: Literary Analysis

Vocabulary and Grammar

12. ANS: D	DIF: Easy	OBJ: Vocabulary
13. ANS: D	DIF: Easy	OBJ: Vocabulary
14. ANS: B	DIF: Easy	OBJ: Grammar
15. ANS: A	DIF: Easy	OBJ: Grammar

Essay

16. Student essays should note that Walt has to overcome cold, exhaustion, and the fear of being pursued by ruthless, violent men. Students may note that Walt's desire to help his neighbor and to fight injustice probably

keeps him going. He is smart enough to outwit the claim-jumpers, strong enough to endure the trip, and fearless in danger.

Difficulty: *Easy*

Objective: *Essay*

17. Student essays should include the qualities of Walt's "good heart," the strength and bravery he inherited from his father, his refusal to tolerate injustice, and several examples of his courage. Essays should include the bad qualities of the claim-jumpers' determination to steal what others have worked hard to earn and their willingness to shoot Walt to keep him from ruining their plans.

Difficulty: *Easy*

Objective: *Essay*

18. Student essays should say that good does come from the conflict: Walt saves Loren Hall's claim and he gains great respect from the men of the Yukon. Some students might mention that Walt gains more confidence from the experience. Most students should say that Walt would behave in the same way again because he hates injustice and has the self-confidence that he can succeed.

Difficulty: *Easy*

Objective: *Essay*

Selection Test B, p. 181

Critical Reading

1. ANS: D	DIF: Challenging	OBJ: Interpretation
2. ANS: A	DIF: Average	OBJ: Literary Analysis
3. ANS: D	DIF: Challenging	OBJ: Reading
4. ANS: D	DIF: Average	OBJ: Literary Analysis
5. ANS: A	DIF: Average	OBJ: Interpretation
6. ANS: B	DIF: Challenging	OBJ: Comprehension
7. ANS: C	DIF: Challenging	OBJ: Literary Analysis
8. ANS: B	DIF: Average	OBJ: Interpretation
9. ANS: C	DIF: Average	OBJ: Comprehension
10. ANS: B	DIF: Average	OBJ: Interpretation
11. ANS: B	DIF: Average	OBJ: Comprehension
12. ANS: B	DIF: Challenging	OBJ: Interpretation

Vocabulary and Grammar

13. ANS: C	DIF: Average	OBJ: Vocabulary
14. ANS: D	DIF: Average	OBJ: Vocabulary
15. ANS: D	DIF: Average	OBJ: Grammar
16. ANS: C	DIF: Average	OBJ: Grammar
17. ANS: B	DIF: Average	OBJ: Grammar

Essay

18. Student essays may say that Walt was born with a sense of justice and bravery; that his ability to react quickly in a crisis and to keep functioning through a

long, difficult night are qualities that may be inborn but are also brought out in a harsh and demanding environment. Essays might include that Walt developed qualities of independence and being able to take care of himself because of the demands of his environment.

Difficulty: *Average*

Objective: *Essay*

19. Student essays should note the extreme nature of the Klondike climate: the bitter cold and the constant presence of snow and ice. Essays should include that there are no people around, no law enforcement, and no modern communication. Prospectors have a long trek to Dawson to register a claim; cold and ice make the claim-jumpers' pursuit of Walt especially exciting; lack of surrounding community makes the threat posed by the claim-jumpers much more menacing.

Difficulty: *Challenging*

Objective: *Essay*

20. Student essays should mention that Walt was in mortal danger while being pursued by the claim-jumpers. Things could have turned out very badly for Walt. However, the new respect he gains from his actions is a very positive outcome, as is the fact that he saves Loren Hall's claim. Some students might mention that Walt gains more confidence from the experience. Most students should say that Walt would undertake such a conflict again since he hates injustice and has the self-confidence that he can succeed.

Difficulty: *Average*

Objective: *Essay*

"Aaron's Gift" by Myron Levoy

Vocabulary Warm-up Exercises, p. 185

A. 1. shack
2. properly
3. series
4. thrashing
5. genius
6. miserable
7. soothe
8. heal

B. Sample Answers
1. F; Big dogs bark; they don't coo.
2. T; A few spoons of rice wouldn't keep hunger away for a long time.
3. F; Aviators leave the ground in planes.
4. F; On the contrary, a frenzied person would be frantic.
5. T; Mud is soft; pavement is hard and better for roller skating.
6. T; If the joke is unusually funny, people may laugh a whole lot.

7. T; Since they are birds, sparrows probably would enjoy bird food.
8. F; *Boring* is a better word for watching someone park a car than *fantastic*.

Reading Warm-up A, p. 186

Sample Answers
1. being smart; A *genius* is someone who is incredibly smart.
2. (practice medicine); *Properly* means "correctly."
3. from dogs to chickens to monkeys; A *series* is a group of related things in order.
4. (calm down); A vet can *soothe* a hurt and angry horse.
5. (a cat); *Thrashing* means "moving about in a wild way."
6. on the edge of a field; A *shack* is a small, poorly built house.
7. (animals); *Heal* means "to recover from an injury or a wound."
8. happier; *Miserable* means "very sad or uncomfortable."

Reading Warm-up B, p. 187

Sample Answers
1. pigeons hop around; *Pavement* gets very hot in the summertime.
2. (fight for food); People lining up to get tickets to a concert might act *frenzied*.
3. (permanent); *Temporarily* means "for a short time."
4. a flock of migratory birds flying overhead; I would call a fleet of monster trucks a *fantastic* sight.
5. (the city); *Sparrows* are a kind of bird.
6. crows, sparrows, and blackbirds; You might hear *doves* or *gulls* cooing.
7. It turns out that the ledges of city buildings provide homes that are just as good as the cliffs that these birds normally live in.
8. Birds can cause big problems for airplanes. An *aviator* is someone who flies a plane.

Writing About the Big Question, p. 188

A. 1. argue
2. issue
3. defend
4. convince

B. Sample Answers
1. A parent might disapprove of a friend because the friend takes up too much time or tries to talk the child into doing something he or she knows not to do.
2. I would **defend** my choice of a friend by explaining the friend's good points and trying to **convince** my parent that the friend would not cause problems.

C. Sample Answer

Children may not always agree with their parents, but it is important for them to discuss their issues and to try to resolve their conflicts reasonably. If the conflicts are resolved,they are not really bad.

"Aaron's Gift" by Myron Levoy

Reading: Use Prior Knowledge to Draw Conclusions, p. 189

Sample Answers

A. 2. *Prior knowledge:* Someone whose parent is very proud might call his child a genius.

Conclusion: Aaron's father is very proud of him.

3. *Prior knowledge:* Parents worry about gangs bringing harm to their children.

Conclusion: Aaron's mother worries that the gang will harm him.

4. *Prior knowledge:* You give a wonderful present to someone you love a lot.

Conclusion: Aaron loves his grandmother very much.

B. Aaron's grandmother knows the importance of freedom, and she wants others to enjoy freedom. Aaron believes his grandmother, who lived through a Cossack pogrom, would have let the pigeon go free. Those who have had their freedom denied know the importance of freedom for all.

Literary Analysis: Setting, p. 190

A. Answers

1. New York City; details include Tompkins Square Park, Second Avenue, and references to Brooklyn and the Lower East Side

2. sometime in the past; details include references to peddlers, roller-skates rather than roller blades, and that Aaron appears to be a first-generation American

3. The Ukraine

4. the time of Alexander the Third of Russia

B. Sample Answer

The setting is important because pigeons like Pidge are readily found in cities; many recent immigrants settled in cities; Aaron's grandmother's survival of a pogrom in the Ukraine between 1881 and 1921 is a historical experience that is very important to the story.

Vocabulary Builder, p. 191

A. Sample Answers

1. Scared; *Thrashing* means "squirming wildly."

2. No, he paused before climbing.

3. No, you *console* someone who is upset.

4. A lot; you *plead* by begging.

5. Gentle; you *coax* by asking gently.

6. Soon; *temporarily* means "for a short time."

B. Sample Answers

1. The road will probably be fixed soon.

2. It means you have to make it up on the spot.

3. They are clothes that are in style right now.

Enrichment: Becoming a Veterinarian, p. 192

Answers

A. 1. C; 2. C

B. Sample Questions

1. Why do you want to be a veterinarian?

2. What kinds of courses have you taken?

3. Do you have experience working with animals?

"The King of Mazy May" by Jack London
"Aaron's Gift" by Myron Levoy

Integrated Language Skills: Grammar, p. 193

A. Answers

1. had traveled

2. has remained

3. will have resided

4. has lived

5. had proposed

6. will have finished

B. Guidelines for evaluation: Students should write a paragraph that correctly uses several verbs in perfect tenses. They should use the past perfect, present perfect, and future perfect tenses at least once.

Open-Book Test, p. 196

Short Answer

1. The phrase "in those days" suggests that the story takes place sometime in the past during hard times.

   Difficulty: *Easy*   Objective: *Literary Analysis*

2. Aaron is a kind, thoughtful boy. This description is also supported by the thoughtful gift he wants to give his grandmother.

   Difficulty: *Easy*   Objective: *Interpretation*

3. Aaron loves and respects his grandmother, but he does not always understand her. He knows he can count on her to accept the pigeon because she is a kind person, but he does not know why she talks to the birds outside the window.

   Difficulty: *Average*   Objective: *Interpretation*

4. Mr. Kandal expresses pride in how Aaron dressed the pigeon's wounds. He is more impressed with Aaron's skill than he is upset about having a pigeon in the house.

   Difficulty: *Average*   Objective: *Reading*

5. Aaron's mother refuses to let Aaron join Carl's "gang." She thinks "those boys" are bad news and doesn't want Aaron to be around them.

   Difficulty: *Easy*   Objective: *Reading*

6. The word *consoled* means "comforted." Aaron's grandmother consoled him by kissing him and thanking him for his present, "which was even better than the pigeon."

   Difficulty: *Average*   **Objective:** *Vocabulary*

7. Sample answers for web: no peace; boots pounding on the floor; everything breaking and crashing; people and animals lying on the ground. Students might describe the setting as grim or cruel.

   Difficulty: *Challenging*   **Objective:** *Literary Analysis*

8. The Ukraine is where important events from the life of Aaron's grandmother took place. It is because of what happened to her goat at the hands of the Cossacks that Aaron wants to give her Pidge.

   Difficulty: *Average*   **Objective:** *Literary Analysis*

9. The word *hesitated* means "stopped because of indecision." He hesitated because he was unsure that bringing the pigeon to Carl was the right thing to do.

   Difficulty: *Challenging*   **Objective:** *Vocabulary*

10. Aaron's grandmother is very pleased with his gift and wants him to see how beautiful and wonderful he is to her.

   Difficulty: *Challenging*   **Objective:** *Interpretation*

Essay

11. Student essays should note that both experiences involved cruelty to animals. However, the grandmother's experience was far worse because people were also harmed. Also, Aaron is able to save Pidge, while his grandmother could not save her pet goat. From her experience, Aaron's grandmother learned the value of freedom. From his experience, Aaron learns the importance of standing up to cruelty.

   Difficulty: *Easy*   **Objective:** *Essay*

12. Student essays should note that Aaron means that Pidge can take the place of the goat in his grandmother's heart: Pidge's escape can free the goat in her memory. Students may point out that to Aaron's grandmother, the goat represents the past, while the pigeon represents the present, in which freedom had been obtained.

   Difficulty: *Average*   **Objective:** *Essay*

13. Student essays should show an understanding of the story's main idea: Aaron's gift to his grandmother is Pidge's freedom, which helps her get over the death of her pet goat at the hands of the Cossacks. Students should point out that the title includes the word *gift*, but it is not a material gift that Aaron's grandmother receives. Rather, it is the gift of peace of mind. In this way, the title does express the most important idea of the story.

   Difficulty: *Challenging*   **Objective:** *Essay*

14. Most students will probably indicate that Aaron would not think that conflict is always bad. He does get beaten up by Carl's gang and loses Pidge. However, the pigeon flies free, providing the best gift for his grandmother

that she could receive. Some students might indicate that Aaron would think that conflict is always bad. His grandmother's conflict with the Cossacks led to grief. His conflict with Carl's gang leaves him beaten and without Pidge. Things would have worked out fine if he had been able to give the pigeon to his grandmother so she could set it free.

   Difficulty: *Average*   **Objective:** *Essay*

Oral Response

15. Oral responses should be clear, well organized, and well supported by appropriate examples from the selection.

   Difficulty: *Average*   **Objective:** *Oral Interpretation*

Selection Test A, p. 199

Critical Reading

1. ANS: D	DIF: Easy	OBJ: Interpretation
2. ANS: A	DIF: Easy	OBJ: Reading Skill
3. ANS: C	DIF: Easy	OBJ: Reading Skill
4. ANS: C	DIF: Easy	OBJ: Reading Skill
5. ANS: A	DIF: Easy	OBJ: Comprehension
6. ANS: D	DIF: Easy	OBJ: Literary Analysis
7. ANS: D	DIF: Easy	OBJ: Interpretation
8. ANS: A	DIF: Easy	OBJ: Interpretation
9. ANS: B	DIF: Easy	OBJ: Reading
10. ANS: B	DIF: Easy	OBJ: Comprehension
11. ANS: B	DIF: Easy	OBJ: Literary Analysis
12. ANS: C	DIF: Easy	OBJ: Literary Analysis

Vocabulary and Grammar

13. ANS: A	DIF: Easy	OBJ: Vocabulary
14. ANS: B	DIF: Easy	OBJ: Vocabulary
15. ANS: B	DIF: Easy	OBJ: Grammar

Essay

16. Student essays should tell that the pogrom took place in the Ukraine, sometime about fifty or sixty years before the main story. Essays should note that the grandmother's pogrom experience shapes the characters and the action of the story. For example, the loss of a pet in the pogrom explains the grandmother's attitude toward animals and is why Aaron wants to give her the pigeon. The loss of freedom during the pogrom explains the importance of freedom for the pigeon.

   Difficulty: *Easy*

   Objective: *Essay*

17. Student essays might say that the gift in "Aaron's Gift" stands for the actual pigeon that is meant as a birthday gift. It also means a different kind of gift: an action that helped ease his grandmother's mind and the gift Aaron

receives, which is a better understanding of his grand-mother and of the meaning of freedom.

Difficulty: *Easy*
Objective: *Essay*

18. Most students will probably say Aaron would not think conflict is always bad. He does get beat up by Carl's gang and loses Pidge. However, the pigeon flies free, and Aaron's grandmother says that is the best gift she could receive. Some students might say that Aaron would think conflict is always bad. His grandmother's conflict with the Cossacks led to grief. His conflict with Carl's gang leaves him beaten and without Pidge. Things would have worked out fine if he had been able to give the pigeon to his grandmother so she could set it free.

Difficulty: *Easy*
Objective: *Essay*

Selection Test B, p. 202

Critical Reading

1. ANS: B	DIF: Average	OBJ: Literary Analysis
2. ANS: C	DIF: Average	OBJ: Literary Analysis
3. ANS: A	DIF: Challenging	OBJ: Reading
4. ANS: B	DIF: Average	OBJ: Interpretation
5. ANS: A	DIF: Average	OBJ: Comprehension
6. ANS: C	DIF: Challenging	OBJ: Reading
7. ANS: C	DIF: Challenging	OBJ: Reading
8. ANS: D	DIF: Average	OBJ: Literary Analysis
9. ANS: A	DIF: Average	OBJ: Comprehension
10. ANS: A	DIF: Average	OBJ: Interpretation
11. ANS: C	DIF: Challenging	OBJ: Interpretation
12. ANS: A	DIF: Average	OBJ: Comprehension

Vocabulary and Grammar

13. ANS: D	DIF: Average	OBJ: Vocabulary
14. ANS: A	DIF: Average	OBJ: Vocabulary
15. ANS: B	DIF: Average	OBJ: Vocabulary
16. ANS: D	DIF: Average	OBJ: Grammar
17. ANS: D	DIF: Average	OBJ: Grammar

Essay

18. Student essays should note that Aaron means that Pidge can take the place of the goat in his grand-mother's heart and that Pidge's escape can free the goat in his grandmother's memory. Students may point out that to Aaron's grandmother, the goat represents her family and her past, while the pigeon represents the present, in which freedom has been attained.

Difficulty: *Average*
Objective: *Essay*

19. Student essays should show an understanding of the story's main idea: Aaron's gift to his grandmother is Pidge's freedom, which helps the grandmother get over her

hurt from long ago when the Cossacks cruelly killed her beloved pet goat. The title, which includes the word *gift*, makes the reader think about the story's idea, because Aaron has no physical gift to give his grandmother.

Difficulty: *Challenging*
Objective: *Essay*

20. Most students will probably indicate that Aaron would not think that conflict is always bad. He does get beat up by Carl's gang and loses Pidge. However, the pigeon flies free, providing the best gift that his grandmother could receive. Some students might indicate that Aaron would think that conflict is always bad. His grand-mother's conflict with the Cossacks led to grief. His conflict with Carl's gang leaves him beaten and without Pidge. Things would have worked out fine if he had been able to give the pigeon to his grandmother so she could set it free.

Difficulty: *Average*
Objective: *Essay*

"The Fun They Had" by Isaac Asimov
"Feathered Friend" by Arthur C. Clarke

Vocabulary Warm-up Exercises, p. 206

A. 1. inspector
2. scornful
3. obvious
4. sensible
5. absence
6. geography
7. progress
8. permanent

B. Sample Answers
1. If I detect the smell of smoke in my house, I will leave the house.
2. A mask is usually concealing a person's face.
3. No, because the remainder or other half might melt in my pocket.
4. If I were charged too much, I would dispute the bill and have it corrected.
5. You must insert a key into a locked door to open it.
6. Satisfactory work is good enough but probably not my best.
7. I would not like to have a mechanical pet; a live animal is better than a machine.

Reading Warm-up A, p. 207

Sample Answers
1. A person who examines; The *inspector* looked for rust on the bottom of my car but did not find any.
2. whether the work is going as it should; We made *progress* this morning; we finished painting three of the five rooms.

3. (whether something is wrong with wires inside a wall); *Obvious* means "something that is easy to see or understand."

4. A floor tile; The opposite of *absence* is *presence*.

5. hard, dirty work on your hands and knees; My brother gave me a *scornful* look when I said I was scared of the dark.

6. damage, the parts of a building that cannot be fixed; I don't think this *permanent* marker will wash off my jacket.

7. (reasonable); He is a *sensible* person who makes practical choices.

8. Climate can have a big effect on a building. So can location. After I studied the *geography* of Mexico, I knew where mountains were located in that country.

Reading Warm-up B, p. 208

Sample Answers

1. discover; I can *detect* when food has spoiled; it gives off a bad smell.

2. (magnetic pumps, solar-powered engines, and fuel rods containing energy-producing chemicals); *Mechanical* means "something that is operated by using a machine."

3. (new wires into the chambers containing the fuel rods); I would like to *insert* an extra sentence into this paragraph.

4. (Word of the situation had spread from person to person in a matter of hours.) *Concealing* my diary from my little brother is very important.

5. arguing; *Agree* is an antonym for *dispute*.

6. all of them, or Earth, Venus, and Jupiter; Everyone who does *satisfactory* work will be rewarded.

7. (voyage to Earth); We each took a slice of pie and then wrapped up the *remainder*.

8. (settlement or colony); The settlement is *vacant* because everyone had to leave.

Writing About the Big Question, p. 209

A. 1. issue
2. defend
3. oppose
4. convince

B. Sample Answers
1. At camp, a boy tried to take candy and money from the other boys.
2. To stop bullying, you can join together with other kids to **defend** others. You can also **challenge** bullies because they are often cowards and will back down.

C. Sample Answer

When humans rely on animals or computers to do their work, they are avoiding the challenge of doing the work themselves and are more likely to lose control of the product. These possible conflicts could be bad.

Literary Analysis: Theme, p. 210

Sample Answers

A. Future
Margie's schoolroom
A weekday, during the day

B. Detail: Narrator feels the effects of a lack of oxygen.
Detail: Narrator realizes there's an oxygen shortage.
Detail: Narrator remembers that canaries warn miners.
Theme: Small, low-tech animals can help get an important job done.

Vocabulary Builder, p. 211

Sample Answers

2. Synonym: figured
Sentence: I figured the amount of food each guest would eat.

3. Synonym: proudly
Sentence: Jerome spoke proudly about his fancy new bike.

4. Synonym: casually
Sentence: Tyra walked casually through the crowds at the theater.

5. Synonym: rule
Sentence: The city has a rule against riding bicycles on sidewalks.

6. Synonym: joining
Sentence: The welder began joining two metal bars with a blowtorch.

7. Synonym: stopped
Sentence: When the rain stopped, we went back outside.

Open-Book Test, p. 213

Short Answer

1. *Loftily* means "in a superior way." The word suggests that Tommy thinks he is smarter than Margie and looks down on her.
Difficulty: *Average*   **Objective:** *Vocabulary*

2. Some students will respond that Tommy does not care about the book or its description of schools. Near the beginning of the story, he states that books are "a waste." He is also "nonchalant" as he walks away. Other students may respond that the way Tommy explains the concept of a traditional school to Margie and talks about his father's intelligence shows that he respects the past.
Difficulty: *Challenging*   **Objective:** *Interpretation*

3. Margie seems to dislike the lack of human interaction. She envies the old schools, where "teachers were people" and children talked to one another about school-work.
Difficulty: *Easy*   **Objective:** *Interpretation*

4. Sven probably waits in order to see how other crew members react to having a bird on board. It turns out that everyone has accepted the bird as "a general pet" by the time Sven confesses that Claribel is his.

   Difficulty: *Average*   **Objective:** *Interpretation*

5. *Ceased* means "stopped." The air filter stopped working, so the air the crew was breathing was not providing the necessary level of oxygen.

   Difficulty: *Challenging*   **Objective:** *Vocabulary*

6. *How Claribel Helps:* Claribel's fainting spells lead the narrator to realize that the bird is reacting to a lack of oxygen in the space center's atmosphere.

   How Narrator Views Claribel at the End: The narrator recognizes that Claribel has saved their lives and that no space center should be without a pet bird.

   Students' answers will vary. They may suggest, for example, that human beings are not self-sufficient or that technology alone cannot protect people.

   Difficulty: *Average*   **Objective:** *Interpretation*

7. Both stories seem to take place some time in the future.

   Difficulty: *Easy*   **Objective:** *Literary Analysis*

8. In "The Fun They Had," Margie is taught by a mechanical teacher in a schoolroom in her home, but she wishes she had a human teacher. In "Feathered Friend," the crew of the space station cannot survive without technology, but a malfunction almost kills them.

   Difficulty: *Challenging*   **Objective:** *Literary Analysis*

9. The comparisons show that the old ways may be better than the new. In "The Fun They Had," Margie thinks she would prefer the old schools to her mechanical teacher. In "Feathered Friend," the canary, and not technology, saves the crew, just as canaries saved miners in the past.

   Difficulty: *Average*   **Objective:** *Literary Analysis*

10. Both stories point out the drawbacks in depending on technology. Technology fails the crew in "Feathered Friend" when both the air purifier and the alarm malfunction. The mechanical teacher in "The Fun They Had" does not provide the human interaction Margie wants.

    Difficulty: *Challenging*   **Objective:** *Literary Analysis*

Essay

11. Students should indicate that the central message of "The Fun They Had" relates to the superiority of old schools over new schools. The title conveys that message by referring to the fun that students in the old schools presumably had. Students should note that the central message of "Feathered Friend" relates to Claribel's part in rescuing the space-station crew. Students might say that the word *friend* expresses the crew members' feelings about Claribel after she saves their lives.

Difficulty: *Easy*   **Objective:** *Essay*

12. Students should point out that in "The Fun They Had," details about Margie's daily life allow the reader to feel what Margie is feeling. For example, the description of the mechanical teacher as "large and ugly" and the reference to the punch code Margie uses allow the reader to understand Margie's dislike of school. In "Feathered Friend," the details about the construction work make the space station seem like a real place. The reader can imagine the crew members as real people and therefore worry about them when they face the life-threatening problem with the air purifier.

    Difficulty: *Average*   **Objective:** *Essay*

13. Some students may say that "The Fun They Had" is more believable. With computers in wide use and home schooling fairly common, the idea of a mechanical teacher in each family's home may not seem far-fetched. The character of Margie is believable because a girl of her age would want to have human interaction. Students who take this point of view might point out that "Feathered Friend" is less believable because it is unlikely that technology would fail as completely as it does in that story. Other students may indicate that "Feathered Friend" is more believable because space stations are already in place. Students who take this point of view might find "The Fun They Had" unrealistic because society is not likely to totally abandon teaching in a group setting and without any human intervention.

    Difficulty: *Challenging*   **Objective:** *Essay*

14. Students may argue that Margie would not likely agree that conflict is always bad. She dislikes her form of education and might realize that she is in conflict with it. If she realized that, she would not likely think her protest—a form of conflict—is bad. She might also come to realize that in the kind of school she envies, there is bound to be conflict because people with different ideas come together in one place. She might consider that conflict is a healthy part of group interaction. Students might recognize that the narrator of "Feathered Friend" might be more likely to see conflict as a negative because of the need for close cooperation on a space station.

    Difficulty: *Average*   **Objective:** *Essay*

Oral Response

15. Oral responses should be clear, well organized, and well supported by appropriate examples from the stories.

    Difficulty: *Average*   **Objective:** *Oral Interpretation*

Selection Test A, p. 216

Critical Reading

1. **ANS:** C   **DIF:** Easy   **OBJ:** Comprehension
2. **ANS:** A   **DIF:** Easy   **OBJ:** Interpretation

3. ANS: B DIF: Easy OBJ: Literary Analysis
4. ANS: D DIF: Easy OBJ: Comprehension
5. ANS: A DIF: Easy OBJ: Comprehension
6. ANS: B DIF: Easy OBJ: Interpretation
7. ANS: B DIF: Easy OBJ: Comprehension
8. ANS: C DIF: Easy OBJ: Literary Analysis
9. ANS: D DIF: Easy OBJ: Literary Analysis
10. ANS: A DIF: Easy OBJ: Interpretation
11. ANS: B DIF: Easy OBJ: Literary Analysis
12. ANS: C DIF: Easy OBJ: Literary Analysis

Vocabulary

13. ANS: D DIF: Easy OBJ: Vocabulary
14. ANS: C DIF: Easy OBJ: Vocabulary
15. ANS: A DIF: Easy OBJ: Vocabulary

Essay

16. Student essays should propose a theme for "The Fun They Had" that relates to Margie's wish that she could have fun. Essays might say that the title helps communicate the theme because it suggests that Margie longs for the world of the past. A proposed theme of "Feathered Friend" should relate to the rescue of the crew members. Essays might say that the title helps communicate the theme because the word *friend* expresses the crew members' feelings toward Claribel.

Difficulty: *Easy*
Objective: *Essay*

17. Student essays should address the idea that "The Fun They Had" describes Margie's individual effort to excel at schoolwork, and that "Feathered Friend" describes the group effort to solve the mystery of the unconscious bird. Lessons learned from "The Fun They Had" should include the idea that work is more fun with others. Lessons learned from "Feathered Friend" should include the idea that all members of a team have an important contribution to make.

Difficulty: *Easy*
Objective: *Essay*

18. Students will probably say that Margie would not agree that conflict is always bad. She envies the old school-children for the fun they had in school and probably recognizes that even conflicts with friends and teachers would be better than the school she has now. Some students may say that the narrator of "Feathered Friend" also will recognize conflict as a good thing because without the conflict about what was happening with the bird and the oxygen, the crew would have died. Others may say the narrator would see conflict as a bad thing in a small space station.

Difficulty: *Easy*
Objective: *Essay*

Selection Test B, p. 219

Critical Reading

1. ANS: B DIF: Average OBJ: Literary Analysis
2. ANS: C DIF: Average OBJ: Comprehension
3. ANS: A DIF: Average OBJ: Interpretation
4. ANS: D DIF: Challenging OBJ: Comprehension
5. ANS: A DIF: Average OBJ: Interpretation
6. ANS: D DIF: Average OBJ: Comprehension
7. ANS: B DIF: Average OBJ: Comprehension
8. ANS: B DIF: Average OBJ: Interpretation
9. ANS: A DIF: Challenging OBJ: Comprehension
10. ANS: C DIF: Challenging OBJ: Literary Analysis
11. ANS: D DIF: Challenging OBJ: Interpretation
12. ANS: B DIF: Average OBJ: Literary Analysis
13. ANS: A DIF: Average OBJ: Comprehension
14. ANS: A DIF: Average OBJ: Literary Analysis
15. ANS: C DIF: Challenging OBJ: Interpretation

Vocabulary

16. ANS: D DIF: Average OBJ: Vocabulary
17. ANS: A DIF: Average OBJ: Vocabulary
18. ANS: B DIF: Average OBJ: Vocabulary

Essay

19. Student essays should propose a theme for "The Fun They Had" that relates to Margie's loneliness and longing for the past. Essays should suggest that the title expresses the idea that Margie longs for fun. A proposed theme for "Feathered Friend" should relate to the canary's rescue of the space station crew. The word *friend* in the title expresses how the crew feels about Claribel.

Difficulty: *Average*
Objective: *Essay*

20. Essays should note that "The Fun They Had" describes Margie's individual effort to learn and do schoolwork; "Feathered Friend" describes the group effort of the crew to solve the mystery of the unconscious bird.

Difficulty: *Average*
Objective: *Essay*

21. Student essays might say that Margie faces loneliness and boredom and the space station crew work under difficult circumstances. Both are challenged by their situations. Essays might say that the characters' jobs are different because Margie faces loneliness and boredom alone, whereas the crew must rely on one another. Opinions about which character or characters face the greater challenge will differ but should be soundly supported.

Difficulty: *Challenging*
Objective: *Essay*

22. Students may argue that Margie would not likely agree that conflict is always bad. She dislikes her form of education and might realize that she is in conflict with it. If she realized that, she likely would not think her protest—a form of conflict—is bad. She might also come to realize that in the kind of school she envies, there is bound to be conflict because people with different ideas come together in one place. She might consider that conflict is a healthy part of group interaction. Students might recognize that the narrator of "Feathered Friend" might be more likely to see conflict as a negative because of the need for close cooperation on a space station.

Difficulty: *Average*
Objective: *Essay*

Writing Workshop

Short Story: Grammar, p. 223

A. 1. present; 2. past; 3. future; 4. past
B. Sample Answers

1. While Luz practices her lines, she learns the cue words. While Luz practiced her lines, she learned the cue words.

2. All of the actors were nervous because they wanted to do well. All of the actors are nervous because they want to do well.

3. The performance will take place on Saturday if all goes as planned.

4. Everyone expects a large audience, but we never know for sure. Everyone expected a large audience, but we never knew for sure.

Vocabulary Workshop—1, p. 224

Sample Answers

1. E
2. F
3. G
4. C
5. D
6. B
7. A

Vocabulary Workshop—2, p. 225

Sample Answers

1. E
2. B
3. A
4. C
5. D

incredible, incurable, incriminate, increments, incubating

Benchmark Test 4, p. 227

MULTIPLE CHOICE

1. ANS: D
2. ANS: B
3. ANS: C
4. ANS: C
5. ANS: A
6. ANS: A
7. ANS: B
8. ANS: B
9. ANS: A
10. ANS: C
11. ANS: C
12. ANS: D
13. ANS: C
14. ANS: D
15. ANS: A
16. ANS: B
17. ANS: C
18. ANS: D
19. ANS: B
20. ANS: D
21. ANS: C
22. ANS: A
23. ANS: D
24. ANS: A
25. ANS: B
26. ANS: C
27. ANS: D
28. ANS: B
29. ANS: C
30. ANS: D
31. ANS: A

ESSAY

32. Students' descriptions should discuss the character's personality, actions, achievements, and/or appearance. They should state characteristics of the person and then provide details that support their general statements.

33. Students' narratives should recount the experience in chronological order. They should include the details of the experience as well as their thoughts and feelings about it.

34. Students should outline the exposition, conflict, rising action, climax, falling action, and resolution of the plot of their stories. Outlines should also briefly describe the setting or settings and the main characters, giving details of characters' situations and personalities and perhaps their dialogue and actions.

Vocabulary in Context, p. 233

MULTIPLE CHOICE

  1. ANS: B
  2. ANS: C
  3. ANS: A
  4. ANS: B
  5. ANS: D
  6. ANS: D
  7. ANS: C
  8. ANS: A
  9. ANS: B
10. ANS: D
11. ANS: A
12. ANS: B
13. ANS: D
14. ANS: B
15. ANS: C
16. ANS: C
17. ANS: A
18. ANS: D
19. ANS: B
20. ANS: B